T0246143

'Few ministers have such influence and make the impact and contribution Steven Joyce did. We knew him as Mr Fix-It; the press gallery called him the Minister for Everything; but the public saw it more simply. He was the guy who got the stuff they wanted done, and he did it in spades and with style.'
— SIR JOHN KEY

'Steven Joyce was at the heart of the sustained policy and political success of the John Key government. He has a unique combination of discipline, positivity and political acumen. He got stuff done.'
— SIR BILL ENGLISH

Steven Joyce
On the Record

ALLEN&UNWIN
SYDNEY•MELBOURNE•AUCKLAND•LONDON

First published in 2023

Copyright © Steven Joyce, 2023

Unless otherwise credited, photographs in the picture section
are from the collections of the author and his political office.

All rights reserved. No part of this book may be reproduced
or transmitted in any form or by any means, electronic or
mechanical, including photocopying, recording or by any
information storage and retrieval system, without prior
permission in writing from the publisher.

Allen & Unwin
Level 2, 10 College Hill, Freemans Bay
Auckland 1011, New Zealand
+64 (9) 377 3800
auckland@allenandunwin.com
www.allenandunwin.co.nz

83 Alexander Street
Crows Nest NSW 2065, Australia
+61 (2) 8425 0100

A catalogue record for this book is available from the
National Library of New Zealand.

ISBN 978 1 99100 646 2

Design by Kate Barraclough
Set in Adobe Caslon Pro and Big Caslon
Printed in Australia by Pegasus Media & Logistics

5 7 9 10 8 6

This book has been printed using sustainably managed stock.

MIX
Paper from
responsible sources
FSC® C008194
www.fsc.org

The paper in this book is FSC® certified.
FSC® promotes environmentally responsible,
socially beneficial and economically viable
management of the world's forests.

To my dad, Peter, and my late mum, Lorna,
and to Suzanne, Amelia and Tommy

Contents

Chapter One
Energy FM

I NEVER REALLY SET OUT to be a politician. I did have an interest in politics growing up, but all the way through school I had my heart set on one thing, being a vet.

We had animals all around when I was a kid. Dogs, cats, goldfish, a budgie at one point, and even a goat called Paddy McGinty. My sister Diane and I were into horse-riding, and by the time I was in high school I had responsibility for two large thoroughbreds with variable showjumping ability, one of my own and one handed down from Diane. We kept them on rented grazing at Ōtaihanga on the Kāpiti Coast. I took both horses with me to Massey University and grazed them on a farm at Linton, biking each day between the paddock and campus.

Growing up, our household was a busy one. My parents both left school at fifteen and they married when my mum was twenty and my dad twenty-one. They scrimped and borrowed and bought a Four Square store in New Plymouth, working really hard to make a go of both their shop and their family. They ran a seven-days-a-week business and brought up five kids at the same time. We moved to Kāpiti when I was fourteen, after Dad was given the opportunity to purchase the Self Help supermarket in Coastlands, which later became a New World. The grocery trade was a good business, and I know Dad was keen for one of us to follow in his footsteps, but my ambition was to be a vet and I set off to Massey to pursue my dream.

Competition to get into vet school proper at the end of the first, intermediate, year was intense, and unfortunately I didn't make the cut. I was told I missed by about sixteen places, but I met a number of other people who'd been told something similar. I didn't have a plan B, and seriously considered giving up university at that point and heading home. A wise careers adviser suggested I study another degree, 'any degree', through which I would learn how to learn, and while I was doing that I should keep my eye out for something else that might interest me.

I duly studied a BSc in Zoology (my school subjects were all maths, English and sciences) and had a lot of fun over the next two years. While I completed my degree, I explored other subjects like psychology and economics, the latter of which I particularly enjoyed. But I really wanted to 'have a go' at student radio.

I loved listening to radio growing up. I listened to it more than anyone I knew. I knew all the stations, all the formats, and the schtick of all the announcers. It was a magical medium and I wanted to be part of it. But I was also shy. Student-radio people were all very cool and superior and difficult to approach, so it took some prodding from my university girlfriend for me to summon the courage to go to Radio Massey and ask if I could have a shot at being a DJ.

It was a shaky start. From the beginner's mistake of leaving the microphone on after I'd finished talking, to playing records at the wrong speed, my first attempt at radio announcing had it all. However my tutor, Radio Massey manager Maxine Parker, who was rostered for the shift I was practising on, seemed happy enough with my progress. After helping me for half an hour, she considered me duly trained, and announced she was heading off for coffee with a friend on the other side of campus. I could play anything I liked from the box of records to my right, and I was to have a good time.

Immediate problem. A quick look through the box revealed no artists or songs I knew. This was alternative radio after all, and at that stage my knowledge of British and American alternative music was laughably thin. After panicking for a few seconds, I decided to play side one track one from each album in turn, reasoning that the artists must have believed they were good songs to place them up the front. It all worked very well until I got to a track which sounded particularly melancholy and seemed to take an inordinately long time to play. A listener soon called to point out that it was designed to be played at 45 rpm, not 33.

Radio Massey was a mostly voluntary station which seemed to operate on the principle that if you hung around you got a bigger job. I hung around a lot. I loved radio and everything about it. I wanted to learn everything I could. I became the station's news hound in that first year, a role which seemed to be mostly about transcribing the work of other news outlets and reading it on air. I was programme director in 1984, and then station manager in 1985, when we greatly extended the station's hours of operation.

In 1984 a few mates at the station and I started to discuss what we would do after university. All of us had the bug and wanted to work in radio commercially, but none of us had much confidence in the two career paths on offer. These were doing midnight–dawn shifts on one of the private radio stations around the country and probably waiting years to be promoted, or becoming a trainee announcer for the government-owned Broadcasting Corporation of New Zealand (BCNZ), and being sent to Timaru or Tokoroa to earn our stripes.

1984 was the year of Muldoon's 'schnapps' election, and when it was called we decided Radio Massey would do some documentaries on key election issues, in the style of the new TV current-affairs shows which spliced different interviews together into a single narrative. We raced around the lower North Island interviewing local luminaries like MPs Trevor de Cleene and Bruce Beetham, and University of Victoria political scientist Dr Rod Alley. The Radio Massey election specials were uncharted territory for student radio, and probably attracted an audience you could count in the tens, most of whom would have preferred listening to music. But we enjoyed making them.

While we were working on the election specials, we started to discuss launching our own radio station as a short cut into the industry. Rob Muldoon's government had haltingly allowed the development of private radio over the previous few years. There had been new stations like 89.8 FM in Hamilton, 2XS in Palmerston North, as well as 91 FM and 89 FM in Auckland. Why shouldn't we start one too?

We were an eclectic bunch. What united us was a belief in our own talent, matched with the fear no one would recognise it. Besides me, there was Quentin Bright, who was the Radio Massey station manager in 1984, breakfast announcer Jeremy Corbett, Post Office computer programmer Peter Noldus, who we called Grandad because he was 29 while the rest of us were only 21 or 22, and a bit of a drifter called Darryl Reid, who loved to party.

New Plymouth and Gisborne were the largest remaining North Island towns without a privately owned radio station. We eventually settled on New Plymouth, primarily because both Quentin and I originally came from there. We then spent an inordinate amount of time brainstorming the name of the new radio station; we considered Milk FM and Mountain FM, before settling on Energy FM, for the energy province. It sounded great. It worked for Taranaki and for music. We patted ourselves on the back for such an excellent choice.

The Broadcasting Tribunal, which controlled the allocation of frequencies in those days, allowed short-term summer broadcasts on FM frequencies in 'holiday spots' to test the market for local FM radio stations. These were stations like Fifeshire FM in Nelson and 2XX on the Kāpiti Coast. We decided that running a summer station in New Plymouth would be a manageable first step towards our dream. We could lease the Radio Massey gear, as that station wouldn't be on air, and see how our plan played out.

We went on a reconnoitre to Taranaki to check the lie of the land and work out where we might operate from. There we learnt we weren't going to have the FM radio waves to ourselves. Somewhat undercutting our marketing brilliance, there was not one but two other potential licence bidders called Energy FM and Radio Energy. There was also a third crowd called Peak FM, who were planning a summer station, just like us.

With no time to waste, we put together a company called Energy Enterprises Ltd with $500 capital, $100 each from the five of us. We didn't have much money — I had to loan one of the guys his $100. We then prepared and lodged an application for a summer broadcast, at the well-known holiday hotspot of New Plymouth, in doing so extolling our virtues against the nascent Peak FM. With the wisdom of Solomon, the Broadcasting Tribunal gave both stations a 28-day 100-watt FM summer warrant, and let us duke it out on the airwaves. On appeal they gave us an extra two weeks of non-commercial broadcasting.

That first summer was quite a crazy time. We set the station up in a little old two-storey weatherboard building in the central city on Powderham Street, and tacked egg cartons on the wall to provide some sound-proofing. Pete arranged to have our broadcast aerial located at Taranaki Polytechnic, which provided reasonable coverage across the city. I designed the original logo, and Jeremy and Darryl spent way too many hours painting it on the roof of the building. We went to air with a mix of rock music and top 40 with the strapline 'Hot Summer Music'. The station was a popular success, especially with the younger market.

Peak FM, on the other hand, struggled. It was owned by a radio engineer called Malcolm Hay, who was more of an enthusiast than a broadcaster, and it showed. He hired popular DJ Muzza Inglis back home to Taranaki to do breakfast, but after that the station slipped backwards. There was no on-air discipline — everybody pretty much played what they liked. It also had poor transmission coverage. After that first summer, it was announced that Peak wouldn't be back. Round one to the Massey students.

Our first broadcast stint felt like it was over almost before it began. We hardly made any money, but off the back of it we had the right mix of experience and naivety to believe we could make a good fist of a full-time station. We went back to Palmerston North determined to redouble our efforts to secure an FM warrant.

The process was very bureaucratic. Applicants had to wait until the Broadcasting Tribunal was ready to call for applications for an FM licence for a region. There would then be a tribunal hearing, and at some point after that there would be a decision. We had no idea when that would take place.

We decided in the meantime to run a second broadcast, in the summer of 1985–86. The tribunal had made it very clear it didn't want summer stations running in the lucrative pre-Christmas advertising period, because it would take revenue away from the established local BCNZ station, which apparently needed to be protected. So we came up with a cunning plan to run commercial-free prior to Christmas so we could have a longer time on air, and to use that time to promote a huge concert at the Bowl of Brooklands, making our money from that.

The tribunal accepted our plan, and gave us an eight-week broadcast from the end of November to the end of January, with the three weeks prior to Christmas to be commercial-free. Energy FM was back, this time with a transmitter on the New Plymouth power-station chimney, and Summer Rock 85 was born. There was quite a lot to juggle, because the tribunal also announced that applications would close for a full-time licence at the end of November. A few all-nighters were pulled in the service of getting the station going, getting the application lodged and preparing for the concert.

The plan worked. We had most of the top pop bands in New Zealand at the time — Dance Exponents, Netherworld Dancing Toys, The Narcs, Midge Marsden and Peking Man — all at the Bowl for one afternoon and evening. Some 5000 people came and we netted $20,000, which was an exciting amount of money for us students. The less exciting bit was having to give half of it to charity, as we'd rashly promised the Broadcasting Tribunal we would.

Our second broadcast period was more profitable than the first, and effectively paid for our full-time application and hearing costs. We were still living hand to mouth but we were making some headway.

A BROADCASTING TRIBUNAL HEARING IN the mid-1980s was a unique and curious thing. Firstly, you had to turn up with your fully formed business plan. The tribunal wanted to see who was going to run the station, who the owners were, and who would be on the board of directors. We had been able to convince prominent local businessmen Norton Moller and John Armstrong to be chairman and a director respectively. Us boys would own 51 per cent of the company, and a range of Taranaki shareholders would own the other 49 per cent. We weren't sure where we were getting the funding for our 51 per cent from; we would work on that.

We secured the services of a young broadcasting lawyer called Brent Impey to represent us before the tribunal. He was able to arrange Radio Pacific CEO and former Hauraki pirate Derek Lowe to meet us, and Derek too came on board as a director to provide the necessary broadcasting experience. Brent's offsider at the hearing was another young lawyer called Simon Dallow, who went on to ditch the law for television news.

There were three applicants for what we assumed to be one FM licence for Taranaki. As well as us, there was one of the previous Energy FM promoters, renamed as Action FM Ltd. Action FM was backed by a sizeable chunk of the private radio industry, including Brierley Investments who were big radio owners at the time, and the team from Magic 91 FM in Auckland, notably Trevor Egerton and Rob McKay. The government-owned BCNZ had an application in for a satellite ZM station as well.

We had a memorable meeting with the Brierley representatives, as they sought for us to join forces with them rather than running separate applications. We met in our accountant's boardroom, with all the suits filing in down one side, and the Massey boys in our jeans down the other. Their representative cleared his throat and said they were keen to work with us and were happy with a 70:30 shareholding split. Jeremy Corbett immediately deadpanned, 'Yes, that's what we thought too. Us 70, you 30.' They quickly moved their proposal to them owning at least 51 per cent, but Jeremy pointed out it was like they were trying to sell us a minority stake in our own radio station. The meeting was over in about ten minutes.

The tribunal held a full three-day hearing for the applications in the New Plymouth courthouse, complete with briefs of evidence, cross-examination by lawyers, and reporters in attendance. There were some unintentionally hilarious moments. One of the things the tribunal was required to consider was whether the new warrant-holder would have an undue commercial impact on the established local radio station owned by the government. The BCNZ witnesses spent half the hearing arguing we would slaughter them commercially if we were given a warrant, while we had to argue that our target market, people aged under 35 who liked music, was a different market entirely and we'd have no commercial effect whatsoever. All of this evidence was given under oath.

Pete Noldus and I were listed as joint managing directors, and we gave evidence for the five of us. The Brierley/91 FM team decided to ignore us as much as possible. They wanted to give the tribunal the sense that we weren't up to running a radio station, and they were concerned that if they cross-examined us we may manage to give an impression of competence. Happily the BCNZ lawyers hadn't received the memo, and they proceeded to ask us all sorts of questions about how we would run a radio station. After managing a student radio station and two summer broadcasts, we knew enough to sound knowledgeable, and passed that test. At one pivotal moment, tribunal chairman Bruce Slane asked Derek whether he thought I would be able to be both the programme director and financial controller of the new station. Derek helpfully replied that he thought I could do both standing on my head.

The hearing wrapped up with the tribunal reserving its decision, and we settled down to wait. Surely it wouldn't be long.

We decided to apply for and run a winter broadcast in the meantime, on the rather dubious claim that Taranaki, and the small local Manganui ski field, was a snow mecca and winter wonderland. The tribunal gave us another 28 days, which kept the wolf from the door. When it became clear that there wouldn't be a decision before the end of that year, we applied for and ran a third summer broadcast as well.

The delays were taking their toll. We had all now given up the first two and a half years of our post-university careers, and we still didn't know whether this dream of owning a radio station had any chance of coming to pass. Gradually the partners started bowing out, unwilling to put their lives on hold any longer for what seemed a mirage. Jeremy got married and went to live in Perth as a computer programmer, before ultimately returning to New Zealand for a successful career on radio and as a comedian. Quentin decided to go down one of the more traditional career paths and get a steady job in government-owned radio. Darryl just got on his motorbike and left town. It was down to Peter and me, and a new recruit who'd been there or thereabouts since the start, Don Raine. Don was at least a commercial broadcaster, having worked at 2XS before he was unceremoniously fired by their station manager, Larry Summerville.

As the third summer broadcast wound down at the end of January 1987, all three of us had an acute need to get a job and start making some money. We agreed to start applying for full-time jobs. If the curly question 'What about Energy FM?' came up, we'd say that if the decision was positive then the station's operation would be left to the other two. It was a bit fast and loose, but needs must. Pete took a job in sales for Radio Avon in Christchurch, Don was hired as an announcer at Hot 93 in Hawke's Bay, and I started work as an account manager for PR firm Consultus in Wellington.

As luck would have it, I was called into the Broadcasting Tribunal office on The Terrace a week after I started at Consultus. Fifteen months after the tribunal hearing, and three years since we had formed the company, Energy FM was given a full-time warrant to go to air in Taranaki. We were on cloud nine. BCNZ was also given a ZM warrant, but it wasn't allowed to launch until at least a year after we had started broadcasting.

Finally we were away and running. We all quit our jobs and returned to Taranaki. We had to collect our capital, build some radio studios, and hire some staff. It wasn't easy, happening as it did against the backdrop of the Black Monday stock-market crash in October, but we did get it all done inside five months. Energy FM, the full-time station, went to air for the first time on 30 November 1987. We started with fifteen staff, and our average age was 24.

I DON'T THINK IT'S TOO much to say that the new station was an immediate ratings success. We had been priming the market for three years, so it wasn't a surprise that Taranaki people were ready to switch to FM. We ran a launch campaign called 'The Big Switch is On' with an AM amnesty, where people could exchange their old AM radios for an Energy FM T-shirt. On a Saturday a few weeks after we went to air we placed all the old radios in a car park and brought in a steam roller to flatten them.

That first summer was hugely successful. We ran all the events we'd run through previous summers, plus a few more, and had a great time doing it. One highlight was an Icehouse concert at the Bowl of Brooklands in front of 12,000 people with yours truly as the MC. I was the afternoon-drive announcer on the station, programme director and part-time bush accountant.

Our competitors never really knew what hit them. Radio Taranaki was on AM, playing a lot of old music interspersed with horse racing and 'buy, sell and exchange', and with a character on the breakfast show called Yudi the Yeti. We played pop and rock music on FM. It was hard not to do well. At the first audience rating period, five months after we went to air, Energy FM rated a 37.9 per cent share of the Taranaki audience, against Radio Taranaki's 36.7 per cent, and 2ZH Hāwera's 10.5 per cent. It was the highest-ever debut by an FM radio station in Australasia.

That first year wasn't all plain sailing, though. In March, Cyclone Bola hit, and while it is most remembered for the havoc it caused in Gisborne and Hawke's Bay, it made a mess in Taranaki as well. It lifted the roof off our new radio station and nearly destroyed it, just months after we had gone on air. Thankfully, Civil Defence and the fire brigade considered us an essential service, and put the roof back on before we were literally blown out.

We also weren't making a huge amount of money. While we were proving pretty good at playing bands like R.E.M. on the radio, we had a fair bit to learn about advertising sales and accounting. Our patient board of directors helped us fill the gaps, but it was still another year before we were consistently making the sort of money that our ratings suggested we should.

Eighteen months after we went on air, we picked up three awards at our first-ever New Zealand radio awards: Jana Rangooni for best new broadcaster, my brother Rodney and his offsider Cliff Joiner for best news story for their Cyclone Bola coverage, and yours truly for Programme Director of the Year. We were making our mark in the radio industry. I remember Derek telling me to enjoy that first awards evening because most people waited years for that sort of recognition, and it might be a while before it came around again. He was right. As far as radio awards were concerned, for Energy FM it became a long time between drinks.

The fairy tale couldn't last, and it didn't. BCNZ hit back at us, firstly by hiring away our breakfast announcer Darren Mills to Classic Hits in Auckland, just prior to our second annual audience survey. That led to me taking on breakfast anchoring duties as well as my other jobs. I loved the breakfast shift, and threw myself into it. I partnered with co-host Andi Brotherston and we ran a high-tempo show with features including Fun Cash Tuesdays (where we gave away envelopes of cash to people prepared to do things like take a cream pie to their face on the way to work), Battle of the Sexes and wacky 60-minute challenges. In our 'early-morning wake-up calls' we would prank one or two unsuspecting listeners each day with an increasingly implausible scenario. Favourites included persuading All Black Kieran Crowley's sister to audition for a laundry detergent commercial in an Australian accent ('Fabulous clean, fabulous soft') and getting the local Westpac bank manager to rush downtown, convinced that his ATM machine was spitting out $20 notes onto the footpath. My stint doing breakfast was a real highlight among all my time in radio. We had a lot of fun, and it seemed infectious. In our second survey, Energy FM widened its lead over Radio Taranaki.

Then the other shoe dropped. The same government-owned

Radio New Zealand (now split off from BCNZ) launched a new automated music station on their ZM frequency at the end of 1989. Q90 FM was designed as a loss-leader, playing very similar music to our station with much less advertising. The plan was clearly to starve us of ratings or revenue or both.

It was a very tough fight for the next eighteen months. While Energy FM stayed number one, the combined ratings of the two Radio New Zealand (RNZ) stations were well in excess of ours. Derek rightly saw RNZ's attack as an existential threat to our little company, and encouraged the board to back the fight with extra marketing money, which they did.

I gave up the breakfast show towards the end of that time so I could revamp the station's format to compete more effectively with Q90. In any event, getting up at 4 a.m. and working a normal business day after the breakfast show was wearing me out. The new format worked, and the threat began to recede.

RNZ more widely was in financial trouble, and had appealed to the government to bail them out. Misadventures like unprofitable music stations in Hawke's Bay, Manawatū and Taranaki were symptomatic of a more general approach of playing fast and loose with the cheque book. The new Bolger government refused to help, telling them they had to cut their coat according to their cloth.

In late June 1991 RNZ waved the white flag in Taranaki. They took Q90 FM off air, instead simulcasting Radio Taranaki on both FM and AM. That repaired their profitability in the region, and it also repaired ours. Our market position grew again and the revenue started to flow. We'd been through the fire and survived.

With Energy FM now back and growing, our thoughts turned towards expansion into another market. We decided we didn't want to be as vulnerable to attack a second time, and we needed to spread the risk. The board also decided that, after four years, one radio station was getting a bit small for Pete, Don and me. They believed we needed to take advantage of the skills we'd built and get out of each other's pockets.

It was easier said than done. There simply weren't that many independent private radio stations around for sale, and those that were available were being quickly snapped up by the expansionist listed company Radio Otago. Otago had bought stations in Hawke's Bay, Rotorua and Taupō, and then whipped Star FM Whanganui out from under our noses while we were talking to its owner about a possible sale.

There was, however, one station that even Radio Otago had been unable to buy. The *National Business Review*'s publisher Barry Colman had purchased a Tauranga-based start-up station called Coastline FM, and was known to be having problems running it. He didn't want to sell, but he was happy to talk to us about managing it for him. One thing led to another, and we were halfway through negotiating a management agreement with a minority shareholding when he finally decided it was all too hard and he was willing to sell.

That was a fantastic breakthrough and we wasted no time doing the deal, just in case Radio Otago got wind of it. We took over in October 1992, and Pete Noldus went to Tauranga to run the station. He arrived for the handover, only to find that nobody from Auckland had remembered to tell the staff that the business was being sold. Pete had to call his own staff meeting to tell the Coastline team we had purchased the station.

We hired back Jana Rangooni as marketing and operations manager and worked quickly to reformat Coastline to an Energy FM-style music mix. Peter did his magic on the sales side, and our second station was up and running. I took up managing Energy FM, with Don Raine leading operations.

Five years in and Energy Enterprises was running along nicely with stations in Taranaki and the Bay of Plenty. Life was good.

Chapter Two
Building RadioWorks

THE BIG NEWS IN NEW ZEALAND RADIO in the early 1990s was deregulation. In 1989 Broadcasting Minister Jonathan Hunt decided to do away with the old Broadcasting Tribunal and the associated 'fashion parade' approach to allocating radio frequencies, and instead sell frequency rights to the highest bidder, initially by tender, and later by auction. This was a much more radical reform than anything adopted in the UK, the US or Australia. Broadcasters had been accustomed to a highly limited number of frequencies being available, and the granting of a frequency effectively providing a franchise to the broadcaster. This new approach could change the whole industry.

The impact was gradual in the early days of the new regime. The Ministry of Commerce told everyone they were releasing pretty much all the available frequencies for tender, which amounted to some 35 around the country. But then things started to warm up. As more people asked for more frequencies, more seemed to be able to be engineered. While the number of FM frequencies wouldn't be infinite, it was apparent there were many more that could be allocated than had been originally thought possible.

At Energy FM, we experienced early the sort of competition we might see under the new regime. In 1991 an entrepreneurial type called Joe Dennehy got together with Grant Hislop, the founder of Coastline FM, and set up Rock 93 FM in Hamilton using one of the new frequencies. Rock 93 played nothing but rock music, and it quickly made big inroads in that city against the more broadly targeted legacy stations, Kiwi FM and Radio New Zealand's 1ZH. The Rock guys then purchased a bunch of odds and sods frequencies from the Christian Broadcasting Association, including one which was licensed to broadcast in Ōakura, down the Taranaki coast from New Plymouth.

We thought we were fine, because the 100 FM frequency was nowhere near New Plymouth. Imagine our surprise when Nevada Resources (the formal name for the Rock 93 crew) managed to have the Ōakura frequency re-engineered into the New Plymouth market without it being returned for a new tender. They simply had to pay the ministry for the increased audience value of the shift. In 1993, just after seeing off Q90 FM, we were faced with a new rock station, Rock 100 FM, competing with our mother ship in the middle of New Plymouth.

We decided it was time to test out this new regulatory regime and arm ourselves with new frequencies before more people came after us. We asked for two new frequencies in each of Taranaki and the Bay of Plenty. In response the ministry came up with three full-powered frequencies in Taranaki and one in Tauranga. We were able to secure two of the Taranaki frequencies, and Radio Pacific won the other one. We missed out in Tauranga, but weren't too worried because we'd received a second frequency when we bought Coastline.

It was time to do some strategic thinking. What did all this mean for the shape of radio in a decade's time? Peter and I got together and whiteboarded some options with our directors. By now we were learning there was no shortage of FM frequencies, with potentially ten or more available in each regional market. We also knew that audiences loved choice, so new stations would continue to enter each market and fragment audiences. No matter how good your top 40 station was, some people would prefer a rock station instead, or an easy-listening station, or country music. The days of radio stations with audience shares of 30 to 40 per cent in regional markets were numbered.

Our third truism was that fragmentation was bad for advertising sales. As radio audiences fragmented, our old foes in the newspaper industry rubbed their hands with glee. They would be able to sell far bigger audiences to advertisers than any individual radio station. That was troubling for radio's financial viability.

We weren't able to look for inspiration overseas because New Zealand was in uncharted territory. I tried to explain the situation once at a National Association of Broadcasters convention in the US, and was looked at like I was from another planet.

The more we thought about it, the more the answer seemed to be to 'multiplex' radio stations, effectively housing two or more radio brands under one roof with a common sales team, creative team and support services. It seems obvious now but at the time it was revolutionary. A Brierley's guy in Auckland, Josh Easby, was trying it with Radio Hauraki, Radio I and some other Auckland stations, and getting slammed for it by the traditionalists, who called it 'the Warehouse model' of radio, after the eponymous red sheds. While that might have been a reasonable debate to have in Auckland, in regional markets it seemed likely to be the only way to survive and thrive.

We decided to set up a new station in each of Tauranga and Taranaki, targeting 35–54-year-olds, with what is known as adult contemporary, or easy-listening, music. They would complement the pop/rock format of Energy and Coastline. Taranaki's Easy 98 FM and Tauranga's Bay 99.8 FM were launched in 1993, and the

RadioWorks-branded sales team was launched at the same time as the umbrella brand for the two stations in each market. They were an instant success with advertisers.

The Nevada boys were attracting a committed audience with Rock 100 in Taranaki, but obtaining advertising revenue was much more difficult. In fact we heard they were financially stretched in a number of ways. They'd launched a second station in Hamilton called The Buzzard, which was designed to take audience share off Kiwi FM. They'd also bought 50 per cent of a third station, Radio Waikato, and built an expensive recording studio. We decided to approach them to see if they were interested in selling.

In short they were, although it didn't end up being straight-forward. We did a deal, with payment in two instalments, and it turned out their financials were worse than they had realised, or had represented to us. We took over in mid-1994 with Joe and Grant staying on to run Hamilton, but things were going from bad to worse. Once we had more accurate accounts, it was clear that Nevada was losing around $30,000 a month, which was a lot for our company to bear.

We sorted out Taranaki first of all, moving Rock 100 into the RadioWorks Building on Devon Street. It was a tight fit running three radio stations from a studio complex built for one, but it did work. From an advertising perspective it was a little monster; the three stations covered the market under 50 years, and our revenue climbed significantly.

To sort out Waikato, the board agreed that I should go to Hamilton and work with the guys to turn things around, while Don stayed to run Taranaki. The very day I arrived, Joe Dennehy resigned, and Grant Hislop did the same a short time later.

Turning around the Hamilton operation was a huge effort. We had to terminate the Radio Waikato arrangements, which were a big financial drain every month. Many of the clients had ceased advertising and trust had to be rebuilt. The Buzzard was not a financial or ratings success. We decided to relaunch it in the style of Energy FM and Coastline FM, but targeting a slightly younger demographic. In late 1994, The Edge was born, with Martin Devlin and Taranaki girl Jay-Jay Feeney on breakfast.

Jay-Jay was a home-grown Energy FM talent, the first of a bunch we developed over the years, including The Rock's Brad King, The Edge's Leon Wratt, and Jolene James from The Breeze. Jay-Jay came to work for us while still a student at New Plymouth Girls' High School, starting off by sorting records. She graduated to midnight-to-dawn shifts and then to nights, before moving to Hamilton for a slot on Kiwi FM, and then back to us when we launched The Edge.

The Edge was deliberately colloquial and anarchic. It was the antidote to the jolly-hockey-sticks style of the RNZ ZM stations, and was full of talented young broadcasters pushing the boundaries to find the line of acceptability. I was regularly drawn in to solve issues raised by those slighted by their antics, including unplanned promotions like 'National Fill Up and Drive Away Free Day' (exactly as it sounds), 'National Free Smokes Day' (ditto), and 'Nude Tennis' on Victoria Street (thankfully not quite as it sounds).

The Edge's most famous sanctioned promo was 'Two Strangers and a Wedding' which was a huge success over several years. But the one I remember most was the day Jay-Jay and her long-term co-host Brian Reid (who went by the pseudonym Butt-Ugly Bob) rang Paul Holmes while he was on air on ZB and Jay-Jay pretended to be Paul's then girlfriend, fearful of the paparazzi. Paul fell for it hook, line and sinker, clearly believing the call was genuine. The ensuing conversation between Paul and his presumed lover was priceless radio, and such a successful prank that Jay-Jay and Bob became nervous and hung up before the great reveal. Afterwards there was a stunned silence, before Bob said to their audience, 'Okay, nobody tell Paul Holmes that was us!' Needless to say, the legal letter arrived in my office before the team came off air, threatening all sorts of dire consequences including criminal charges. Paul only calmed down weeks later when journalist Brian Edwards wrote an opinion piece, reminding Paul that he himself had behaved similarly back in the days of shows like the Coca-Cola All Nighter.

The more time I spent in the Waikato, the more it became clear that the company should be run from there. It was twice the size of Taranaki or Tauranga by population, and roughly halfway between them geographically. It was a much more competitive market and it needed serious attention, but it would likely also generate serious returns once we got everything right. We rebranded as RadioWorks Waikato, and the board and I agreed I'd base myself in Hamilton.

I really enjoyed my time there. Once we got The Edge and The Rock honking along equally, they monstered the Waikato radio market for the next several years, scoring a lock on the under-40s, in a region with a young population. The entry into our third market was rough at the beginning, but it ultimately came right.

Our second big strategic step after embracing multiplexed radio stations was to help pioneer the digitisation of radio in New Zealand. In the early 1990s, radio studios were still being run on analogue tapes and cart machines, which played professional tape cassettes in quick succession. The only nod to digital technology was playing some music on CDs, and every studio still had at least one turntable and a couple of reel-to-reel tape machines for pre-recording phone calls and news bulletins.

Running three analogue radio stations in one organisation was proving hellishly hard in a region as small as Taranaki but, fortunately, the world was just beginning to explore digital storage and playback. We'd been impressed with a young guy working for Radio Otago in Dunedin called Craig Vause, who was at the leading edge of computer automation in radio. We decided to hire him to digitise and automate our three stations in Taranaki.

Craig did a great job. I will never forget the tower of computer cases needed to stack together what was at that time an almost unheard of 27 gigabytes of data needed to store the music and ads for Energy FM, Easy 98 and Rock 100. Craig went on to digitise the whole RadioWorks operation over seven years. He ultimately blotted his copybook getting into legal trouble with RadioWorks well after I left, and that was a real disappointment. He was a great talent and a secret weapon in the growth of our business.

THE OLDER, MORE TRADITIONAL RADIO companies balked at buying the new frequencies that came up for tender, seeing the outlay as another government tax on their business. They also believed in the power of their brands to repel all comers. We, on the other hand, embraced the opportunity. In one memorable tender in 1995 we picked up three Manawatū frequencies, one from Waikato, one from Tauranga, and three from Rotorua, all for less than $600,000. The three Rotorua ones cost us $45,000 all up. A few months later we bought a Hawke's Bay one for $45,000. They really were ridiculously cheap prices. The challenge would be coming up with the cash to light up these frequencies.

The biggest radio industry news in 1996 was the sale of the government's commercial radio stations to a consortium part-owned by US radio giant Clear Channel Communications. They also purchased the old Brierley assets in Auckland and Hamilton, giving them something like 60 per cent of the New Zealand radio market. That sent a shiver through the rest of the industry. How would we all compete with a leviathan like that? Not long after, Doug Gold's More FM network was sold to the Canadian broadcaster CanWest Global, and Brent Impey left Radio Pacific, where he was general counsel, to become chief executive.

For our part, we'd been working on a deal to buy the North Island stations of Radio Otago. They were in a messy state. Radio Otago was making a small profit in each of Tauranga, Rotorua and Taupō, and losing all of that and more in Hawke's Bay, which had become a disastrous radio market with advertising being sold well below cost. We were about to put real pressure on Radio Otago in Tauranga, and we had three frequencies up our sleeves in Rotorua.

I got on well with Radio Otago's new chief executive Sussan Turner, and I met her in Tauranga to show her around the new multiplex studios we were building. Part of the tour was having another chance to chat with her, and the other part was a not-so-subtle attempt to show her we had big plans in the town. I needn't have worried. Sussan was receptive. Our challenge was how to fund a purchase.

It was about this time that Derek Lowe and I started to have discussions about merging our two companies. Radio Pacific was publicly listed on the New Zealand Stock Exchange and was an excellent financial performer. It had one networked talk station with frequencies the length and breadth of the country. Its success was underpinned by a cornerstone shareholding held by the TAB, and an agreement which gave Pacific the sole right and responsibility to broadcast horse racing on radio, in return for a sizeable fee. Pacific was throwing off cash, but acknowledged that its operating model was approaching its limit.

RadioWorks, on the other hand, had more opportunities to grow than we had funds to deploy. Our three music formats were very popular in the three regions we operated in, and we had all those frequencies in Rotorua, Palmerston North and Hawke's Bay. It made strategic sense to bring the two companies together. One thing led to another, and we merged RadioWorks into Radio Pacific in April 1997.

Derek and I were very careful to keep the culture of the two companies separate in those initial stages. RadioWorks would be a separate subsidiary with a separate board, while Norton Moller and I would also sit on the main board, which would make the final investment decisions. With Radio Pacific's cash, the RadioWorks growth plan could really take off.

Before the ink was dry on the merger deal, we completed a cash deal with Radio Otago to buy their North Island stations. In one transaction, RadioWorks was now in seven North Island regional markets. Over the first 36 hours Sussan and I did a quick tour of the five Otago stations to meet the new staff. Most were happy, except the Classic Rock team in Tauranga, who were very worried for their futures given the RadioWorks operation there. We solved that by taking on the Classic Rock manager John Bedford as the head of the combined operation in the city, while my business partner Pete took on a group sales role.

The next part of the strategy was to start networking the more niche music stations via satellite. We'd been planning to do that for some time but had held off, partly to maintain a strong local presence for The Rock in Hamilton, which was now our largest local market. With all the new markets coming on stream, and Radio Pacific's networking guru John Haynes now part of the wider RadioWorks family, the time was right. We announced the launch of The Rock network in July 1997, initially networking from Hamilton into Tauranga and Taranaki, and then Rotorua, Taupō and Hawke's Bay in quick succession, all before the end of the calendar year.

The Rock was an immediate ratings success in every market it entered, but the politically incorrect style of the breakfast show, The Morning Rumble with Nick Trott and Roger Farrelly, encountered a few serial complainants as it fanned out across the country. While Waikato audiences were accustomed to their earthy 'shock jock' humour, in some regions the show was confronting to new listeners, and that resulted in regular visits to the Broadcasting Standards Authority. At one stage we hired former prime minister Geoffrey Palmer to run a free-speech argument for The Rock with the

BSA. He met with the station's whole on-air team, and expressed enthusiastically, in his academic style, how much he loved their station. 'But if you could just tone down some of the rough edges while I am working with the Authority that would be helpful,' he said. Pressed to be more specific, he said, 'Well, if we could just drop the jokes on bestiality, necrophilia and defecation that would be great.' There was a long pause before Nick said, 'Well, that's basically the whole show.'

We now had a template for the ideal shape of each market we would operate in. There would be one big mid-market local radio station, locally branded, targeting the 25–44-year market and the vehicle for most of the local promotions. Around it we would group the music networks and Radio Pacific, piped in from elsewhere but filling the niches which complemented the big 'LocalWorks' station. The local RadioWorks sales team would sell ads on all the stations. That structure would provide the greatest breadth of audience in the most cost-effective way, and with only one set of local programme costs.

Under the Clear Channel / Brierley merger, the Commerce Commission had forced the new company, The Radio Network, to sell off frequencies in each of Auckland and Hamilton, to ensure fair competition in both markets. TRN sold us two of their Hamilton frequencies, but in Auckland they had been leasing two frequencies, so they simply gave those back to their respective owners. One of the owners was Rob McKay, who we'd come up against back in the days of the Energy FM tribunal hearings. Rob was keen to sell his frequency, but also keen to sell me on the idea of an oldies format of hits from the sixties and seventies targeting the baby boomers. I listened carefully and bought the idea. Solid Gold was born.

Solid Gold was a network from the get-go. We hired some of the old Hauraki stars out of retirement, and launched with the legendary Blackie (Kevin Black) on breakfast and Tony Amos on drive. We pumped it into Waikato, Taranaki, the Bay of Plenty, Rotorua and Hawke's Bay as well as Auckland. In doing so we were able to close the second local station in each of those towns, and that both improved our cost structures and allowed us to better resource our lead stations. Solid Gold was an instant ratings and revenue hit, and partnered well with Radio Pacific to target the 50-plus market.

Our third music network would be The Edge, which we announced in January 1998, with a roll-out around the country. This one was a little more contentious internally because it required our legacy stations like Energy FM, Coastline FM, Hot 93 FM and Lakes 96 in Rotorua to 'move over' and make room for the more youth-oriented Edge format. It couldn't help but cannibalise the younger end of their audience, but we believed it was better we do it to ourselves than have another network like ZM or CanWest's Channel Z do it to us.

As if that wasn't enough, we were having a long on-again off-again courtship with XS Radio in Palmerston North, which owned the legendary 2XS, plus Hitz FM in Wairarapa and 2XX on the Kāpiti Coast. They could see our plan unfolding, but also had great confidence in 2XS to repel all comers. That purchase ended up co-inciding with a somewhat surreal Ministry of Commerce frequency auction where we were both bidding for one Manawatū frequency. The 2XS board ended up pulling out of that auction midway through and selling us their business. That deal was completed in June 1998.

The pace was exhausting, but in a nice touch I was given the Radio Broadcaster of the Year Award that year for our work merging with Pacific and launching the Rock and Solid Gold networks. It was great to receive the recognition.

Awards nights were always fun, but also busy. We were constantly fending off TRN people seeking to schmooze, and likely hire, our key on-air talent. The Rock boys were reasonably safe because their style was unlikely to be suited to any of the TRN networks.

Jay-Jay Feeney was a different story, and she was constantly being wooed by the programmers at ZM. At one point during one awards evening I was talking with TRN boss Joan Withers, when across the room I could see ZMers swarming around Jay-Jay once more. In desperation I came up with an idea. 'Joan,' I said, 'you know your boys are wasting their time, don't you? Jay-Jay is my niece.'

'Ohhh,' said Joan, the penny dropping. 'That explains it.'

I'd driven Jay-Jay up to Auckland for that awards night, and the next day on the drive home I confessed my sin. Thankfully she saw the funny side, and has been known as my niece ever since.

At the end of 1998 I made another move north, into Auckland, and Derek and I started talking about a new working arrangement. I would become managing director of both RadioWorks and Radio Pacific, and Derek would become the chair of the combined company.

The final piece of the puzzle was the South Island, and the prospect of doing a merger deal with Radio Otago. Since selling the North Island stations, Otago had consolidated in the south, purchasing Fifeshire FM in Nelson and C93 FM in Christchurch. We were having regular catch-ups with Sussan Turner and her board in early 1999, and they could see the logic of bringing the two companies together in a single nationwide network. The sticking point, as always, would be the price.

By then I felt I was becoming more a mergers-and-acquisitions guy than a radio guy. Derek and I, and our numbers man Colin Giffney, worked hard to land on a deal with Otago. It took time, but on 1 August 1999 we completed an all-shares agreement, where Otago shareholders exchanged every four Radio Otago shares for three Radio Pacific group shares. We were there.

Twelve days later the combined group was renamed RadioWorks New Zealand Ltd, and we were off, introducing the RadioWorks network brands around the South Island. The combined entity was a juggernaut in the south, with six stations in each of Christchurch and Dunedin, five each in Invercargill and Nelson, and a mixture of stations in Central Otago in Queenstown. Overall, we had leaped to 650 staff, across eighteen markets.

Notwithstanding all the headlines about buying this and launching that, I was well aware the big job was moulding all the cultures of ten disparate radio companies together under the single umbrella brand of RadioWorks. Fortunately we had been forced to do a lot of work on a RadioWorks system when we first moved into Waikato back in 1994, and as a result had a very useful set of manuals we could pass around that laid out 'how we do things around here'. However, there is no substitute for regular face time and making the effort to explain why you do the things you do.

I was very conscious that once I got on a plane and left, say, Invercargill, the team either would have bought into the plan or would say 'That was a nice visit' and go straight back to doing what they had always done. I therefore spent every spare day I had in 1998, 1999 and 2000 crisscrossing the country visiting and revisiting the managers and staff in each town, selling the vision and embedding the RadioWorks style. We also picked up one more region, buying KCC FM in Northland and a bunch of associated frequencies.

FINALLY THINGS WERE STARTING TO settle down. We could all take a breath and focus on consolidating the programming and sales side of the business. In May of 2000, I headed to Christchurch to guest-lecture at the CPIT Broadcasting School, and then stay on for the national radio conference and that year's radio awards. I liked to meet with the students each year because the school was a rich source of talent. While I was there I got a text message that shocked me. CanWest had launched a raid on the company's shares. They had bought just under 20 per cent from two fund managers, NZ Funds and Spicers, and were seeking to build a 44.8 per cent stake by standing in the market and offering $8.25 a share.

The price was a 23 per cent premium on the overnight closing price of $6.70, which on the face of it looked positive. But we had yet to announce the first full-year results for the merged company, and we knew they would push the value of the company up significantly. Even those results would only include eight months of the Radio Otago South Island stations. The timing of the raid was very opportunistic.

We held a board meeting by phone conference and agreed to immediately release our preliminary full-year results, which showed profit up 41 per cent over the previous year. However, Derek as chair equivocated about issuing a 'Don't Sell' notice, and refused to say whether he might sell some of his own 5 per cent stake, which he had been building up over the previous year. That felt a little ominous to me.

Once I got over the shock, I wanted to fight the takeover. We had just put the company and the new operating model together and there were huge opportunities to grow it further, particularly in Auckland and Wellington, and perhaps ultimately in Australia. I also felt huge loyalty to the staff of the enlarged company who had come on the journey with us. Whether they had started with Energy FM thirteen years before or had joined through one of the mergers, they had all bought into the plan and were making their futures with RadioWorks. We couldn't just sell them down the river.

Unfortunately, fighting back would prove difficult. Many of our new Otago shareholders saw the RadioWorks play as their exit point, and our rapid growth had left the share register open to attack. I myself owned only around 8 per cent. A number of the core Otago shareholders, who had arrived only nine months previously, decided to cash up, and before long CanWest was up to its target of 45 per cent.

Then a further shock. Derek had decided to pull the pin, or more aptly the rug, from under our defence. He announced he was selling his 5 per cent, and that led to another 6 per cent of shareholders selling. Derek's decision was very disappointing. Given he'd been such a huge supporter of me and of the plan, I couldn't help but feel let down, and right at the wrong moment.

CanWest was then up to 56 per cent, and they announced a new bid to go to 70 per cent. It remained a hostile takeover all the way through. They refused to talk to the board or the remaining key shareholders. We had no idea whether they wanted to go to 100 per cent, which seemed increasingly likely, or stop at a majority stake.

Their approach of accumulating one target and then announcing a bigger target was working. At each step of the way, wavering shareholders were told they would miss out if the quota was filled without them. Some would sell, and the offer was then extended. These sorts of tactics were one reason why the New Zealand Stock Exchange was called the Wild West of stock exchanges, and they were prohibited in the new Takeovers Code adopted one year later. Unfortunately, that was too late for us.

The TAB had been holding out with their 12 per cent, but finally they sold. Their RadioWorks shares had become a big investment for them as the share price had grown, and the racing industry wanted the money for its own capital spending. CanWest reached 70 per cent, but were still short of two important targets, the 75 per cent required for a special resolution, and the 90 per cent required to make a compulsory acquisition of the remaining shares. We circled the remaining wagons and refused to sell. It was a stalemate.

The two sides settled into an uneasy truce. I undertook to show the new majority Canadian owners around, and I spent some time explaining what they had purchased. I sensed the smaller local More FM group, under Brent Impey, were a bit dismissive of RadioWorks and some of the people, and I wanted the Canadians to understand how it all worked, including its strengths and the risks.

CanWest was impatient to integrate its 70-per-cent-owned asset RadioWorks with their 100-per-cent-owned one, More FM. Their New Zealand directors told me they didn't want RadioWorks competing with More FM — the common enemy was TRN. The problem with that instruction was that the directors of RadioWorks clearly had to act in their company's interest, not CanWest's. CanWest placed a majority of directors on the RadioWorks board and I had to regularly remind them they didn't own 100 per cent of the company. They also put together an 'operational committee' to assist with the integration, loaded with More FM executives, who were given access to sensitive sales data.

I worked hard to keep the place together, while behind the scenes CanWest and their advisers went to work on me to sell the rest of the shares. Goldman Sachs made a couple of attempts, as did the lawyers, and Impey as well. They tried cajoling, they tried threatening my employment, they cancelled the company's dividend. Every story was basically the same. There was no more money so I should do the 'decent thing'. I said no. By then I was starting to realise the game was up, but I needed to extract fair value for the remaining loyal shareholders plus decent recognition of the value of RadioWorks staff. Various senior execs at More FM were running around talking to RadioWorks people with a 'we won, you lost' attitude, which was very unsettling.

It was a seven-month war of attrition and it was exhausting. I was accused of being obstructive, betraying the staff and shareholders, and so on. Then, finally, a breakthrough. Realising we weren't going anywhere, CanWest agreed to talk.

The upshot was a new offer of $9.35 a share for the remaining shares they didn't hold. With a total of around 12 million shares, that valued the whole company at $112 million. The revenue for the full 2001 year was predicted to be $57 million with a pre-tax profit of around $10 million. It wasn't perfect but it was probably enough.

My sense was that we had done all we could to halt the original rush of blood to the head for the conquering managers. We decided it was time to stop standing in the path of the inevitable and agreed to sell.

It all happened very quickly after that. CanWest offered to keep me on to head up the combined radio business, but I was done. I resigned, effective the first week of April. I did a tour of the country, personally thanking the staff, and then left the building on Friday, 6 April 2001, one day before my thirty-eighth birthday.

The radio dream had been a wonderful seventeen-year roller-coaster ride. It had taken me to places I had never dreamed of back when we had wanted to just play some decent music on the radio. But it was clearly over.

Chapter Three
After radio

IT WAS TIME TO TAKE STOCK. What did I want to do for the next stage of my life? I'd never had time to think much about my 'future plans' as they had always involved building the radio company. It felt like I'd been motoring along happily and then someone had pulled the handbrake on, real hard.

To say I was discombobulated was an understatement. I was very confused. I still had adrenaline flowing, but there was nothing to fight for. I suddenly had no direction, compared with the absolute mission I had been on before. I was a bit stuffed.

CanWest were keen to offer me a new role, but I was too bruised to work for them. I tried to consider it. They wanted me to run their billboard company in Australia, and flew me across to Sydney to discuss the idea.

I don't remember much about the interview, but I do remember the feeling I had walking through the city afterwards. It was a busy afternoon and I became caught in a crowd of people in the underground walkway that leads to the Queen Victoria Building. I felt claustrophobic and hemmed in. It wasn't Sydney — I love that city. I had the presence of mind to realise this was my visceral reaction to the idea of taking up a leadership role with the Canadians after everything that had happened. I couldn't do it. I rang and turned them down before I flew back to Auckland.

I made myself busy in the meantime renovating my house in Bayswater. It was a lovely 1920s French villa on the cliff looking back over to the city — reputedly once the French Consul's summer house. It didn't make the most of the south-facing city views, so I had a new two-storey verandah built with French doors, as well as an in-ground swimming pool and new gardens. The pièce de résistance (or folly, if you will) was a circular wrought-iron staircase between the upper and lower verandahs.

My then partner, Vicky, had stayed working at RadioWorks after I left. She said the busyness I had generated at the office had been transferred to our home; where previously she had come home to relax, now she went to the office.

I was all at sea about what to do next. I had a few sessions with Steve Saunders, a psychologist colleague in Hamilton who had helped with motivational training for the RadioWorks sales team, to try to identify some priorities. He started off talking to me about learning to relax, and suggested I sit in a cafe and read a book mid-morning on a Monday and marvel at everyone scurrying about. I did that, once, and it was great — but not a solution.

I made a list of things that I'd never had time to do in those seventeen hectic radio years. The list included travelling overseas, joining a gym, having a family and joining a political party.

The gym part was quite straightforward, apart from not having done any exercise at all since varsity days. I found an excellent trainer and, after a very slow start, eventually ended up fit enough to run half-marathons, which I enjoyed, and which lasted until I found my next mission in life.

Travelling was high on the list. I loved travelling and had never done an OE. Apart from a few trips to radio conventions in the

US, I'd only had one holiday of any length, in all my time in radio, to England and France in the mid-nineties. I took a seven-week trip around the US and parts of Europe in late 2001, coincidentally leaving New York just a few days before September 11, and being grounded in Los Angeles for a week while it all unfolded. A second trip in 2002 covered France and Spain.

Another thing on the bucket list was finally graduating from Massey University. I had completed my zoology degree nearly twenty years ago, but never bothered to collect the piece of paper proving I'd done it. There was a bunch of us who professed at the end of their degrees, as only twenty-year-olds can, that graduating was all very passé and bourgeois, and we would pass on it. It turns out I was the only one who had followed through on that agreement. All my friends meekly went home and turned up the following May with their families for graduation. By the time I realised they had capitulated it was too late for me to apply, so I missed out.

I then got swept up in radio and the importance of actually graduating receded, until here we were, nearly twenty years later. I had by now realised that graduating wasn't just about me, it was also for my family, and my parents in particular. I had, after all, been the first in my family to attend university, and Mum and Dad were very proud, or would have been if I'd given them the opportunity.

That's how I found my 39-year-old self walking through the streets of Takapuna in the Massey University capping parade in 2002, in front of my parents and a few close friends, very much standing out from the crowd of early twenty-somethings, finally graduating with a BSc in Zoology.

A few of my fellow graduands asked me about my degree and why they hadn't seen me on campus at Albany, as there weren't many zoologists there, and I seemed, well, older. I started to tell them but it was a long story.

Having a family wouldn't be straightforward. My relationship was deteriorating, and my partner wasn't keen on more children anyway, already having a teenage son. We were to eventually embark on a tortuous break-up.

Joining a political party was easier. I'd always had an interest in politics and in helping the country and its people be more successful. Like many people, I was frustrated at some of the political decisions made on our behalf. It seemed to me that most politicians had their hearts in the right place, but their actions, particularly in the economic space, often made things worse rather than better. They seemed unaware of the law of unintended consequences. I was also frustrated at the state of our infrastructure, and our education and health systems. Surely we could do better than we were doing?

The question was, which party? Given my background and beliefs about things like individual freedom, personal responsibility, and people being rewarded for their effort, it boiled down to a choice between National and ACT.

While I was attracted to some of ACT's policies, it could be a little uncompromising and doctrinaire, and in my experience the world was a little more complicated and nuanced. Ultimately ACT's role was to be a fringe-ideas party, like the Greens but on the right. National was more mainstream, and a bit more likely to compromise and accept that the world often wasn't as simple as it seemed. It was also more likely to be in a position to get things done. On the other hand, National had a reputation for considering itself the natural party of government, and its critics said its philosophy in government was nothing more than to 'keep the other guys out' and maintain the status quo.

I even ummed and ahhed about joining a political party at all. I had never really been a 'joiner' and until then my politics had been very personal. It felt uncomfortable signing up to a party and waving my flag publicly as a member of that tribe. I was conscious that once I joined a party, a whole bunch of people would simply discount my views because of the logo on my shirt.

I experimented with forming a lobby group instead, and got together with some like-minded centre-right types to form a group called 'Silent Majority', with the express aim of developing and advocating for sensible policies which would improve New Zealand, without participating directly in the process. We launched a rather over-engineered blog-type website to convey our ideas and views, but to me it felt a little too 'one step removed' from the political process.

I think a lot of people have apprehensions about joining a political party, but parties also need members, and, after all, politics is real. If parties don't have ordinary people as members they risk becoming echo chambers for fringe and extreme views. Swallowing my reservations, I met my local MP, Wayne Mapp, and signed up for National.

The next question was how to contribute. As a result of the sale of my RadioWorks shares I was in the fortunate position of not needing to work for some time, and I was quite keen to 'give something back' to the country which had provided me my opportunities in life. I considered standing for Parliament in the 2002 election. Steve Saunders was not keen on my behalf. His pithy advice was that if I wanted to 'do' community service I should get married and have kids, and that would involve me in all the community service I could handle.

Wayne Mapp put me in touch with East Coast Bays MP Murray McCully, new National Party President Michelle Boag and Northern Regional Chair Scott Simpson. Scott suggested that if I was thinking of standing I should have a chat with the Helensville electorate people, who were underwhelmed with their existing MP, Brian Neeson, and considering selecting someone new.

I trekked out to West Harbour to meet with Beverley Revell, who was a bit of a mover and shaker in the electorate. We had a good chat, and she confided they already had their candidate, a merchant banker returning from overseas by the name of John Key. I had no idea who he was, but they seemed pretty enamoured with him. I left realising that Helensville would likely not be an option for me.

I knew Murray from my radio days, and he and Michelle suggested I put my name forward as a list candidate. The party had a quaint idea about list candidates at that point, with every electorate able to nominate a list candidate as well as an electorate candidate. I was duly nominated by the North Shore electorate as their list representative. Whether I made it into Parliament would depend on the all-important ranking of the party list.

As 2002 began, National had high hopes for the election. It had a new leader, Bill English, who had replaced Jenny Shipley in September the previous year. Bill had an initial bump in the polls pre-Christmas, but Helen Clark's government steadily reasserted itself in the first quarter of 2002, regularly polling above 50 per cent.

Meanwhile I was having second thoughts about standing for Parliament. I had been slowly adjusting to a more relaxed pace in my post-radio life. I used to describe the experience of de-stressing like peeling an onion. Each month I would feel more relaxed and healthy, so much better than the month before. And then a month later I would feel even more healthy, and I'd look back at the previous month thinking how wound up I had still been.

I was happier, calmer and in a much more positive frame of mind. Diving into Parliament now, should I be successful, would feel a lot like jumping back into the fire. After lots of thought and a couple of chats with Murray and one with Michelle, I withdrew from the list. As it turned out, it wouldn't have made any difference. The result of the 2002 election meant it was virtually impossible for me to have been given a winnable position on the list wherever I'd been placed, so angsting over whether I should have stood was a bit academic.

Helen Clark took advantage of Labour's high polling and in

mid-June called a snap election for 27 July 2002. She didn't achieve the absolute majority she was looking for, but she did succeed in making the election all about who would be Labour's coalition partner rather than who would win the Treasury benches. With that framing, the National Party was superfluous, and also ill-prepared for the campaign. In a calamitous result it sank to its lowest-ever share of the vote (20.9 per cent), and its lowest number of seats in Parliament, just 27 out of 120. It was a train smash.

The media was brutal, and Labour was triumphant. It certainly wasn't a good time to be a new member of the National Party. With the rise of New Zealand First (thirteen seats) and United Future (eight seats), plus ACT's retention of nine seats, there was even some public debate, slightly mischievous perhaps, about whether National could truly be considered to be leading the Opposition. A crestfallen Bill English immediately committed to a full and honest campaign review, and the party got on with organising it.

Michelle Boag called me a few days later and asked me to chair the 2002 campaign review. She told me the party's National Management Board believed I was the ideal person to lead it given my background in business, marketing and advertising. It would be a three-person review, and I would be assisted by the former Awarua MP Jeff Grant and Auckland barrister Denese Henare, who was also the spouse of Wayne Mapp. I had the time, so I agreed to do it. We were given six weeks.

The three of us wasted no time, going up and down the country meeting the National Party faithful wherever we went. I had the most unencumbered diary, so I ended up talking to pretty much every member who wanted to have their say; sometimes with Denese alongside, sometimes with Jeff, and sometimes on my own.

I was under no illusions about how I came to get my role. There were two factions around the presidency of the National Party at that time. Michelle Boag had beaten John Slater in a rancorous election in 2001. John broadly represented the 'East Auckland' establishment wing of the National Party, centred around Rob Muldoon's old Tāmaki electorate, plus Remuera, Pakuranga and Howick. Michelle, on the other hand, represented the upstarts of the North Shore electorates, predominantly centred around wily East Coast Bays MP Murray McCully. The party was still bruised from that presidential contest, and the wounds had been reopened by the 2002 election debacle. I realised I had been chosen, as much as anything else, because I was a political clean skin with no allegiance to either side.

Jeff, a fellow Southlander to Bill, was at least partly there to protect Bill's interests, while Denese was there on behalf of the North Shore wing of the party. That's not to denigrate their role — they were both and are still very much their own people. It's just the way political parties and many politicians think.

The party was very badly damaged by the mauling it had taken in the election. Volunteers and party staff poured their hearts out about the state of the campaign. I took an early trip to Wellington where I was greeted by Bill's chief adviser Tim Grafton, and Deputy Leader Roger Sowry. Tim gave me a detailed and cross-referenced dossier that amounted to his own review of the campaign, while Roger took me over the road to the Backbencher pub, bringing along some staff to tell their stories. I'll never forget sitting between two intense and passionate National Party staffers, a young woman called Megan Campbell, and another called Nikki Kaye, as they laid out their frustrations and concerns for the party. My overriding memory was their relentless advocacy for their points of view, a relentlessness I would have cause to recall in later years.

Up and down the country the story was different versions of the same narrative. The party was broken and at a loss about how to rebuild. After a couple of weeks of listening, I realised we would need to be very careful with our report as we risked completely breaking up this organisation. It was that vulnerable. We needed to meet the expectations of members that the review be thorough and unflinching, while not taking sides or fuelling internal debates.

Within six weeks we had a draft document, largely authored by yours truly. The three of us then gathered in Wellington at the InterContinental Hotel at about six o'clock on a Friday evening to review the manuscript and make final changes, before I was to brief Bill over breakfast the next morning. We turned our phones off and meticulously massaged our language and the recommendations, to make sure the report truly reflected our thoughts.

We knew both Michelle's position as president and Bill's as leader were hanging by a thread. We didn't want our words to be used to kick off a putsch against them, either in the caucus or in the wider party. Our emerging view was that the party's problems were bigger than any individual, and a quick attempt to change personnel would not solve the problem. While not arguing against any particular change, we didn't want this report to be the cause of it. It was a very fine line we were walking.

We finished our editing and polishing at about 10 p.m. and turned our phones back on. They all started pinging immediately with a string of voice messages. While we had been obliviously beavering away, Michelle Boag had gone on *Holmes* at 7 p.m. and announced her resignation as party president.

At one level all our thoughtful massaging of the report was instantly for nowt. The report's mere existence had helped precipitate Michelle's resignation. We sat down and discussed our conclusions one more time. We decided they would stand. The report was the report.

The next morning I met with Bill and took him through our summary. I had only met him once before, when he came to see Derek Lowe and me when we were chair and CE of RadioWorks. At that stage it was late in the term of the Bolger / Shipley government and they were casting around for ideas to hold back the tide of Helen Clark and Michael Cullen. He wanted to test the idea of National endorsing Labour's bid for a non-commercial youth radio network, which would have played havoc with our commercial Edge and Rock networks. Our feedback was unvarnished and uncompromising — we thought it was a crappy way to waste public money and we said so.

Bill listened carefully that Saturday morning as I took him through the key conclusions of the campaign review. Over the preceding three years, the party's brand had become confused and voters no longer knew what it stood for. The party had clearly been caught unprepared for the snap election, and its fundraising, policy and candidate selection were underdone. The campaign management and governance had been muddled and had collapsed under pressure. Slogans were switched and advertising material was inconsistent.

There had been no discernible campaign for the party vote, with candidates doing too much of their own thing. In a memorable example, former Party President Sue Wood, campaigning in the Mana electorate, hadn't even used the party's logo and colours in her campaign billboards or collateral. She wasn't the only one. It was as if many candidates were embarrassed to be associated with the National Party. Finally, and most importantly, we believed the party structure was unsuited to campaigning in the new MMP era. A full structural review of the party organisation was needed.

Bill took all of this pretty well, coming as it did from a party neophyte. He took a few notes, and was unflinching in his self-criticism. He thanked me for the report and told me the job of the party was to act on it.

I met the party's National Management Board the following Tuesday and presented our formal report. They had hastily elected Central North Island Regional Chair Judy Kirk as president to replace Michelle Boag. Judy received the report and thanked us for our assistance. That night an opinion poll was released saying the National Party was polling at 18 per cent.

A few days later I left on a long-planned holiday to Europe.

Chapter Four
Party rebuild

THE PHONE CALL CAME WHEN I was travelling through France on a train. It was Judy Kirk. The National Management Board had decided to proceed with the structural review and they wanted me to come back to run it, this time on my own. I arrived back in New Zealand in late October 2002 and launched into it shortly afterwards. The board had released a first discussion document in my absence. My job was to collect feedback and shape a solution.

By then the party was picking itself up off the floor and ideas for change were coming thick and fast. All sorts of things were being proposed, from changing the brand and the party colours through to giving up the tradition of mass membership. There were proposals to allow people to be 'supporters' rather than 'members', or to relax the rules to permit members to belong to any number of parties, in a belief that it was consistent with MMP. Internationally, there was a trend towards giving party members a say in choosing the leader of a political party, and party pollster David Farrar was part of a group seeking that change as part of the review.

I went around the country a couple of times, firstly collecting a round of submissions based on that first discussion document, and then again to collect reactions to a set of draft recommendations. I interviewed hundreds of people individually or in groups, and received 150 written submissions. With the help of President Judy and the board, I distilled all the ideas and feedback into five groups of changes.

Firstly, we had to modernise and simplify what the party stood for. Over time National had built up a long, rambling list of written principles, full of clauses and sub-clauses no doubt wrangled over for years at annual conferences. It ran to one and a half closely typewritten, and sometimes contradictory, pages. At some point members had even added a summary list which read differently to the main list. It was highly unlikely anyone had ever read them in full, and nobody much referred to them at all.

We distilled them down and proposed a simplified list of nine values and an overarching vision for a 'prosperous and successful New Zealand which provided opportunities for all New Zealanders to reach their goals and dreams'. The aim was not to change the National Party's DNA but to make it clear and visible to members. We were under no illusion that a stated set of principles was a substitute for the actions of the caucus, but we felt that without that base there was no strategic underpinning for the party's existence.

Secondly, we proposed to reaffirm the party as a mass membership political movement which was focused on strengthening the value of party membership. We wanted to do that by giving members a greater say in the development of policies they were interested in and in the selection of candidates. The world was entering a period of flatter structures and individuals having more say. Nobody was likely to be happy any more to simply elect a delegate who then selected a candidate on their behalf. Electorates should be given the option of using universal suffrage amongst their members to select candidates, as an alternative to the old branch delegate system. We also sought to affirm the condition that party members must not belong to any other party at the same time as being a member of the National Party. We wanted to strengthen the party, not weaken it.

The next important change was to strengthen the role of electorate organisations and the national body in running the party and fighting election campaigns. This was crucial in the new MMP environment. Over the years, the party's power had become concentrated in five regional divisions, led by all-powerful regional chairs and regional councils. These regional powerhouses all had different views on marketing, campaigning, candidate selections and party lists. Regional organisations were stuffed full of regional delegates made up of former electorate officials who had 'done their time' and were now content with attending regional meetings and mentoring (read as holding up scorecards on) new officeholders, leaving the actual electoral work to the newbies.

All the money and people power was currently collected at the one level within the organisation that had the smallest role in actually fighting and winning elections. It had worked fine under the first-past-the-post electoral system when there were many more electorates and national election results were determined electorate by electorate. Regions helped electorates to succeed, and supported the most important electorates.

Under MMP the only vote that determines the make-up of Parliament is the nationwide party vote. MMP elections are fought nationally first and then on the ground at electorate level, not in the regions. Yet the National Party head office at that time consisted of a sole director-general, a receptionist, an IT person and a part-time semi-retired accountant, with most staff employed by the regions. At the national level, all meetings were a trade-off between the interests of the different divisions and myriad special-interest groups. The only person with any sort of nationwide mandate to represent the party interests as a whole was the directly elected president.

We proposed a number of rule changes that would strengthen

electorate organisations, and drive senior volunteers back into helping in their electorates. Regions would still exist, but as collections of electorates working together, not a tier of the party in their own right. All party staff would be run by a strengthened national office working under a general manager, geared to fight a nationwide MMP campaign. The upgraded national office would run in semi-permanent campaign mode, growing the membership, fundraising and supporting the electorates.

The biggest organisational change would be to the party's board. Instead of a large management board where each person was elected by and accountable to a different chunk of the party, all board members would be elected by the party membership at large, so their accountability would be to the whole party. The board would include the party leader and a second representative from the caucus. The elected board would then choose one of their number to be president, in a 'chair of the board' type model.

I was particularly hot on the changes needed to the party's governance and staff. In my view, for National to operate and campaign successfully under MMP, it needed a singular nationwide focus, with all board members representing the party at large. I'm a great believer in form following function, and if you believe that the first role of a New Zealand political party is to win MMP elections, then the resources and effort need to be focused on where that is done, nationally first and then on the ground in electorates.

It was also clear that over the years, and not just in 2001, the party membership had wasted huge energy pulling itself apart internally over who would get to be president of the party. The president was, after all was said and done, the administrative head of the organisation, not a politician. Their job was to get the fundraising done, support the members and get the party elected. The party was wasting too much time arguing amongst itself about who got to be the administrative leader.

A 'first amongst equals' party president, elected by the board, would lower the significance of the presidential role relative to the board as a whole. The party would likely operate more professionally and evenly, without swinging wildly from president to president. Board members would also develop a good understanding through attending meetings as to who amongst their number was best placed to lead them.

These governance changes were consistent with reforms being made by many volunteer-based non-profit and charitable organisations around that time.

Policy development was the fourth area of change. While the old-fashioned conference remit system was retained, it was clear the party needed a better mechanism for involving party members in broader policy development. We came up with the idea of policy advisory groups, where like-minded party members and those with specific knowledge of a policy area would get together and work with caucus spokespeople to help develop the party's policy for that area. The Bluegreens, the National Party's advisory group on environmental issues, are a particularly good example of that approach.

Finally, there were changes proposed to the candidate selection process. The critical change was limiting each electorate to one candidate, who would be required to stand as both the electorate candidate and the list candidate. Under the old system roughly 130 candidates, two per electorate, would be ranked just prior to an election, with the majority of them having no show of being elected, even in a good year. This would leave 70 to 80 people with their hopes dashed just at the time the organisation needed all its able-bodied volunteers working on the election campaign. At a time of heightened media interest, there was every chance at least one of the disappointed candidates would 'go rogue'. Far better to have a more realistic number being nominated into the top of the funnel, rather than disappoint everyone later.

Including all electorate candidates on the list would also stop independent-minded MPs or candidates seeking to shun the party list, something which had become a popular sport. Having a significant number of senior people refusing to appear on the list couldn't fail to make the party look disunited at the wrong time.

We proposed up to five board-nominated list-only candidate positions. These could be reserved for exceptional individuals or senior MPs seeking to retire from their electorates to focus on their national responsibilities.

A key personal initiative of Party President Judy Kirk was setting up a candidate college to develop and train prospective candidates. The plan was to socialise potential candidates as much as possible with party stalwarts before they were selected as a party candidate. This would help them to get to know the party and the party to get to know them, minimising the chance of candidates getting selected who were unaware of their obligations, or who wouldn't fit with the party's values.

We proposed leaving the mechanical process by which candidates were selected largely unchanged, aside from the option of allowing all electorate members to vote for their preferred candidate. Selections have always been proudly led by each local electorate, and that principle was retained along with associated rules which had been sharpened over time through a series of legal challenges. We just didn't have time to start playing around with those. A number of people have commented since the reforms that the party's selection methods were compromised through the reform process — which simply wasn't the case.

We did seek to introduce a minimum membership threshold for each electorate (200 members), below which a candidate would be chosen primarily by the party board rather than the local electorate organisation. This was to prevent electorates with tiny memberships foisting a completely unsuitable candidate on the wider party.

We thought this rule would also serve to encourage a focus on membership growth in small electorates, and that turned out to be the case. Plenty of strongly Labour-held electorates were suddenly able to muster 200 National Party members so they could have a say in the selection of a candidate to represent them.

I went on a roadshow to discuss the changes with as many party members in as many electorates as possible. As a political newbie it would amaze me how members could spend their evenings passionately debating the different governance and operating models. Sometimes I'd pinch myself when it was after 9.30 p.m. before I'd completed a particularly lively meeting in a draughty hall miles from anywhere.

There was a rearguard action by a number of people to take up the idea of members being given a vote on who the party leader should be. It was thoroughly debated but ultimately not adopted. I, for one, was uncomfortable with it. The only time it would have an impact would be when the party membership took a different view to the party caucus on who the leader should be. If that happened, the caucus would be being led by someone they didn't respect enough to elect as leader themselves. I thought that way led to a divided caucus and instability.

The caucus choosing the leader wasn't a perfect system — mistakes could no doubt be made and have been from time to time. The frequent changes in National's leadership following Bill English's retirement in 2018 are examples of how fraught this decision can be. Nobody would argue that moving from Simon Bridges to Todd Muller and on to Judith Collins all within three years was ideal preparation for the 2020 election campaign. But at least the caucus would have it within its power to correct mistakes. It was surely a 'least worst' system.

The Labour parties in New Zealand and Australia, and both the Conservatives and Labour in the UK, all eventually adopted the approach of membership (and in some cases union) representation in leadership contests. Most of those selections haven't proven to be successful (think Bill Shorten, Jeremy Corbyn, David Cunliffe, Andrew Little and Liz Truss), and that particular fad seems likely to be waning now. Interestingly, the change from Andrew Little to Jacinda Ardern was not subject to a membership vote — because it was too close to an election.

The strategic review came to a head at a special constitutional conference held on 12 April 2003 at the old Overseas Passenger Terminal building in Wellington. In the lead-up to the day, Judy Kirk worked the phones, calling in favours from all over the party to support the reforms. It was my first chance to watch a true political operator in action, and it was impressive. Importantly, Bill English and the caucus supported the changes. As the day of the conference dawned, we were as ready as we would ever be.

The Overseas Passenger Terminal building, since turned into swanky apartments, was a long, narrow, draughty affair, with large clear glass windows down either side. It wasn't the perfect venue, but the poor state of the party's finances meant the options were limited. Around 560 delegates turned out to debate 85 separate motions for change to the party's rules and constitution.

Some of the proposals were amended slightly, but most were going through. The governance changes were the most contentious. Each member was given five minutes to speak and they were lining up to debate the relevant remits. It was at that point that former party president Sir George Chapman staged an intervention with an impassioned plea for change. Although he had been president in the seventies and eighties, he was not an old-school conservative. He believed the party needed to move with the times, and set itself up better to fight MMP elections.

I subtly checked my watch a couple of times during Sir George's speech, for that's what it was, and it went well past five minutes, and indeed ten. The timekeeper afterwards told me they didn't have the courage to interrupt him. Anyway, it did the job. The waverers and the old school melted away, and the reforms proceeded.

Judy Kirk chaired the meeting masterfully, ensuring all board members had the opportunity, and responsibility, to move the adoption of different parts of the reform, and calling on suitable speakers, like Sir George, at opportune moments. But the party was ready for change, too. The 2002 result had shocked the members. They collectively knew they had to modernise or be crushed.

That conference adopted the biggest reforms the National Party has seen since it was first created in 1936. All 85 resolutions were passed, either as proposed or amended. The party had started a new chapter.

EVEN BEFORE THE CONFERENCE, JUDY had been floating the idea of me becoming the inaugural general manager of the new party organisation, should the changes be successfully voted in. The pitch went along the lines that I would have helped create the new machine, and I should help teach the party how to drive it. The party's previous director general, Allan Johnston, had not been in the job long and had struggled with the weight of all the reform happening around him. He had left back in December, during the review process.

There was a saying in the National Party around that time: if the president rang you and gave you the speech about 'stepping up for your country', it was called 'being Judy-ed'. I was being relentlessly Judy-ed.

I had definitely not set out to become the chief administrator for a political party, but I had to acknowledge the logic of recruiting one of the architects of the reform to get it underway. I had no pressing family commitments and no time-consuming private-sector role at the time. I agreed to run the party on a four-day-a-week basis for a year, spending about half my time each week in Wellington and half in Auckland. I signed an employment contract on 14 May, a month after the constitutional conference.

I travelled back to Wellington again and quickly realised that the task ahead of me was even bigger than I had thought. The party's professional structure was almost non-existent. It had one receptionist / secretary, Brenda Toner, who was expected to do everything from supporting the president and board through to providing administrative support to the general manager and organising party conferences. Brenda had been a stalwart of the organisation for a long time but had clearly run out of puff.

The party had a part-time financial controller, Barry Jobson, who came in for a couple of days a week and oversaw the party's antiquated manual accounting system, and Ross Browne, who was nominally in charge of the party's IT systems. I say nominally, because in a huge volunteer organisation there was an incredible range of computer systems, and Ross simply didn't have the resources to do much more than be the *piñata* when something went wrong, as it invariably did.

There were seven other staff around the country tied to the various regions. They saw themselves as conference organisers and administrative assistants to the volunteers. Nearly every system was manual, from collecting donations and memberships to registering people for conferences. The party was at least twenty years out of date.

There was nothing to do but roll my sleeves up and get on with things. We needed to reorganise the professional staff, modernise the party's financial management, start fundraising, run membership drives, conduct a policy process and, yes, prepare for an election campaign.

The next election was in a little over two years.

Chapter Five
Getting the machine going

MY FIRST CHALLENGE WAS TO prepare for the party's annual conference at the Hotel Grand Chancellor in Christchurch in July 2003 — just a couple of months away. Organising the constitutional conference in April had almost exhausted the party staff, but this was to be the first big one of the new regime. It would include the first election for the new party board, and the first opportunity to look forward to 2005 with a new structure in place. It had to be a success.

A small group of us effectively bootstrapped the conference, sweating every detail. I had been to only one National Party conference before, which had been hastily arranged in the lead-up to the 2002 election. That was a desultory affair, full of foreboding about the election result, and not much of a model for my first conference as GM. I leaned heavily on Judy Kirk and others for their knowledge in bringing it together.

On the day, it all started well. The organisation wasn't perfect but there were no visible slips. With the help of some comprehensive discussion documents, an excellent line-up of speakers and a great turnout of members, it was proceeding well despite the drubbing the party had received just twelve months before.

Unfortunately, none of that had any chance of being seen beyond the conference hall. Despite a clear sense that the party organisation had turned a corner, a number of delegates obviously believed the parliamentary leadership needed a revamp as well. Chief among them was Pakuranga MP Maurice Williamson, who embarked on a one-man kamikaze mission to disrupt the weekend and attack Bill English's leadership. He was a wrecking ball through the conference, at one stage memorably heading into the lift like a pied piper with his trailing media pack, after declaring 'the boy was still standing on the burning deck'.

The conference media coverage was all about Maurice going feral, and his verdict on Bill English's leadership. Opposition leaders don't get many set-piece opportunities to speak to the public, and the annual party conference is one of them. Maurice's actions were clearly designed to prevent Bill from having that platform.

Much of the party was horrified. Bill had been doing good work steadily rebuilding the party and many wanted to give him more time to turn things around. National had recovered somewhat in the polls from the nadir of 21 per cent at the previous election, reaching 28 per cent by the time of the conference. However, it was still well behind Labour, who were polling between 48 and 50 per cent.

Judy Kirk and I were personally dismayed that our plans to present a more organised, positive National Party had been trashed. There were immediate demands across the party to suspend Maurice from caucus, and that duly happened ten days later.

Judy and I were sent to talk to Maurice's electorate organisation, and we attended a rowdy meeting on a cold Monday night in Pakuranga. There I experienced one of the fundamental truths of politics: the local party organisation will always back their MP. If the relationship is good between the MP and his or her local party members, then the MP can generally do no wrong. If they are having a stoush with Wellington, Wellington is clearly not doing right by their MP. And so it was with Maurice.

It was a torrid discussion. Judy was read her pedigree and the pedigree of Bill English and his deputy, Roger Sowry. It was clear the electorate supported Maurice, but they did respect that Judy had fronted up to talk with them.

One of my enduring memories of that evening is how we finished up with a cup of tea and a biscuit, and people who had been forcefully arguing their case just moments before were suddenly friendly and solicitous as if nothing had happened. As a political novice I was taken aback by the sudden change of temperature. It surprises me even now that people can turn from fiery debaters berating you one minute to being as nice as pie in person to you the next.

It became clearer in subsequent weeks that Maurice's actions were part of a deliberate destabilisation campaign to weaken Bill's role as leader and Roger Sowry as deputy. Roger did himself no favours. His demeanour in caucus and around the party was to tell what he saw as the truth and damn the torpedoes. He wasn't the sort to seek to win a popularity contest, and as a result he wasn't about to. At times his approach could be seen as endearing and funny. Some of his policy speeches were devastatingly accurate and achieved excellent cut-through. At other times he came across like an imperious sergeant major.

One night during the regional conference season in May, there were two conferences on the same weekend. On the Saturday evening Judy and I were driving between Timaru, the location of the Southern conference, and Ashburton, the venue of the Canterbury–Westland conference. The idea had been to have dinner with the good folk of Timaru, and then supper and a drink with the team at Ashburton.

Sowry was in Ashburton and got on the phone to us, providing a colourful blow-by-blow account of what was and wasn't happening at the dinner. Much to Roger's amusement, the entertainment was an old-style accordion orchestra, where the average age of the players would have been about seventy, with some in their eighties. Tongue firmly in cheek, Roger wanted me to see the band so I could hire them to play at the new-look annual conference, but he was concerned they would have retired for the evening, and perhaps permanently, before I arrived.

The conference had the last laugh, though, presenting a jokey horse-poo cake to Roger at the end of the evening to 'thank' him for his service.

Inevitably the party dropped in the polls again after the national conference. The public hates disunity and messiness, and the National Party of 2003 had no political capital in the bank to draw on. Talk turned to leadership change, and after a particularly bad poll in October, former Reserve Bank governor and MP of one year Don Brash announced he was challenging Bill for the party leadership.

Bill and his team were confident they could hold off Don, but Don, in his bookish way, also appeared confident. For my part, I was surprised to start receiving calls from caucus members asking what I thought they should do. Conscious of my new role heading up the professional wing of the party, I carefully played it straight down the line. For the sake of the party organisation, I couldn't have a dog in this fight. It had to be the caucus's call.

Judy and I went to caucus as usual and waited in the Leader's Office while the vote was taken down the hall in the Opposition caucus room. While we sat there I marvelled, not for the first time, at how much my life had changed in only two years. It was quite a switch from running a radio company to witnessing up close the internal machinations of New Zealand's leading conservative political party and, historically at least, its most successful political brand.

Word came back up the hallway. There had been a surprise result. Don Brash would be the new leader of the National Party. The office was in shock and so was Judy. It seemed nobody had truly expected Don to win.

Bill reappeared, looking stunned. In a rueful tone he said something that I have never forgotten: 'In politics, it's always later than you think.' It certainly was for Bill that day, and there have been many times since where I have seen political protagonists fail to recognise an opportunity slipping away before it was too late.

It appeared Team Don hadn't been that organised either. They had no idea who they wanted as deputy leader. After hurried discussions it was proposed that Nick Smith's name go forward as an olive branch from Don's supporters to the freshly deposed 'Brat Pack' — a uniting move, if you like.

The only problem was that Nick was in completely the wrong head space. He had been running the numbers for Bill, had clearly got them wrong, and felt very guilty about it. Yet here he was, being asked to be the deputy to Bill's political nemesis. He accepted the position but it was immediately clear he wasn't emotionally able to execute the role. He took Judy and I to dinner that evening and talked at a hundred miles an hour. The next day he was worse, and Judy and others were called on to make an intervention. Within a few days Nick had stepped down, and Gerry Brownlee was asked to take on the role of deputy leader. The new team of Don Brash and Gerry Brownlee would be tasked with leading the National Party forward to 2005.

I was five months into my new role running the National Party, and the leadership had changed in tumultuous fashion. While I didn't know Bill that well, it was all a bit disconcerting for someone more used to business life, and a more settled business life at that. But there was nothing for it but to drive onwards. I decided to hang on for the ride.

INITIALLY, IT WASN'T CLEAR WHETHER Don Brash wanted change in the party, but we were soon introduced to an Australian political operative called Bryan Sinclair. Bryan was a young thruster of the type you might see on British political comedy *The Thick of It*. He turned up to see me in his sharp suit, pretty much declaring he and the Leader's Office were going to run things from here on in, including all the fundraising and campaign planning, and I should get with the programme. I heard him out and felt the need to acquaint him with the difference between the party organisation and the caucus in New Zealand politics, including who does what and why. I was particularly pointed on fundraising. Politicians don't lead the fundraising effort, for obvious reasons.

Young Bryan, in my opinion, had a remarkable knack for rubbing people up the wrong way. I was one of the easiest people he had to deal with, given I had only been around for all of five minutes. Yet still he made it difficult. He quickly fell offside with experienced politicians like Gerry Brownlee and Murray McCully. Gerry developed a distaste for all things Bryan and pretty much froze him out. Once, when Bryan had obviously been talking up his role with members of the press gallery, Gerry responded to a journalist's query with the memorable quote, 'Bryan, oh yes, he puts out the chairs for us at public meetings.'

Gradually the new team settled down and got on with the business of preparing for the election, now in just eighteen months' time. One of the big challenges was candidate selection. The party had been decimated in the 2002 election, and was down to 27 MPs. With the change of leadership, Roger Sowry and Lynda Scott decided to retire at the 2005 election, so that left 25.

Judy Kirk was passionate about rebuilding the party in the regional seats it had lost in 1999 and 2002. She spent much time looking for strong centre-right candidates for electorates like Napier, Tukituki, Wairarapa, East Coast, the two Hamilton seats, New Plymouth,

Ōtaki, Rangitata, Otago and Invercargill. She set up the candidate college as planned and ran four meetings over an eighteen-month period, training prospective candidates, testing their aptitude and attitude towards a political career, and introducing them to party grandees.

Judy was also passionate about our stated mission of elevating the importance of electorate chairs and electorate organisations in the party structure. She introduced awards to celebrate high performance, and new touches like the annual Electorate Chairs Breakfast with the leader to lift the chairs' status and mana.

Electorate organisations in the National Party have always cherished their role in selecting their candidate, and Judy certainly wasn't about to disrupt that process. Her approach was to talk, listen and cajole, matchmaking people she saw as MP material with their prospective electorate organisations.

I lost count of the number of times I met prospective candidates as Judy's wingman all over the country. Judy wanted candidates that looked like middle New Zealand and were reliable and dependable. She didn't succeed with her preferred choice in every case, but her batting average was very good. She played a very significant role in the composition of the large 2005 and 2008 cohorts of new National MPs, who ultimately formed the basis and the political ballast of the Key government.

My scheduled year at the top was rapidly passing. I recruited hard to put together a strong central team that would be the backbone of the party's fight in the 2005 election. I hired a talented young person from outside politics named Greg Sheehan as my deputy and eventual successor, and first Megan Campbell then Jo de Joux as party operations manager. Deborah James was brought in as the party's development manager, and a team of customer service officers was recruited. At last the party had some professional resources to get things done.

What we didn't have was a campaign manager. National had made do with a string of campaign chiefs in recent election campaigns, generally dragooning in a senior volunteer. There was no programme to develop campaign managers within the party, and we didn't have anything like the union movement with its professional staff which Labour could and did draw from.

A plan had taken shape to hire an experienced campaign director from Australia to run the 2005 campaign. Judy and I had travelled to Australia in September 2004 to both observe the Liberal Party's federal election campaign and meet our prospective campaign director.

I really enjoyed my few days in Melbourne following the progress of the federal campaign. The Liberals were very good to us — inviting us to sit in on their daily meetings, to follow their team leaders through the day and have dinner each evening — even though hanging out with a couple of Kiwis ten days out from an election they looked likely to lose was probably the last thing they wanted to do. I struck up a friendship with the Libs' pollster, Mark Textor, and Judy and I got on well with both Brian Loughnane, the party's long-standing federal director, and Party President Shane Stone.

I took a lot of notes, copied the campaign structure diagrams, and noted the professionalism of the organisation and the structured approach they took to each day. Those few days made a lasting and positive impression on me. Judy and I then headed to Sydney to look in on the New South Wales campaign, and meet our candidate for campaign director, a guy called Scott Morrison.

Scott was at that stage the Liberal Party's New South Wales state director, and he'd previously spent some time in New Zealand working on tourism in the office of Tourism Minister Murray McCully — so he wasn't completely unknown to the National Party. Scott and I hit it off pretty well, and both Judy and I returned to

Wellington thinking he would be a good fit for our campaign.

Our time in Melbourne turned out to coincide with the nadir of the Liberals' 2004 election campaign. The mood had been pretty dark over dinner both evenings, with our hosts seemingly convinced Prime Minister John Howard was heading for a loss. In the following days, however, their relentless pressure on Labor leader Mark Latham and his suitability or otherwise for high office started to pay dividends, and he ended up imploding spectacularly. John Howard duly won his fourth election that November, on his way to the second-longest prime ministership in Australian history.

That was great for the Liberals but led to the wheels falling off our grand plan. After the election Scott Morrison was encouraged to stay in Australia, as a federal seat would be coming available in South Sydney as the result of a retirement. It was an offer he couldn't refuse, and he duly made himself unavailable to be our campaign director for the 2005 election. He went on to become the member for the federal seat of Cook, entering Parliament in 2007.

As for me, I was Judy-ed again. In the interests of doing it for my party and my country, and there being no one else around, I agreed to stay on up to the election and be the National Party's campaign director for the 2005 campaign. Just as well I'd taken good notes in Melbourne.

THE FIRST BIG SHOT FIRED in that campaign in fact occurred at the beginning of 2004, a full eighteen months ahead of the likely election date. It was to be Don Brash's first big speech as National Party leader, the traditional Opposition leader's State of the Nation speech.

Back in the day, Rob Muldoon used to give an annual State of the Nation address at the Orewa Rotary Club. Muldoon had a bach up the road at Hatfields Beach where he'd spend the summer holidays. He would pop down to Ōrewa towards the end of January and give his view of the world. Don liked the political symbolism of using the same location, even though there had been no love lost between the two men, and their political philosophies were hardly similar.

Rob was an economic wet and a social conservative, while Don was an economic dry and a social liberal. Rob presided over mounting inflation and ended up regulating the New Zealand economy to within an inch of debt default, while Don was the flinty Reserve Bank governor who was set free to tame inflation.

There was personal history as well. Rob had, by some accounts deliberately, scuppered the young Don Brash's first attempt at a political career as a National candidate in the East Coast Bays by-election back in 1980, by raising the Harbour Bridge tolls at an inopportune time.

Ōrewa it would be then, and the location would undoubtedly raise interest in the speech. The topic was the next issue. A range of ideas were discussed, with the economy being a perennial favourite, but Don and his close team kept coming back to the Treaty of Waitangi and the trend of Māori separatism under the Clark government.

There was a lot of public disquiet at the time about government policy decisions providing preferential treatment to Māori in order to address areas of social disadvantage. While most New Zealanders wanted Māori to succeed, large parts of the electorate found the trend towards positive discrimination in favour of Māori and the pace of change unsettling. Don had a fairly straightforward view. He believed there should be one law for all and no preferential treatment for anyone, and he articulated that view in his Ōrewa speech.

The effect was dramatic and almost instantaneous. He had struck a chord, particularly in Auckland and across regional New Zealand. While the ACT party and Winston Peters had been saying similar things for some time, Don was the first person in a mainstream political party to take the issue on. Social progressives hated the speech and piled onto Don, which gave him even more airtime.

The polls turned around virtually overnight. Labour dropped from the mid-forties to the high thirties, while National shot up from 28 per cent to 45 per cent, moving consistently ahead of Labour for the first time since the 1996 election, eight years previously.

Some of National's rise in the polls came at the expense of the smaller parties that had done so well in the 2002 election; not for the last time, the party was criticised for cannibalising its smaller potential partners. We weren't so worried. To have any chance in the upcoming election, we had to consolidate much of the centre-right vote back together again. We knew that would bruise the likes of ACT and New Zealand First, but we really didn't have a choice. There was nothing we could do that would make them happy beyond staying in the twenties, and that wasn't an option.

The sudden lift in the polls following the Ōrewa speech put us in the game, but many pundits argued that the party had gone too early and would not be able to sustain the momentum. They were right of course, but nobody, not even Don, had anticipated the impact of the Ōrewa speech.

Throughout 2004 the caucus and the party slogged away to stay level with Labour, while preparing for the election campaign behind the scenes. Don and the MPs, with our help, landed on five key policy themes on which to fight the election: the Treaty, education, welfare, law and order, and the economy. We knew from our research that those areas resonated most strongly with the public, and were where the public believed National had a better approach.

Judy Kirk and I attended caucus almost weekly, laying out the campaign plans and reporting on the party's research. I was able to bring my radio experience to bear on the research programme, and with the assistance of Australian lobbying firm and political consultancy Crosby Textor I developed it into a bit of a speciality. Many people are quite cynical of political party polling and focus groups, but to me it is the stock in trade of listening to your voters.

Without it you would be adrift on a sea of MPs' anecdotal reckons, which may — or more likely may not — reflect the views of the wider public.

Campaign planning was the most challenging part of the story for me, as people were still deeply scarred from the 2002 campaign and fearful that the party hadn't fully learnt its lessons or wouldn't be able to run a successful nationwide MMP campaign. Judy and I had to be very patient in seeking to earn the trust of the caucus, in the face of some quite testy exchanges from time to time.

I had to remind myself regularly that these people had their political lives on the line every day. One way I coped was to keep a private spreadsheet of the people in caucus I was happy to work for from week to week. I said to Judy that if the number on the negative list ever outweighed the number on the positive list, we would need to talk. Fortunately that didn't happen.

Milestone by milestone, we built a campaign machine from scratch: a new party website, better canvassing systems, more unified branding, and so on.

We sustained a poll lead through to mid-2004, before Labour moved in front again. They ran through until Christmas with a four- or five-point lead, which they carried into the start of election year. While we would have rather been ahead, we were all thrilled to at least be back in the game. The party had come a long way since 2002, and we had every reason to be optimistic for the upcoming contest.

Things were advancing for me, too, on the personal front. Judy had introduced me to Suzanne Booth at a caucus function in 2003, and we had steadily got to know each other. Suzanne was a National Party member from Wellington, and, like me, had been nominated as a list-only candidate in 2002, before pulling out. We got on really well, and one thing led happily to another.

We got engaged on a holiday in Prague in mid-2004, and married on Waiheke Island at the start of 2005. It was a stunning day, with a full turnout of family, friends and key National Party figures whom we both knew. Don put in an appearance and entered family folklore when he mistook one of my brothers for me, his diligent campaign director, and wished him all the best for his wedding day. To be fair to Don, Kevin was suited up as my groomsman, and had a similar follicly challenged hairstyle to mine.

Suzanne and I had a wonderful time, and an excellent honeymoon in Hawai'i. I knew that even if nothing else positive came from my involvement in politics, I would have always met my future wife through the National Party.

Chapter Six
The Brash brigade

THE 2005 CAMPAIGN WAS WARMING UP. Judy Kirk, Jo de Joux and I had put in a lot of effort putting the building blocks in place. The campaign strategy team had been meeting regularly for a year, and all the key roles had been filled. I sensed the effort taken to build those relationships would stand us in good stead when the pressure came on. I didn't want a repeat of 2002, when the team clearly self-destructed under the duress of the campaign.

After the stunt Helen Clark pulled calling an early election in 2002, there was quite a lot of wariness she might play the same game in 2005. One of our strategic objectives was therefore to push her to settle on a predictable election date that we could plan towards, on the grounds it was too risky for her to go any earlier. That meant maintaining sufficient momentum in the polls in the first half of the year to prevent her pulling the pin.

We had built up quite a campaign war chest, so we made the decision to deploy some of it early. It was a risky approach — we could end up firing our shots before it really mattered, but on balance we thought it was worth it.

The advertising medium we settled on pretty much picked itself.

We were not permitted to use radio or TV until the campaign proper, and newspapers were a bit blah. We chose billboards to convey the immediacy and visibility we wanted. An experienced creative guy, John Ansell, who was a fan of Don Brash, had joined the team. It was he who came up with the simple and arresting concept of the red-and-blue billboards, with one or two words describing Labour on one side paired with a slightly grumpy photo of Helen Clark on a red backdrop, and a contrasting phrase describing National on the other side, with a blue background and a smiling photo of Don.

The red / blue billboards were an instant hit, clearly contrasting the policies of Labour and National. The first three were the self-explanatory 'Tax / Cut', the controversial 'Iwi / Kiwi' to describe race relations, and one headed up 'Education Priorities' with 'PPTA, NZQA, NZEI, NCEA' on the Labour side and 'KIDS' on the National side. People weren't going to die wondering what National stood for in 2005.

Suzanne and I were away for a weekend in Gisborne just after the early ads had been provided to the weekend newspapers. The media went nuts analysing them. We sat in a cafe reading through something like four or five pages of coverage of the new campaign across the Sundays, all seeking to assess the effectiveness or otherwise of National's approach. I had launched a few advertising campaigns in my time but this was next level. Talk about cut-through.

You can never tell in advance when something like the red / blue billboards will come along and capture the public or the media's imagination. I liken such moments to the America's Cup red socks campaign. Nobody would have expected a simple pair of red socks to take off like they did. When you discover a marketing device like that your job is to ride it for as long as you can — and we did.

John Ansell was a prolific creative, and came up with hundreds of ideas for the red / blue billboards, some of which we used but most of which died on the cutting-room floor. For me as campaign director, it was great to have a constant stream of options. We produced postcards of the billboards, corflute versions for electorates to use, and even an online generator for people to make their own. What was intended as a short-term pre-campaign marketing blitz ran all the way to election day.

The battle had been joined, and the Labour team was clearly rattled. The polls started to narrow.

The next opportunity pretty much fell into our laps. Michael Cullen's Budget in May 2005 was a shocker. Despite rising surpluses as a result of a relatively strong economy, Cullen offered very little in tax relief to ordinary New Zealanders, proposing only a shift in tax thresholds three years away in 2008, which wouldn't even match the rate of inflation. In many ways he would have been better off doing nothing. John Key had become National's finance spokesperson when Don Brash became leader, and he coined the phrase 'chewing-gum tax cuts' to describe Cullen's changes, and the moniker stuck.

We rode the tax theme all the way to election day, placing a huge amount of pressure on Labour, including teasing an announcement of significant tax cuts that would come into effect should National win the election. They responded first by wiping the interest off student loans while a person is studying, and secondly by announcing significant increases in Working for Families payments in mid-July — four days before National's tax package was due for release.

The Working for Families changes nearly stuffed up our tax announcement. We had carefully designed our tax package, and for the first time ever we had accompanied it with an online tax calculator to allow people to see quickly what they would receive under National versus Labour, depending on who won the upcoming election. The website also used the red / blue motif. While we weren't particularly concerned about the revamped Working for Families package, we did need to factor it in to both our tax-cut package and the tax calculator, and quickly. And we were a tiny team.

Don and John's economic adviser set to work on the spreadsheets, making the necessary adjustments while the campaign team waited to adjust the calculator. Labour's announcement had been on the Wednesday and we were due to release our tax package the following Monday. The package was updated by the Friday, but the calculator still had to be amended and tested before it went live after Monday's announcement.

I wasn't sure where 'tax calculator' came in the campaign director job description, but it was all hands on deck over the weekend to amend and test the calculations. It all seemed to be going well until mid-afternoon Sunday, when political adviser Sarah Boyle found a series of examples which incorrectly spat out negative numbers, suggesting tax increases rather than decreases. We painstakingly trawled through the calculations and eventually found the error in the relevant equation, but by now it was early Monday morning.

The whole thing was getting pretty nerve-wracking. I didn't sleep much at all that night. The calculator had to work and work well — because we knew the media would be throwing all sorts of scenarios at it as soon as it was released. It would be a disaster if there was a flaw that we hadn't detected.

That next day, Monday, 22 August, was the day I first saw John Key flourish under pressure. He got off the plane in Wellington, came to the office, and was briefed by members of the team as to the final changes and what it all meant. He arrived no more than a couple of hours ahead of the announcement. It can't have escaped his attention how wired everyone was, but he was unflappable. He took it all in, processed it, and declared himself ready to make the announcement.

He then went out and nailed it.

The tax policy was launched, and then we waited with our fingers crossed. Journalists rang with queries, some quite detailed, but nothing appeared broken. Gradually, over a couple of days, we learnt to breathe again.

The tax debate led to the second great piece of creative in the 2005 campaign, the 'Taxathon' TV commercial. We were looking for a way to highlight the gulf in tax policy between the two major parties, and John Ansell came up with the idea of commandeering the old Telethon 'Thank you very much for your kind donation' song and turning it into a Labour Party attack ad, substituting 'high taxation' for 'kind donation'.

The concept was brilliantly simple and we pounced on it. It was produced using the newly fashionable JibJab animation style with real faces placed on cartoon characters. The ad starred Helen Clark as the Prime Moneywaster and Michael Cullen as the Wastemaster General, and it highlighted that government tax revenues had increased by 50 per cent over the six years of the Labour Government.

We had a deliberate strategy to introduce some humour into our political advertising in the 2005 campaign. Both party leaders had quite severe reputations, Helen Clark in particular. We wanted to lighten the mood and tease and lampoon Labour, who were a bit prone to bossiness and arrogance, while appealing to a younger generation of voters who wouldn't necessarily warm naturally to our leader, the former Reserve Bank governor.

The final piece in the 2005 campaign strategy was to make sure our campaign collateral was completely consistent, and that voters understood it was the party vote that we wanted. We needed to be clear that it was solely the party vote that determined the composition of the Parliament and who would win. That part was successful, too. The party was completely united in its branding and its commitment to winning the party vote. It had been two years' hard work, but organisationally everyone was marching together.

I ran a series of daily conference calls throughout the campaign with every MP, candidate and senior campaign worker. It was a trick

I had picked up from the Liberal Party in Australia. The calls started with the leader at 6 a.m. and finished at 8.15 a.m. each morning, by which time everyone understood where we saw ourselves ahead of that day's events, what the leader was doing, what the key messages were, and what to watch out for. The idea was that nobody would feel out of the loop, everyone would feel part of the team, and it would be less likely anyone would go rogue. It was a massive daily commitment for all involved but it worked very well and became the internal communications template for the next four elections.

LABOUR WAS STRUGGLING AGAINST THE focused attack on our five campaign themes. By mid-June they were starting to fall a little behind in the polls, so they 'went negative' and pulled out some personal attacks. These included a baseless suggestion that New Zealand's nuclear-free stance would be sacrificed by a Don Brash government, and a wild accusation by senior minister Trevor Mallard that the National Party was being bankrolled by a mysterious American bagman. It was all rubbish, but they were determined to demonise Don and put doubt in the voters' minds about whether he could be trusted.

While Labour's attacks were ham-fisted, it had to be said that Don didn't help himself or the party with some of his behaviour, notably around the Exclusive Brethren, a secretive and highly conservative patriarchal religious group that approached Don early on to offer help with his campaign. Quite oddly, the Exclusive Brethren didn't vote on principle, but they were prepared to work behind the scenes to do all they could to get rid of the Labour Government.

Don was keen for them to help. His view was that he'd take help from anybody, but he really didn't think through how a close association with the Exclusive Brethren might be seen by voters in middle New Zealand. Richard Long, Don's chief of staff and the former editor of *The Dominion Post*, did understand the risk, so he sought to place himself between Don and the religious group, meeting with them as an alternative. I too, as campaign director, sought to channel their 'help' in positive directions.

When Richard sent them over to meet me, I referred them on to get advice from the Electoral Commission on appropriate campaigning. It made no sense to me for National to be closely associated with their campaigning, and anyway I had plans for us to use up most if not all of our campaign spending cap. I couldn't afford to have third parties promoting a 'Vote National' message that could be seen by electoral authorities as part of National's campaign and place us over the threshold.

Sadly, we learnt later that Don was still meeting with the Exclusive Brethren during the campaign without telling us. It was during one of those meetings he learnt of their plan to put out attack pamphlets targeting the Greens. Attack pamphlets are legitimate political activity, but the Brethren were secretive about it. All political advertising has to have an authorisation statement on it, and while they had one it didn't identify them and didn't provide a contactable address. That naturally led to a media witch-hunt for the secretive pamphleteers and an eventual admission that the Exclusive Brethren were indeed the authors. There was a memorably disastrous live TV interview where a dozen or more of the key Brethren activists, all middle-aged blokes in white work shirts and no ties, lined up in a row to be interviewed together and defend themselves. It all looked very odd, and it was.

When Don was first approached about their campaign, he denied all knowledge of it. His key spokespeople all followed his lead, only to be completely wrong-footed when he casually admitted in an interview on Radio bFM a few days later that he in fact might have been aware of the campaign before it happened, and even seen the brochures.

That day on the trail we were running a 'First ten things'

announcement outlining our top priorities should we win the election. Don was flanked by deputy leader Gerry Brownlee and the local MP, in this case Murray McCully. Both were key members of the campaign team, and both were unaware of the interview that had just taken place on bFM; well, they were unaware until the media stand-up unfolded.

The media pack launched into Don, peppering him with questions about the Exclusive Brethren, how long he had known about their campaign, and why he hadn't admitted it previously. Watching the video of the press conference back at campaign HQ, I could see the surprise in both Gerry's and Murray's faces as the train wreck occurred in front of their eyes. Needless to say, the first ten things National would do if elected were the last thing on the media's minds as that day's stories were filed.

There were too many moments like that on the campaign trail. Despite his bookish personality, Don did have a gift for the memorable soundbite, only often not one which would deliver what you wanted to say to voters.

Soon after he became leader, Don had met a mother of four children who was upset that three of the four had moved to Australia. The media had picked up her story as an illustration of the wider trans-Tasman migration issue, which we had sheeted home to the weakness of the government's economic policies. This same lady had recently written to Don, saying the fourth child was now leaving, and Richard Long came up with the idea of Don going to Hawke's Bay during the campaign and meeting the woman with his press pack in tow, to highlight the need for economic change. It was a good plan, and the campaign duly headed to Hawke's Bay.

Around the same time we had been having trouble with our new Tauranga candidate, the well-known local property developer Bob Clarkson. Bob was on track to win the Tauranga electorate over long-time MP Winston Peters, which was great. Unfortunately, he was also a walking colourful quote machine, and his often inflammatory and always politically incorrect quotes were regularly sucking the oxygen out of the central campaign.

Bob wasn't prone to listening to his support team, or the nationwide campaign, so neighbouring senior MP Tony Ryall was asked to spend a bit of time with him, helping with his media appearances and the like. The immediate challenge was that TV3 had sent a camera crew and a political reporter to interview Bob, and that was quite high-risk. Who knew what Bob would say?

Bob and Tony sat down with the reporter and had a good and sensible chat, but just when Tony was getting ready to declare victory, Bob stood up and announced he needed to go outside and 'drain the spuds', visibly rearranging himself in the process. This clip duly played on the evening news, complete with a shot of Tony with his head in his hands.

There it might have ended, as perhaps the second or third political story of the day, but for Don's reaction when doing his daily stand-up outside the house in Hawke's Bay. Faced with questions from TV3 about Bob's behaviour, Don responded to the press pack with the memorable line: 'I do not wish any candidates to be talking about their testicles, to be quite frank.' His response led every channel's political coverage that night, and another day's message was lost.

As with a lot of politicians, Don's biggest strengths were also his weaknesses. He was unfailingly polite and genuinely interested in discussing whatever subject was raised with him. His approach was to sincerely answer whatever question he was asked, which was good, but he would then not go on to tie his answer back into the messages he and the campaign wanted to give voters, which was bad.

Once, in the last few days of the campaign, I was prepping Don for an extended interview with Leighton Smith on Newstalk ZB. This was not my role, but the campaign was getting exasperated with Don's inability to prosecute his case for election, and it was agreed

I would talk with him. I carefully went through our key messages with Don on the phone and he earnestly agreed with them, and that he should be saying them. Then there was a pause. 'Of course, Steven, I'll only be able to say these things if Leighton asks me the right questions, won't I? I will have to answer his questions.' With a sinking feeling, I tried to explain to Don how he might manage to do both. This was the nub of the issue.

There were plenty of plusses for Don's candidacy as leader of the National Party. He had impeccable economic credentials, and had carefully thought through many issues, knew his mind on them, and was not afraid of arguing his case. Unlike some leaders, he arrived in the role knowing what he wanted to achieve in politics. He gave the party clear definition after the wilderness years from the late 1990s through to 2002. However, he was very dry, fond of quoting figures, and unfailingly logical in his arguments. His politeness could also come across as patrician.

Don was very popular with male voters, but had, as Murray McCully was wont to say, a women problem, meaning he didn't poll strongly enough with female voters. At one point Murray and I met with Sandy Burgham, who was quite a prominent social columnist at the time, to assess what could be done. Sandy quite sensibly told us the public needed to see more of Don the family figure, for example having fish and chips on St Heliers beach with his wife and son. She told us that many women had the mistaken impression of Don 'sitting up late at night hunched over his computer sending out lengthy emails about economic policy in the eerie light of the screen'. Murray and I gave each other a knowing glance. We didn't have the heart to tell her.

We had another problem, too. Somebody, somehow, had got hold of some of Don's emails, and was selectively drip-feeding them to the media. While they were more titillating than particularly concerning — containing, for example, advice from ACT party members encouraging Don to seek the leadership of National — they did distract both Don and the campaign team, and the potential for their leaking to be an inside job was corrosive. Everybody was looking over their shoulder, and everyone had a theory as to who might have leaked them and why.

At Don's urging, I ended up spending much of the last few days of the election campaign working with Parliamentary Service to investigate whether his emails had been hacked. There was no sign of that, and a later police investigation could also find no evidence of hacking. The number of ways the emails could have escaped expanded exponentially when I learnt Don had a habit of printing out his emails and carrying them from Wellington to Auckland or from the office to his apartment in Wellington in large ringbinders. They could have been lost almost anywhere.

It all boiled down to a haphazard campaign. Our five key issues were going well and taking it to Labour with clear advertising and enough successful set pieces to make the point. But our negatives were also visible and not helped by our candidate for prime minister. Some days it felt like we were successfully running both the attack on the government and the attack on ourselves. With all the stuff we had going on it was hard for Labour to even get a word in.

It ended up being a very close election, with the opinion polls see-sawing right up to the day. Of the ten opinion polls taken in the final four weeks, National was ahead in five. Two polls in the second-to-last week had Labour in front by two points and seven points respectively. In the last week the final Fairfax poll and the final *One News* poll had National ahead by a massive six points. We dared to dream we might get there.

AND THEN IT WAS POLLING day. I voted mid-morning at the Albany village booth, which is located at the confluence of three North Shore electorates. I wasn't happy with the vibe; something wasn't quite right. I had nothing to go on beyond the expressions of the booth volunteers for the various parties, as this was my first campaign. I had only ever been a volunteer on a booth once before, in 2002. For what it was worth, my hunch was we hadn't quite got there.

We all went home and waited. In the afternoon, Judy Kirk, Murray McCully and I went to Don's place in St Heliers. Don was feeling quietly confident, but he picked that moment to tell us that if National didn't win he would resign as leader that night. That shocked us, and we spent some time persuading him that would be the wrong approach.

Previously on election nights, Auckland MPs had all stayed in their electorates. We wanted to make sure the whole party was together, and started a new tradition of one large function in central Auckland. Candidates and MPs would have a local function to thank their volunteers and then head into the central function, which was held at SkyCity.

It was a big night. National nearly doubled its vote from three years previously to 39 per cent, and increased its number of seats from 27 to 49. It was the first time the party's vote had been that high since 1990. But it still wasn't quite enough. Labour itself only lost two seats and polled at 41 per cent. In the final wash-up they had 50 seats, while we lost one on the special votes to finish just behind on 48.

Our increase in seats came mainly at the expense of New Zealand First (down six), United Future (down five) and ACT (down seven). We had reunited the centre-right, but not dragged enough centrist votes across from Labour.

With 121 seats in the new Parliament, both National and Labour needed 61 to govern. With Jim Anderton's Wigram seat in the bag for his Alliance party, Labour started from 51. They would need New Zealand First (seven seats) and United Future (three) to get to 61. They could also do it with the Greens (six seats) but would still need New Zealand First, and Winston hated the Greens.

National could count on ACT (two seats), which would get us to 50. Joining with New Zealand First and United Future would provide a four-way coalition, but it still only added up to 60. We'd need the new Māori Party (four seats) as well, making for a highly unlikely five-way coalition. But that didn't stop Don from trying.

After the election I had to go to New York with Suzanne as her partner on a work trip. While there I received a call from Don back home telling me he was still working on the five-way deal. I listened carefully and then asked who was doing the legwork talking to all the parties. He paused, and said the Exclusive Brethren were the go-betweens. I thanked him for keeping me posted and wished him all the best with it.

To be fair to Don, we were very nearly there. If we'd held on to that forty-ninth seat we had won on election night, then the four-way coalition would have been viable and we might just have seen a change in government. However, in those days, Winston Peters had a declared preference to work with the largest party, so perhaps not.

My read of the result was that voters were getting sick of the Clark government, but they couldn't quite bring themselves to trust a Don Brash-led National Party in sufficiently large numbers. There were enough slips, and enough Brethren moments and the like, that Labour's risk message resonated with just enough voters, especially females. Our exit poll confirmed that National won the male vote comfortably (by 43 to 37 per cent) but just as comfortably lost the female vote (44 to 38 per cent). Overall it was very close, but no cigar.

On 17 October 2005, one month after election day, Helen Clark announced she had formed a coalition with New Zealand First and United Future, with the Greens providing support on confidence and supply. The country was consigned to three more years of Helen Clark's leadership, and National was consigned to three more years in Opposition. But it was a much stronger and much more united National Party that started 2006 on the Opposition benches. In many ways, 2005 was the story of the recovery of the National Party brand.

Chapter Seven
Exit stage right

I HAD BEEN CLEAR WITH the party that I was finishing up as general manager at the 2005 election, and I was very happy with that decision. While I had enjoyed the challenge of running both the party and the campaign and I felt we had done a good job getting as close as we did, I was hankering to resume a more normal pace of life and get on with building a family with Suzanne. The election had been an all-consuming whirlpool of Don, the Exclusive Brethren, emails, Labour, tax and everything else, and I wanted a break. I needed to decompress.

I happily handed the keys to my deputy and appointed replacement, Greg Sheehan, and left the building.

In my experience it's never a good idea to completely stop immediately after such an all-consuming time. You can end up in quite a funk. Fortunately, there was lots to get on with. Suzanne had two quick work trips in the diary: the aforementioned week in New York, and a week in Singapore and Vietnam a month later. I went along for the ride as her partner and enjoyed being a tourist.

In between times I'd been approached by Mitch Harris at talkback station RadioLIVE to provide cover on their afternoon-drive show for six weeks. That was a lot of fun, and it proved to be an ideal way to come back to earth. I still loved radio, and getting behind a mike again while talking politics was the ideal antidote for the pressure of an election campaign.

Amusingly, one of the regular weekly guests on the show was one Helen Clark, and for the first week I don't think anyone in her office had clicked that the stand-in host was the campaign manager for National's recent election campaign. We had a great old chat.

I don't think I'd met Helen at that point, so it was perhaps not surprising she didn't twig she was being interviewed by National's campaign manager. For my part, I played it very straight, but at some point in the next week the penny must have dropped. While her office never said anything to RadioLIVE, for the subsequent five weeks the prime minister was either on a plane, caught in traffic, or otherwise unavailable for the scheduled slot.

There was a bit of tidying up to be done around the campaign, and I fitted that in around the trips and the radio commitment. But there was one big problem which needed sorting and it wouldn't be easy. Somehow, between myself and our media agency Rainmakers, there had been a stuff-up over the GST on our television and radio advertising.

Under New Zealand electoral rules, political parties can't purchase their own radio or television advertising. Instead, a pot of taxpayers' money is allocated for television and radio advertising for all the political parties contesting the election. The Electoral Commission ladles it out to individual parties in an arcane and fiercely argued process based on each party's historic vote, its proportion of MPs in the current Parliament, and its performance in opinion polls leading up to the allocation decision. Parties could choose whether to spend all their allocation on purchasing advertising time, or some of it on producing the ads that would then be broadcast.

It's a slightly mad rule, and it gets sillier as each election passes.

While it may make sense to cap party campaign spending overall, and New Zealand does, having specific rules just for television and radio when they are now a small part of the overall media mix is anachronistic. It dates from when radio and television dominated the media, and were seen to be so powerful that sustained use of them could sway elections. Even in 2005 that clearly wasn't the case. In the 2020s, the idea that broadcast television advertising needs to be expressly regulated is laughable, but here we are.

Still, the rules are the rules, and we had every intention of following them.

National had been allocated $900,000, inclusive of GST, for television and radio advertising for the 2005 election. We'd had quite the debate with the Electoral Commission, who had given Labour $1.1 million based on National's poor 2002 election result. It was the first time the money for the two major parties had not been split evenly.

Given our fundraising coffers were full, we decided to pay for the advertising production costs ourselves and spend the maximum amount of the taxpayer funding purchasing advertising time, to get the biggest bang for our buck. We hired the late Marianne McKenzie, whom I knew from radio days, to book and place the advertising. Marianne was a secret weapon for National over the five election campaigns with which I was involved. She was fast, discreet, unflappable, innovative and had great media relationships, dating from her time selling radio advertising for the old Magic 91 FM.

The problem was, she and I had misunderstood each other in that first campaign as to how much advertising we could place. I told her that the amount should be $900,000 including GST, she heard $900,000 plus GST. To be fair to Marianne, anyone in business works with GST-exclusive figures. Talking about costs inclusive of GST is a quirk of government. We had received formal documentation from the Electoral Commission, which in my recollection was forwarded through to Marianne's agency, but the party was still low-flying from an administrative perspective and there is no doubt that we treated the bookings too informally. Marianne went ahead and booked the advertising, and no one was any the wiser until after the election when the error was discovered during the final reconciliation.

The moment I saw it, I had a terrible, terrible sinking feeling. We had effectively overbooked our advertising by the amount of GST, $112,500, and broken electoral law. We couldn't reallocate money out of the production side of the equation as we had spent all the Electoral Commission money on media. We couldn't even pay the media companies (mostly TV3 and TVNZ) the extra amount, as we were prohibited from spending our own money on television and radio advertising. Paying the bill would be breaking the rules a second time. We were stuffed.

I discussed the problem with Judy Kirk and the head of the Rules Committee Peter Kiely, and we agreed that we should immediately fess up to the Electoral Commission, which we did. The Electoral Commission in turn passed the matter (and a number of cases involving other political parties) over to the police, as it was required to do. Marianne and I were now subject to a police investigation.

The police interviewed us both, and then it all went quiet. They had other fish to fry. The Labour Party had made a much more egregious and intentional breach of the law, by spending Parliamentary Service (taxpayer) money on their election pledge card in clear violation of the rule that such money cannot be used for electioneering. There were also a number of complaints to police about the Exclusive Brethren advertising and other third-party advertisements. Still, it was a nerve-wracking time, and I kicked myself on any number of occasions.

Finally, at the end of April 2006, I received a letter from Senior

Sergeant Ian Kain, telling me that the police had declined to prosecute Marianne, the party or me personally for our advertising breach, because it was a result of a misunderstanding between the two organisations. They did, however, make some pointed comments about the lack of documentation, which was entirely fair.

At last the 2005 election campaign was over, and I could get on with life.

I HAD DECIDED DURING THE election campaign that a deeper involvement in politics was not for me, at least not at this stage of my life. It was stimulating, exciting and challenging, and I cared deeply about the future of the country. But it also sucked up all the time I could give it and more. If you were diligent you could devote every waking minute to politics and it still wouldn't be enough.

I remember one particular example during the campaign when the *Herald*'s Jonathan Milne rang me late one Saturday afternoon to seek comment on a scoop he had discovered. Apparently the Exclusive Brethren was using one of its schools and the kids there to run phone banks 'push-polling' for the National Party. Push-polling is when you don't just seek people's views on politics and issues, but tailor the questions to infer negative things about political opponents with the idea that the people you poll might change their vote. It's frowned upon, and rightly so. In all my time running campaigns we never did it — but here I was on this Saturday evening trying to find out what was going on.

I rang around and learnt the school was in South Auckland. I didn't learn much more than that. Jonathan seemed to know a lot more than I did. He kept ringing with more information, and I kept telling him it wasn't a party initiative, which it wasn't. He was still going at 9.30 p.m. — which was a sure sign that the story would be leading the front page of the paper the next day, as all the other pages would have been put to bed.

I tried to talk him down a little, and remember getting off the phone and thinking that politics was completely taking over my life.

Since leaving radio I'd had tantalising glimpses of what a more varied, balanced, richer life might look like. I wanted to explore that. Suzanne and I had only recently married and we wanted to get on with building our life together.

During election year, we had found there were only brief breaks once a week in the relentless news cycle where I had a little down time. These happened after the Sunday papers had gone to print on Saturday night and before the journalists were back on the job on Sunday afternoon preparing for the Monday news round. We used that precious time touring open homes out in the country just north of Auckland. We found the property we wanted in Dairy Flat in June, three months before the election. It had a new house on it, which suited city girl Suzanne, and 2.5 hectares of land around it, which suited wannabe farm boy Steven. We decided to make our home there.

After the campaign we embarked on a frenzy of building and landscaping, adding a swimming pool, a large ornamental vegetable garden and copious other gardens. Broods of ducklings appeared, fences went in, and our tiny herd of three beef cattle arrived. We even flirted briefly with alpacas.

We also travelled some more, going on another long trip to Europe in the middle of 2006, this time exploring Eastern Europe, including Transylvania and Bucharest (Romania), Budapest (Hungary), Sochi (Russia), and the Crimean Peninsula and Odessa (Ukraine). We topped it off by making the pilgrimage to Gallipoli.

On the work front I was eager to get back into commercial life. I had made a few small investments since leaving radio and was keen to do more. I'd been a director for three years of a company called Howard Wright, a hospital-bed manufacturer and exporter taking on the world from New Plymouth in Taranaki. Howard

Wright was in a real David-and-Goliath situation, up against the big multinationals which dominated the industry. It was the definition of a small, plucky Kiwi player having an outsized impact on the world stage.

My Howard Wright involvement was a lot of fun. It was my first foray into manufacturing and engineering. It was also a great way to keep in touch with friends in Taranaki and with the Moller family, as it was owned and led by Norton Moller's son, Bruce. After the 2005 election I was invited to become the chair of the company, and remained in that role for the next three years.

Another investment I had made was in a smallish specialist advertising company called Jasons Travel Media. In 2005 it had listed on the new alternative small listings exchange of the New Zealand stock exchange (NZX), and I joined the board as a non-executive director for the listing.

Jasons was an intriguing opportunity. It had been a very successful print directory business with a dominant footprint across New Zealand, Queensland and the South Pacific. Its motel and caravan park directories were the cash cows of the business. The Jasons motel directory was a Kiwi staple — prior to the internet, there was one in nearly every car's glove box.

Of course, the internet had come along, and new online businesses like Wotif were threatening the directory model. The challenge for the Jasons of this world was to successfully transition into digital without overly cannibalising the legacy business, before the cashflow from the print directories dried up.

It was a race against time, and Jasons was already running behind. It had a very clunky online model with no ability to make bookings, and it performed poorly on search engines. It looked like what it was: a print company trying to do digital. The company urgently needed a better website, a booking module and some decent search-engine optimisation. Unfortunately, the management team was moving slowly on all three. I was worried they didn't realise how little time they would have to get things right.

The company was still led by the founder, John Sandford. While he understood conceptually what needed to be done, he didn't seem to know how to do it quickly. After watching all this unfold in front of me at board meetings for about ten months, I realised we needed a leadership change, and quickly.

I discussed the situation with the other directors, and they asked whether I would step in for a period as chief executive, to help put some momentum into the turnaround and get the company moving forward. John would stay, but as a non-executive director.

I agreed to do it, provided I could buy my way in to a decent-sized chunk of the company. I was happy to pay the listed price (there was no such thing as executive share options!), but I wanted to ensure a good return for my efforts through the share price if the company succeeded. A suitable arrangement was agreed and I lifted my shareholding from half a million shares (worth about $226,000) to 1.9 million shares. I became Jasons CEO in mid-2006.

There was a huge amount to do, and quickly. The role rapidly became all-consuming as we fought to catch up on the Wotifs of the world and fight off the challenge of Expedia, who were just arriving in the New Zealand marketplace.

In short order we purchased a commission-free booking service to integrate with the Jasons online listings. We also bought brochure-distribution businesses in Queenstown, Christchurch and Dunedin, to bulk up our South Island business. Ironically for a New Zealand tourism media company, we'd been weak in some of the biggest tourism markets.

But the big job was rebuilding the Jasons website.

I contracted a company I had used before for both the RadioWorks and National Party websites: Enlighten Designs from Hamilton. Jasons.com was a big job — it took about a year to complete. We added a booking service, interactive maps, and much better site navigation.

I became something of a specialist in website design and search-engine optimisation. Well, enough to be dangerous anyway. We turned the company from a print plus web organisation to a web-first one, and that involved a big culture change. We also restructured the business so we could afford a decent marketing campaign. For the first time Jasons was advertising on television and radio, up against the big international brands.

The results started to come. Website sessions grew 60 per cent and overall traffic grew 40 per cent in just twelve months. Suddenly, from being nowhere in Google Search, we were top three for most properties and regions we operated in. We refrained from a commission model for bookings, believing we should zig while the other guys zagged. By charging an annual listing fee rather than commissions, once advertisers had paid they would be incentivised to direct traffic to our site rather than away from it.

The growing momentum in the business was reflected in the financial performance. In the two years from mid-2006 to mid-2008 our operating profit nearly doubled. It had been a tough couple of years but there was a sense that Jasons had turned the corner. And I was enjoying the cut and thrust of business once more, while living on our lifestyle block out at Dairy Flat. It was all pretty idyllic.

There were developments on the home front, too. Like many newlyweds, Suzanne and I had taken on a dog, a Retrodoodle puppy we called Gemma, at the end of 2006. It was about that time Suzanne learnt she was pregnant with Amelia. Our first child, and the first girl born in the Joyce family since my sister way back in 1961, was born in August 2007.

Politics had taken a bit of a back seat. I'd stayed on as a consultant for Don Brash after the election, participating in a strategy group that was set up to prepare the party for the 2008 election. That involved a fortnightly visit to Wellington during parliamentary sittings at most.

During that time, Wayne Eagleson joined Don's office as his chief of staff, replacing Richard Long, who wanted to retire. While I had enjoyed working with Richard, Wayne was on another level in terms of his organisation and political nous. He had a wonderful manner with people, and dramatically improved the operation of the party in Parliament.

I stayed close to the research programme in particular, and to President Judy Kirk, and I helped Bill English with the policy planning process. But I deliberately stayed out of the daily cut and thrust of the place. And once I took over at Jasons I didn't have the time anyway.

DON BRASH HAD CONTINUED AS National Party leader, and made a pretty good fist of it through 2006, with the opinion polls holding on to the gains the party had made in 2005. But there was a sense around the party that he wouldn't lead it to a further election in 2008. Most people talked privately about the timing of a change, rather than whether there should be one or not. The party's finance spokesperson, John Key, was the obvious candidate for the leadership, but he was happy biding his time and learning the ropes.

That all changed in September 2006 when Don suddenly took leave from Parliament, reportedly to sort out some marital problems amidst persistent rumours he'd been having an affair. There was also a rumoured book from Nicky Hager, highlighting Don's leaked emails. Don's days were numbered, and by the end of November 2006 John Key was the eleventh leader of the National Party and Bill English was his deputy in what was a very smooth transition.

I was a spectator to all this, watching primarily from afar and not knowing a huge amount more than I'd read in the newspapers. Shortly after John became leader, he gave me a call, asking if I would be a consultant for him as he prepared for the 2008 election. I was happy to. I liked John and thought he was very capable and electable. I believed he would make a great prime minister. I also enjoyed working with Bill. While I didn't have a huge amount of free time, I would do what I could to assist.

I helped the party prepare for the campaign while delivering on the day job and building family life in Dairy Flat. Then I took a second call from John in 2007. Would I be prepared to be his campaign director for the 2008 election?

This request was a bit more logistically challenging. I was working full-time running a listed New Zealand travel media company, and although we were out of the worst of the woods, there was still much to be done. We were in a challenging fight for digital market share against a number of multinational brands. We also had plans to grow our footprint in Australia and across the Pacific.

On the other hand, I was keen to help John and the team, and believed I had learnt much from my first experience running a campaign that could be applied to 2008. President Judy Kirk rang and she was very keen as well. I talked it over with my fellow board members at Jasons, and we agreed I could take three months off to run the campaign. I rang John and said I could do it.

John's third call came in early 2008. The bit I remember was 'Why don't you come to Parliament and do a proper job?' It was clear what he meant, even though he couldn't commit to it. The election hadn't happened and the leader can't offer things explicitly ahead of time. But the inference was unmistakable. If National won at the election, then he wanted me in his Cabinet.

This was the biggy. An invitation to stand on the list for National and enter Parliament to become a minister. It doesn't get any more enticing than that. I had a lot to think about. I asked John for some time to consider it and discuss it with Suzanne. He agreed.

This was clearly a brilliant opportunity, just exactly at the wrong time for me. Suzanne and I had just started a family; Amelia was six months old. I had a full-time gig turning an old media firm into a new media one, with a lot of money personally invested in it. We were developing a great life in Dairy Flat, and it was finally looking like I was achieving a bit of work–life balance.

On the other hand, I had clearly always been interested in politics, and would love to have an opportunity to make things happen on a bigger stage. I loved my country and wanted it to do better. Surely I'd be mad to turn this down?

I discussed it with Suzanne, and with Judy. Judy was obviously keen and there was a bit more Judy-ing. Suzanne was also very supportive. She thought it was a mountain I had to climb, and I'd always regret not doing it. Suzanne had been a senior private secretary for two ministers, Roger Sowry and Murray McCully, in the 1990s. Prior to that she'd also done a stint as a nanny for Tony and Cherie Blair in the UK while on her OE. Based on her own experience of politics, she convinced herself it wouldn't be too hard on the family.

I was the least convinced. Yes, it was the opportunity of a lifetime, but I also understood how intense it would be. I also knew my own personality and that I was not the sort to tackle such a challenge in a measured way. There was also much more to be done at Jasons. I thought the decision was more an 'either / or' than an 'and'.

I wrote down a pros and cons list and tried to work out what was most important to me. Finally I made a decision. It was the wrong time. I wouldn't do it. I told Suzanne and she was a little surprised, but again very supportive. I just needed to ring John.

A few days later Suzanne asked whether I had called him. I hadn't. I said I was still thinking what to say and I'd ring soon. She looked at me quizzically. We went through the pros and cons again. The decision was unchanged. I said I'd get on and call him.

A few more days passed. I still hadn't called John. I was clearly having difficulty. I was also very introspective. Finally Suzanne suggested the no decision was clearly not sitting well with me. 'Shall we turn the decision around and try it on as a yes, just as a thought experiment?' she suggested. I agreed and immediately felt happier. I realised that, regardless of logic, it was something I needed to do.

Suzanne and I talked it through some more. We knew this wouldn't be a three-year commitment. Nobody goes into Parliament planning for just three years. It would need to be at least six and possibly longer. Finally we agreed we would give a parliamentary career up to nine years. The idyllic laid-back lifestyle at Dairy Flat would have to wait.

I talked my decision through with the chair of Jasons, Geoff Burns, and he was very understanding. While he and the directors would be disappointed, they also believed New Zealand needed a change of government and in their view I would be a strong addition to the National team. I finally rang John to say yes, and we started recruiting for my replacement at Jasons.

My candidacy was announced in July 2008.

Chapter Eight
A Key victory

WHILE I WAS BUSY VACILLATING about whether to stand for Parliament, there of course remained an election to plan for, campaign for and win.

My involvement was stepping up through the first half of 2008. In a real novelty for the National Party at that time, a lot of the team was the same as it was in 2005. Jo de Joux was back as campaign operations manager and Judy Kirk of course was leading the party as president. Murray McCully was the caucus rep and experienced head on the campaign.

The big change was the impact of John Key as party leader. John had taken over from Don Brash in late 2006, and from the beginning of 2007 National had taken a ten-to-fifteen-point lead over Labour in the opinion polls. That lead lasted through 2007 and into election year.

John was much easier to work with than Don had been. He was sure-footed, decisive and confident. He was also much lower maintenance for the team around him. That freed up everyone's time to get on with their own jobs, and as a result the whole ship ran more smoothly. The rehabilitation of Bill English as deputy had a big impact as well. Bill is an excellent engine-room thinker and is steeped in the party and its traditions. He provided great depth and institutional knowledge to balance John's more free-thinking style.

The third key part of the parliamentary team was Wayne Eagleson. He had stayed on to be John's chief of staff following Don's departure, and his professionalism, organisational skills and quiet diplomacy brought huge stability to the operation.

Our big poll lead through 2008 meant that this was going to be a very different election to 2005. In 2005 we really hadn't been expected to win and Don's near victory was a surprise to all. In 2008 all the commentators were saying the election was ours to lose. Of course that created different pressures, but there was no sense at all of complacency. National had been out of office far too long for anybody to be under the illusion that winning an election would be easy.

In any event, nearly every MMP election is close. The leading party tends to squeeze its support parties, while the weaker main party loses more votes to its support parties than to the other major party. The difference between the two voting blocs always looks bigger than it actually is, and most of the time forming a government comes down to just one or two seats.

We made a strategic decision in 2008 to adopt a much more positive tone in our campaign than in 2005. That was partially because of John's style, and partially because of the research. All our polling was telling us that voters had already written Labour off. Voters were aware of that party's failings and didn't need to be reminded of them. They were ready to consider buying a new government and they didn't want to hear or see lots of clever ads telling them about the problems with Helen Clark and Michael Cullen. They were interested in what we were going to do, and why they should choose us.

There was also much less interest in the contrast between

National and Labour. The 2005 campaign had done the job of clearly defining National in the public's mind, and, if anything, Labour's brand had deteriorated significantly since then. We could focus on what we were going to do if given the job.

A more positive, upbeat message about the future under a National government suited John's personality down to the ground. He is an immensely positive, friendly individual with a genuine interest in how people are going, and in their goals and dreams. Leaders are such a big part of modern election campaigns, and the campaign messages have to be consistent with the leader's personality and style. In 2008 our campaign and leader were completely in sync.

We workshopped some campaign slogans and settled on 'Choose a Brighter Future'. It encapsulated the campaign and the message and set us off on the right track.

Our other strategic decision was to drop the humour we used in 2005. New Zealand was in a more serious, no-nonsense mood as the election approached. Economic storm clouds were gathering, and the Treasury confirmed in early August that the country had entered a recession even before the Global Financial Crisis (GFC) arrived. While we needed light and shade in our campaign, John's sunny personality could be relied on to lighten the mood sufficiently. The campaign voice needed to be businesslike and no-nonsense.

We had a new creative team for the campaign, and they focused on delivering high-quality images which underscored the impression of a professional National Party team, ready for government, while still delivering strong messages. We used a team of independent contractors, who worked together as 'The Pond'. It was my emerging preference not to use a big-name agency. Political campaigns are obviously very high-profile events, and in my observation big agencies were generally very happy to be publicly announced as being involved, but then naturally spent much of the campaign protecting their own reputations. The association of the agency brand with the political party they were working for often led to the announced agency wanting more strategic control over the campaign than any party would be prepared to give them, given the high stakes involved.

Our creatives came up with a set of beautiful billboards, set on a much lighter blue colour than was traditional. They were positive and action-oriented and set the tone well, focusing on our core themes of the economy, law and order, education and health. If anything, they were a bit too busy visually. The television ads followed a similar style with well-crafted cinematic images of John discussing the issues with voters and listening to their concerns. They worked better. All were about encouraging voters to choose that brighter future.

In contrast, Labour went negative and aggressive, largely running a scare campaign about what they believed would be lost if National won the government benches. Their stated theme was trust, and centred very much around Helen Clark, New Zealand's prime minister for the previous nine years. Both Labour and Clark believed she was the better leader, and there was a whiff of disbelief that the public could possibly prefer a beginner like John Key over a serious world player like Helen Clark. I was happy with the differences between our two approaches. Labour looked tired, grumpy and dark. National looked fresh, aspirational and ready to take on the country's challenges.

We were however roundly criticised for running a boring, safe campaign. Many of our core voters wanted us to take the gloves off and attack Clark, or at least respond to their scare campaigns. The media did, too. Naturally they love a scrap, and wanted more of what we dished out in 2005. But all our research and personal feedback told us voters had moved past that. In 2008 they were auditioning us for office, and we needed to focus on that rather than having a mud wrestle with Labour.

In the end we did run a few of what I called 'issues ads', about two weeks out from election day, partly in response to all the criticism we were getting about being too boring. They were a simple series of newspaper headlines cataloguing Labour's failings in government, to remind people where we had been and what was at stake. They were useful in their own right but they also defused the growing criticism of the campaign creative, so we could then get back onto the positive. We ran them for four days and then reverted to the core campaign.

THE SMALLER PARTIES WERE, FOR the most part, not having a memorable campaign. The 2008 election was shaping up as a drag race between the two major parties and that was always going to squeeze the vote for the minors. Winston Peters was having a nightmare. He had spent three years as a minister in Helen Clark's government and had lost any remaining patience he had with the media through that time. He had been exposed as a hypocrite over big business donations to political parties when he failed to declare a $100,000 donation from Owen Glenn, and that was the subject of a complaint to Parliament's Privileges Committee. He was also subject to allegations around New Zealand First using a secret trust to funnel large donations into its bank account, although he was subsequently cleared by the relevant authorities.

Winston was trying to regain his old Tauranga seat from National. Bob Clarkson, who beat Peters in 2005, was retiring after just three years as an MP, having achieved his great aim of deposing Peters. His replacement was a young man called Simon Bridges, and he was threatening to run rings around Winston all over again.

The Greens and ACT were doing a bit better. The Greens ran an arrestingly simple billboard campaign called 'Vote for Me' which featured young New Zealanders in front of stunning New Zealand vistas. Those billboards were easily the best we saw from opponents in that campaign, and John regularly communicated to me how impressed he was by them. I took that to mean that he too wasn't completely in love with our billboards, although he never quite said as much.

For the first time we resolved to try a more robust tactical approach to the televised debates. Wayne Eagleson and I decided we would approach Labour (chief of staff to chief of staff) to see if we could get agreement as to which debates John and Helen would participate in. Our view was that there were realistically only two prospects for prime minister, so they should debate each other, with the minor-party leaders having their own debate. It was a bit cheeky, but we thought we'd give it a shot.

From our perspective, one-on-one debates were crucial as they gave our candidate a chance to be clearly compared to the incumbent. It was John's chance to look prime ministerial and to be measured up against Helen Clark. We had great confidence in him as a debater. He had performed very successfully as finance spokesperson against Michael Cullen in 2005, and we had no doubt he would acquit himself well against Clark.

I'm not sure why Labour agreed to our approach. In some ways it would have been easier for them if it was Helen Clark up against everyone else. She had far greater name recognition, and in a group she could rely on John being attacked by some 'friendly fire' from the likes of ACT, while at the same time receiving grenades from Winston Peters and the Greens. She could have been positioned as above the fray. I think Labour believed Helen would wipe the floor with John on a head-to-head basis, backing her vast experience over that of the new boy.

The leaders' debates are an important part of New Zealand political theatre in the run-up to an election, but the number of debate requests was beginning to get out of hand. Not only did all the television networks want at least two, the radio networks wanted one, and now the newspaper websites were seeking to get in on the act as well. If you agreed to all the debate requests, you would hardly have time to get out around the country and campaign. They were also increasingly unruly. If every leader of every party with a chance of getting a seat was represented, they often ended up being a no-holds-barred political brawl.

For whatever reasons, Labour agreed to three debates, one with TVNZ relatively early in the campaign and one each with TVNZ and TV3 in the last week. Even better, they spun it that they approached us rather than the other way round, which suited us down to the ground. They could take the rap from the media for seeking to restrict the number.

The first debate was on 14 October, and we knew it would be pivotal. John prepped assiduously for it. He reviewed all the videos of Helen's past debates, and we spent a lot of time trying out answers to every possible question he might receive. We did two or three practice debate sessions, using a young woman called Nicola Willis from John's office as a stand-in for Helen Clark. Nicola did such a good job of being Helen that we had to ask her to dial it back a little at one point for fear of denting the candidate's confidence.

On debate night John did very well. The commentariat didn't have high expectations and John comfortably exceeded them and was generally seen as the winner. I was watching from Wellington, and it is always a nerve-wracking time for the campaign director as the candidate gets put through their paces. At each ad break you try and score the previous segment, and wish you had the time to suggest a couple of things. But there is no time. At that point he or she is on their own. I needn't have worried. John passed an important test that evening, which gave the campaign real momentum heading into its last three weeks.

The other event that provided momentum was the pre-election fiscal update on 6 October. It showed a weaker economic projection than had previously been expected and a declining set of government accounts. Helen Clark declared it was not the time to recklessly borrow to offer tax cuts, while John confirmed that while the numbers were worse than he had expected, New Zealanders needed some tax relief. The public agreed with John. They'd heard the argument against tax cuts from Labour for nine years, and they had had enough.

Once again we had to rework our numbers in a hurry, but on 9 October we were able to show a tax cut amounting to $47 a week for average wage earners, balanced with a few changes to key government programmes.

Meanwhile the world economic storm continued to worsen. The international banking system was in crisis. Household names like Bear Stearns, Lehman Brothers, and John's old firm Merrill Lynch were collapsing, along with America's biggest insurer, AIG. Back here, as well as the country already being in a domestic recession, inflation was at an eighteen-year high. Our Reserve Bank decided an economic collapse was now more worrying than inflation, and cut interest rates by 1 per cent on 23 October on top of a 0.5 per cent cut in September.

The risk of a worldwide banking system failure was high, and the government was planning to unconditionally guarantee all bank deposits, to avoid a run on New Zealand banks. Australia was about to do the same, and we needed to follow suit or our banking system would suffer.

Labour announced the move at their campaign launch, which was dirty pool as you are not supposed to use campaign events for urgent government announcements. We learnt later that officials had advised them to hold a separate event but were ignored. Michael Cullen authorised the officials to brief John and Bill, but not until the announcement had been made. Regardless, we supported it. Both John and Bill understood the gravity of what was happening.

We had a great campaign calendar ready for the 2008 election, full of carefully planned policy announcements in different parts of the country in a range of portfolios, all set up weeks in advance. It became clear though about a month out from election day that all people wanted to hear about was the economy and what we were going to do about it.

I'd learnt from my radio days that one of the best things about having a clear plan is that it gives you the head space to change it. If a breakfast show on a given day or week was well organised and planned, it was easier to alter direction as circumstances required to respond to current events. It was the same with an election campaign.

We had the capacity to change around a lot of our announcements and locations to reflect the new reality, and we did. We added new ones like the plan for a transitional relief package, which would provide extra financial support to Kiwis who lost their jobs through the economic crisis. John had a major hand in designing that policy, and it underlined his more centrist credentials. We looked (and were) focused on the issues that really mattered to Kiwis.

We also relentlessly hammered our message that a lot of New Zealand's current economic problems had been around long before the emerging financial crisis, and they needed to be solved by a new National-led government.

Labour, on the other hand, were less fleet of foot. They knew they couldn't announce the big spending proposals they had planned, so they weirdly started to announce things they would like to do but now couldn't because of the financial crisis. Helen Clark went around the country telling people what she would do if she could. It was quite bizarre, and probably didn't help their chances. She also announced there would be a mini-Budget after the election if Labour won, and at that point all bets were off. Labour were asking the public to write them a blank cheque.

HEADING INTO THE LAST FEW days of the campaign we were looking pretty strong, and Labour increasingly desperate. They had been forced onto the back foot over a bureaucratic plan to regulate the size of shower heads and the length of people's showers, which underlined public concerns about their 'nanny state' tendencies. Then the party's president, Mike Williams, went to Melbourne in a last-ditch attempt to smear John Key with regard to an illegal foreign-exchange transaction known as 'The H-Fee'. This involved Allan Hawkins and Equiticorp back in the 1980s, about the time John had worked at Elders Finance. The entrails of the case had already been hauled over twice since John had become leader, and it was clear that he was not involved in it.

Williams and his Labour Party helpers spent several days reading court documents in Melbourne, and discovered what they thought was a signature on a document that bore 'a striking resemblance' to that of John Key. Only it wasn't his signature. On 30 October, the *New Zealand Herald* headline read '"Neutron bomb" on Key proves fizzer for Govt'. John lost no time comparing Helen Clark in the paintergate scandal (where she signed a painting she didn't paint) with her trying to pot him for something he hadn't signed. The egg pretty quickly landed all over the face of Mike Williams, while Helen Clark distanced herself from the 'revelations' as fast as she could.

The last week of the campaign was fairly surreal. While the opinion polls had tightened a bit through the campaign, the final wave of polls widened out to have us between eleven and thirteen points ahead of Labour. The US election campaign was wrapping up at the same time with Barack Obama likely to be elected as that country's first African American president, and that history-making moment was proving a distraction to the New Zealand election. In the very last debate Helen Clark changed tack and started being positive about John, who was a little surprised but reciprocated. By the end of the debate I was getting texts from people asking what had been put in the water.

The left had one last crack at a dirty-tricks attack before the election. Back in August, a Labour Party 'sympathiser' had infiltrated our election conference cocktail party pretending to be a National Party supporter. He used a digital tape recorder to secretly record a couple of hours of conversations with MPs, including Bill English, Lockwood Smith and Nick Smith. He then released some of the conversations to Duncan Garner at TV3.

There had been a story in October, about Kiwibank, and then a second just prior to the election on whether Barack Obama would be enough of a hawk in foreign policy. They were distracting, but didn't cause us any major problems, at least in part because the taper only released one side of the conversation and not what he had been saying to egg the MPs on. Needless to say, access to party functions was tightened up after that.

Election day, 8 November, dawned with us all feeling cautiously positive. All the signs were good, but it had been a long time between drinks for National. I went to the same Albany village polling booth as I had in 2005, and the vibe was much more positive. A good omen, I thought.

In the end the victory was quite convincing. National received a tick under 45 per cent of the party vote, to Labour's 34 per cent. We picked up a number of electorate seats from Labour, including Auckland Central, Maungakiekie, Waitākere, Hamilton West, New Plymouth, Ōtaki, Rotorua, Taupō, and West Coast-Tasman. Seats like Auckland Central and West Coast-Tasman had never been held by National before. Most importantly, we had a total of 58 seats in a 122-seat Parliament, not a majority but with a number of options to form a government.

Six years after an absolute drubbing in 2002 we were the largest party in Parliament, with the highest party vote of any party under

MMP to date. It was a great recovery. And on a personal note, yours truly was a newly minted MP, having been the highest new candidate at number sixteen on the National Party list. A very special night indeed.

Chapter Nine
Newly minted minister

THE VERY NEXT MORNING I was nominated to do the media rounds on behalf of the party as campaign chair, and I started pretty early with *Q + A*, *The Nation*, Radio New Zealand and Newstalk ZB. Then it was straight off to John Key's house in Parnell, where John held a meeting with Bill English, Wayne Eagleson, Gerry Brownlee, Simon Power, Murray McCully and myself, with an obligatory *Herald* photo.

There was much to discuss. John and Wayne had already been on the phone on election night with Peter Dunne, Rodney Hide from ACT, and Tariana Turia and Pita Sharples from the Māori Party. We didn't need coalition agreements with all three but John wanted to be inclusive, and it made sense tactically to have more than one way to assemble a majority in the House. John and Wayne's view was that all three would come together quite quickly.

John was also keen to have some sort of accommodation with the Greens, but we all knew that would be more difficult, and some of the group thought it an impossible ask given some of the Greens' policy positions and their attitude to the centre-right. It would need to go on a longer track.

The immediate question was whether John would be able to get to the APEC Leaders' meeting in Lima, Peru, in just a couple of weeks. It is important for New Zealand to be visible and active in organisations like APEC, but John would need to get the coalition arrangements and his ministry assembled first. That only left around ten days for both, which would break some sort of record under MMP.

I went home for a couple of days' rest and to wait for John's call, as did every other senior MP. When it came, it was friendly and direct. 'I want you to be Minister of Transport and Minister of ICT,' John said. 'You'll also be an Associate Minister of Finance to Bill.' He told me I'd be ranked at number 14 in Cabinet and then semi-apologised for the ranking, saying he didn't want to paint a target on my back too early. I was pretty relaxed about the number.

I was thrilled to be there and thrilled to bits to have the transport portfolio in particular. I'd been fascinated with transport since I was a kid, and had plenty of experience traversing the country's highways in my time growing RadioWorks. Having an opportunity to improve the roading network and everything else related to transport was a dream job. Fantastic.

John, Bill and Wayne did have the coalition agreements and Cabinet appointments all wrapped up in time for an official swearing-in on 21 November. Weirdly, I was a Cabinet minister before I was sworn in as an MP. We held our first Cabinet meeting that afternoon, and then John was off to APEC in Peru, then on to London to meet UK Prime Minister Gordon Brown and have an audience with the Queen. We were off to a rip-roaring start.

I had a million things to do in short order. Because I hadn't been an MP in Opposition, I had no idea what I was doing and no staff to help me get an office up and running. I was starting with nothing. But I had a stroke of luck; Suzanne used to work with and was friends with one of the best senior private secretaries in the business, Kathleen Lambert. Suzanne got on the phone and persuaded Kathleen to be my SPS — a coup for a new mid-ranked minister. Kathleen would have had her pick of at least a couple of the top half-dozen ministers. She had previously worked for a long period for Labour's Steve Maharey before he retired. Kathleen was a real pro, and completely apolitical.

Senior private secretaries are the glue that hold a minister's office together. They run the minister's office, act as a personal adviser to the minister, and are the primary gatekeeper on the minister's time. I had little appreciation of the role they played at first, I just saw that instantly things started to happen once Kathleen became involved. I don't know what she made of her minister on training wheels, but she took control and started to make things happen.

I also needed to find a political adviser and a media adviser. I was learning quickly that the first few days in the forming of a new ministry are a mad dash to grab the best people you can before someone else does. I was lucky again, picking up a senior policy adviser in Kenny Clark, who was related by marriage to Suzanne. He had been working in health in Opposition with Tony Ryall, but was a great generalist who I knew I could rely on. For media I was able to convince Anita Ferguson to leave the Leader's Office and come and work for me.

You can't do much about which physical office you get, you just take it. The allocation of offices is a top-down exercise run by the Leader of the House, in our case Gerry Brownlee. Gerry is a traditionalist for parliamentary protocol, and the Beehive is very hierarchical anyway. The prime minister and their staff are on the ninth floor, the Department of Prime Minister and Cabinet is on the eighth, ministers two, three and four are on the seventh floor, the next five ministers are on the sixth floor, and so on down the building. I started ministerial life with a fifth-floor office as one of six ministers, adjacent to Jonathan Coleman.

I initially thought my office suite was pretty big. It had a big office for me, with quite a large meeting-room table, plus four or five offices for other staff. What would we do with all this space? I didn't want to leap to judgement but it felt like the typical public-service extravagance I'd heard about.

Then I met all the officials. For a start my office had four ministerial advisers. These are normally youngish smart people on secondment from the portfolio ministry, to liaise between the minister and his or her ministries. They ensure all the briefings are done, the minister's work programme and questions are addressed by the ministry, correspondence is responded to, meetings arranged and so on. I found the good ones would have great initiative and work well with the political staff without overstepping their remit.

In my case I started with one adviser from the Ministry of Transport, two from the New Zealand Transport Agency (NZTA), including one to look after correspondence, and one from the Ministry of Economic Development covering the Information and Communications Technology (ICT) portfolio. Once you added the two diary and administrative staff, there were ten people in my office including me.

I was introduced to 'officials meetings', a weekly get-together of the lead officials for the portfolio, the minister and their key staff, and anyone working on a particular issue of the day. It didn't take me long to realise that once all the relevant advisers arrived, they would easily take up all the places at my meeting table, and the couches, and line the walls. Many weeks it was standing room only.

Often agency chief executives would bring along the person responsible for working on a policy or writing a briefing so they could hear the discussion and participate if required. I developed a habit of asking who in the room was actually working on a policy, and invite them up to the table to join the discussion, as they often knew more than the deputy chief executive who might be briefing me.

WHEN THERE IS A CHANGE of minister in a portfolio, whether accompanied by a change of government or not, each relevant agency prepares a briefing for the incoming minister. These are a full catch-up on everything that is happening in the portfolio, what decisions will shortly need to be made, and so on. They are prepared while the politicians are away politicking, and then finalised once the government is determined, with perhaps the addition of a summary of whatever is known about the incoming minister's priorities.

I was starting to work through all those briefings when I took an early-morning phone call on 28 November, which immediately brought home the seriousness of the transport portfolio. An Air New Zealand A320 had gone down at Perpignan, on the border between France and Spain, where it was being tested after being handed back from a charter airline. Five New Zealanders had been on board, and all lost their lives. I was suddenly spokesperson for the government's dismay and sadness, on behalf of the people of New Zealand.

Rob Fyfe, Air New Zealand's CEO, took personal responsibility for supporting the families of those killed, in a very dedicated and selfless way. He flew to Europe with them and stayed with them through all the formalities. Our key responsibility was ensuring a role for the New Zealand authorities in the investigation of the accident, which we were able to do after a few hiccups.

The big news remained the economy, and in particular the impact of the global turmoil in finance markets. A few months previously, inflation had been New Zealand's big problem. Now it was the risk of our recession turning into something worse, perhaps even a crash to rival that of the Great Depression. On 5 December, Reserve Bank

Governor Alan Bollard underlined the severity of the problem by cutting interest rates drastically again, this time by 1.5 per cent, from 6.5 to 5 per cent. It was an almost unheard-of level of rate cut, and it sent tremors through businesses around the country.

I was yet to set foot in Parliament itself, and the challenge of speaking in the House and answering questions on my portfolios was looming. I spent some time drafting my maiden speech, which is a personal statement about what brings you to Parliament, what motivates you, and what you'd like to achieve. I was making good progress on that, but still the 'answering questions' bit haunted me.

Parliament was due to commence sitting on 8 December, and a few days ahead of time I had a knock at the door. It was former PM Jim Bolger, popping by to see how the new boy was getting on. He sat down, gave me a few general bits of advice in his avuncular way, and then asked me whether there was anything I was worried about. I said my biggest concern was Question Time. I'd never asked a question in the House, let alone answered one. Did he have any advice for me?

He thought for a moment, and said, 'The thing you need to remember is that when you are answering questions you always get the last word. They can start the question but only you can finish it. So don't worry. You always have the upper hand.'

It was great advice that served me very well throughout my years as a minister. Something about knowing I always spoke last relaxed me, as I'm sure Jim intended. Sure, my first question or two was probably a bit stiff, but overall I enjoyed Question Time. I treated it as another opportunity to explain my position. I tried to always go in well prepared, because it is much easier to sound like you are across your brief if you actually are. If I was ever trapped by a gotcha question, I'd just use the old standby of asking the member to submit the details to my office and I'd provide a more detailed answer.

New MPs can't speak in Parliament until they have made their maiden statement. As a minister I needed to be able to speak, so I was given the privilege of making my maiden speech second after fellow new MP Sam Lotu-Iiga.

The maiden speech is one of the few times in Parliament when an MP can speak freely and personally about their journey and their beliefs. I thought long and hard about my speech, and decided to focus on what I believed I could bring to the debate in Parliament. I spoke about my family's background in small business, and my own experience in radio and at Jasons. I undertook to speak up for those risking their all running small- and medium-sized businesses around the country, 'people who pay their taxes and want to see them go to a good home', rather than having them wasted with little return. I spoke about playing to our strengths as a small, nimble, innovative country, and the importance of encouraging people who were striving to improve things for themselves and their families.

It was all over in a flash, and I was back speaking in the House for a second time that same evening. The new government had taken urgency to pass the tax cuts we had promised at the election, and as an Associate Minister of Finance, it was my job to promote them in the debate. I made my speech and had a bit of back and forth with the Opposition benches. I'm sure my first debate contribution was a bit amateur, but at least I was blooded and underway.

After a whirlwind week of parliamentary pomp and urgency, the House lifted for Christmas on 16 December, and we could all at last head home for the first real break all year. It was crucial to take time out when we could. With everything that was going on in the world, it wouldn't be a long one.

THAT YEAR I LEARNT THAT the one minister who doesn't tend to get much of a break is the Transport Minister. The Christmas New Year period is always a big one for transport stories. There is the holiday traffic, the holiday road toll, and always some other issues that crop up. Transport is one portfolio which doesn't go to sleep like many of the others. Just two days after Parliament broke for the year, a taxi driver was callously murdered in Christchurch while doing his job late at night. It wasn't the first time taxi drivers had been targeted. I ordered an urgent safety review on things like cameras and panic alarms in cabs to report back in the New Year.

In January the Pūhoi extension to Auckland's motorway was opening and it was being tolled, using a new cashless tolling system. John and I were both concerned about two things: the absence of a cash option for paying the toll, and the fact that the new road would be opened, and tolls would begin, on Auckland Anniversary weekend.

With John's encouragement I hassled NZTA to provide a cash option at booths north and south of the road to take care of those whose approach to tolling was more 'old-fashioned'. We also convinced NZTA to start tolling the road after Anniversary weekend. The effort made on that one road opening was truly sweating the small stuff, and in hindsight I'm not convinced I needed to spend anything like the time I did on it. In our defence, we were new and hypersensitive about not stuffing anything up in our early months in the job.

Through that first summer I built an easy rapport with the media, which I was able to mostly maintain for my whole time as a minister. I think it helped that I had worked in the industry for such a long time, including with many journalists, and had two in my own family: my brother Rodney and sister Diane. I'd also talked behind the scenes with a lot of senior journalists during the 2005 and 2008 election campaigns, which gave me a head start. While some of my colleagues operated from a position of suspicion of the media or of particular journalists, I tried to give them all the benefit of the doubt. My impression was that for the most part they just wanted to do their job, tell the story well and move on to the next one. My job in turn was to get my version of events published as clearly as I could. Sometimes it was easier than other times.

I tried to look at every interview, however searching, as an opportunity to communicate my story. During an interview, a useful mental exercise is to remind yourself that you are talking to the public at home, rather than the journalist in front of you. If you get annoyed at a journalist's questions, then the public will likely interpret it as you getting annoyed with them, and that's very unhelpful. I won't say I remembered this strategy every time, but I think my batting average was reasonable. When the cameras are on you it is very hard to think of all the things you need to think about, but as my friend Wayne Eagleson was wont to say, 'Politics isn't a game of perfect.'

Most of my break was taken up with reading. Lots of reading. There was so much to learn. I likened the flow of paper coming at me like sucking water from a fire hydrant. That remained true for my first years in office; it all just came gushing at you. I made the flow worse by asking each agency for some extra background summer reading to help me get up to speed. That became a tradition for me. It rather stuffed my break, but it helped me stay ahead of the game.

I also had a training programme of my own over that Christmas period. Suzanne had given me the full boxed set of the British comedy series *Yes Minister* and *Yes, Prime Minister* for Christmas, and we watched our way through it. Some of it turned out to be uncomfortably close to the way the New Zealand public service operated, and I had cause to remember it several times in the years ahead.

My favourite example is when something politically contentious is buried way down near the bottom of a briefing, and if you don't read all the way through, you miss it. Then much later, when the proverbial hits the fan, you ask why you weren't told. At that point the officials say, 'But you were, Minister. Here it is on page wherever of the briefing we sent you three months ago.' I learnt to read everything in full.

I'd already experienced one example of an agency attempting to 'manage' me in a different direction to the one I wished to go. I decided when I became minister to break the mould a little and go and visit the agencies in their own buildings, just to say hello to everyone and see where and how they worked. I went to the NZTA building on Victoria Street in Wellington, was shown around and met everyone, and then sat down briefly with Chairman Brian Roche and Chief Executive Geoff Dangerfield before heading back to the Beehive.

Just before they had left office, Labour had signed off the National Policy Statement for Transport, which was intended to serve as the direction of travel for the transport agencies for the next three years. While we were sitting there, Geoff said to me, 'Now there is just one thing, Minister, while you are here. We have completed the Land Transport Programme for the next three years following on from the National Policy Statement, and wondered if you would mind signing it off.'

He slid it over and I had a look. He made it all sound so banal and business-as-usual, just a bit of housekeeping really, but as I looked down the list it looked a lot like a bunch of projects and activity I might have a view on. I looked at Kenny Clark, who had his own copy, and he looked at me. I paused, and said, 'If it's all the same to you, I think we'll take this back to the office and have a more detailed look before signing it.' Geoff was a study in nonchalance. 'That's absolutely fine, Minister. We can send it over to you if you'd like.' I walked out realising that I had nearly signed off the previous government's infrastructure work programme, which would have tied my hands in the portfolio for the next three years. Bullet dodged.

I got on well with Geoff during my time in the portfolio. He was a highly capable chief executive who always got things done. In his defence, on that occasion he probably didn't realise the extent of my ambitions for the portfolio, but he was also smart enough to never let an opportunity go by.

AS THE NEW YEAR BEGAN, the GFC loomed even larger and John's mind was starting to turn to rallying the country to combat the economic fallout. A few ideas were percolating around, and I suggested to both him and Wayne that we call an early meeting of economic ministers, to both show we were focused and active, and bring some order to the various ideas. The meeting was held in John's office on 16 January, and it was then that John fleshed out his idea for an employment summit on 27 February.

There were mixed views amongst ministers about that plan. They were all raring to get into their work. Some of them had been waiting for the opportunity for nine years after all, and some were worried their own ideas and programmes might get derailed by the summit. There were also reservations amongst some about the PM's choice of summit chair, NZX CEO Mark Weldon.

It had a bit of a smell of the Knowledge Wave about it, a conference where everyone gets together and opines and nothing much changes. That sense was perhaps not a surprise, as the idea was cooked up with the same officials, more or less, who had come up with said Knowledge Wave. We wanted to be known as a more action-oriented government that knew what needed to be done and led from the front.

Nevertheless, we all went along with it on the basis we would follow through on all the useful ideas it surfaced. And it did turn out to be a success, both as a rallying point for all the disparate voices in the business sector, and for some of the ideas that came from it. It was a handy political statement as well, showing we were on the job.

Key initiatives flowing from the Job Summit included the nine-day fortnight, a range of government capital projects, the national cycleway programme which John championed throughout his premiership, improvements to the financial bond programme for central and local government, and measures to increase skills training.

One thing was certain. The Global Financial Crisis was now the worst economic shock the world had seen since the Great Depression. The recovery from it would dominate our first years in government.

Chapter Ten
Build more roads

MY MAIN FOCUS AFTER THE Job Summit was to get on with the job of accelerating infrastructure investment in the transport sector, particularly in the roading system.

We had two main transport policies going into the 2008 election, to set up a 'Roads of National Significance' programme, and a specific commitment to complete the Waikato Expressway within ten years. There was much detail to be filled out on both of those two pledges. Beyond the Waikato Expressway it was pretty much a blank canvas.

The New Zealand roading network is the backbone of our domestic transport system. When I became minister it was responsible for 84 per cent of personal journeys each day, whether by car or by bus. It carried 70 per cent of our freight and probably carries more now. It is the primary means of connecting our seaports and airports with their regional hinterlands.

Simply put, the roading system does most of the heavy lifting for transport across New Zealand and will likely do so for the foreseeable future. We are sparsely populated by world standards and, outside of Auckland, people are dispersed across our country. While the propulsion method of vehicles will change from fossil fuels to electricity, hydrogen and the like as we reduce carbon emissions, the need for multi-point to multi-point road transport is unlikely to diminish.

New Zealand's road-building history has been a story of stop-start construction. While a motorway network had been largely built in Auckland and an urban motorway of sorts constructed in Wellington, there were precious few other parts of the country that enjoyed safe, efficient highways in the first decade of the twenty-first century. Most of our highways are still on the alignments adopted when horses and carts were the main means of transport. While the width, construction and surfaces have been progressively improved, the building of new wider, safer roads on better alignments using modern construction techniques is a rarity.

We have also been guilty of building new roads 'a bit at a time', adding a few kilometres here and there, and only building roads just wide enough for current traffic levels. While the most well-known example of not building roads big enough was the Auckland Harbour Bridge, the approach has been endemic.

The very first road I opened was constructed while my predecessor Annette King was minister. The Mangatāwhiri deviation is on a particularly busy and dangerous piece of State Highway 2. From where it begins from State Highway 1 in Pōkeno south of Auckland through to where it splits with State Highway 29 north of Morrinsville, this section of windy road takes huge amounts of traffic to the Coromandel Peninsula, the Bay of Plenty and east Waikato.

The Labour Government built a high-quality road to bypass Mangatāwhiri, but inexplicably didn't make it a four-lane dual carriageway while they were there. It is also inexplicable that they didn't treble the length of it to deal with the similarly dangerous Maramarua section further east, and the Kopu curves after that. With the diggers and equipment already in place it would have made sense to do the job once and do it properly.

I met the local volunteer fire chief at the road opening. Like most Waikato fire chiefs he spent much more time attending vehicle accidents than anything else. While he was happy the road had been improved, he was saddened the government had stopped short of separating the traffic with a proper four-lane highway. 'I'll be back here soon fishing people out of head-on car crashes.' He was right, of course. The project created a small section of road where everyone thought they could get ahead of everyone else before it deteriorated again. While the accident record of that road is better than it was, it could have been far better again.

Funding is one of the big reasons for our poor roading network. New Zealand nearly went broke in the 1980s, and much of the 1990s was spent repairing the government's financial position. There was precious little money left over for roading infrastructure. Michael Cullen continued with infrastructural austerity until the 2005 election, when National was able to shame him into dedicating road taxes towards building and maintaining roads, the so-called hypothecation of petrol and diesel taxes. This led to the commencement of construction of parts of the Western Ring Route in Auckland.

Party politics has also played a part in our stop-start approach to road-building. The political left around the world is much more interested in mass transit (buses and trains) than personal transport (cars). The right is more interested in personal mobility, flexibility and freedom. For the most part the two rub along together. In Australia both Labor and Coalition governments build roads. They also both build mass transit in the main centres. Only in New Zealand is the modern political left so anti road-building. The Greens in particular take a hair-shirt approach to road construction, which at times infects the Labour Party. As a result, the political pendulum contributes to the on-again off-again approach to roading investment, and transport investment generally. With every change of government, plans get ripped up and restarted, wasting a lot of time and money.

I really wanted to move the dial on infrastucture and make some serious investments in improving our main highways, while at the same time improving commuter rail. As a road user, I'd always been critical of all the 'think small' approaches of past governments. This was my chance to really make a difference — to prove what we as a country could achieve if we really put our minds to it.

We needed a plan, and the means to pay for it. A plan without a funding stream is just an announcement of what you'd like to do, and a jaded public would be unlikely to be impressed. The only problem was we were in the middle of the Global Financial Crisis, and Bill English was not inclined to write big cheques for road funding, or anything else. I would for the most part have to do better with what I already had at my disposal.

I went to work trying to shape up a bigger investment in road-building. The previous government had left me a load of problems. Their Government Policy Statement for Transport forecast a funding decline for state highway building from about a third of money collected from petrol and diesel taxes to less than a quarter over the next ten years. Big chunks of the money were being eaten up in all sorts of pet projects, from regional road-safety programmes (in addition to the national one) to public-transport infrastructure and coastal shipping. Officials had voted themselves big increases in planning and administration budgets as well. Meanwhile, Labour had agreed to allow for regional fuel taxes, a piecemeal approach that the Auckland Regional Council in particular was keen to adopt, to fund their commuter-train electrification.

I decided to release a revised Government Policy Statement that reversed what I saw as the foolhardy elements of the most recent one, and restored the investment in roading infrastructure. I also cancelled regional fuel taxes and replaced them with a smaller increase in national taxes, which would top up the National Land Transport

Fund and increase the amounts available for road-building and other activities like road maintenance. Cancelling regional fuel taxes would place the Auckland electrification in jeopardy, so I persuaded Bill and my other colleagues to fund that and other public-transport investments outside the National Land Transport Fund.

We moved fast, because we had to. If you are going to do anything to change infrastructure outcomes within a three-year election cycle, then you only have the first six months in office to make decisions. In March 2009, John Key and I announced a major realignment in transport funding. Our changes to the National Land Transport Fund, together with a $250 million sweetener from Bill and the Treasury to pay for some Wellington commuter-rail investment outside the fund, allowed us to announce a total of $1 billion in extra investment in the state-highway network over the next three years, taking the total up to $3 billion for highway-building.

Importantly the new Government Policy Statement signalled some $11 billion in total for highway construction over the ten years to 2019, just under 50 per cent more than the previous government had projected. That signalling was important. I knew that if we were going to build a decent number of roads then we needed to increase the contractor workforce. That would only happen if companies could see a big pipeline of forward work and had the confidence to invest in the equipment and people they would need. Too often it was easier to grow their businesses in Australia, where the pipeline of big projects was more reliable.

I was thrilled at being able to secure this funding commitment so early in our time in office, and against the fiscal challenges of the time. I was lucky that the bulk of transport funding came from petrol and road-user taxes already hypothecated to the portfolio. Other ministers didn't have that privilege. Now I had to confirm the building plan.

At first glance it wasn't easy. New Zealand has some 11,000

kilometres of state highways, and a case can be made for doing some sort of work on most of them. However, most didn't need big capacity improvements of the type that would mean a new alignment and two lanes in each direction. With the Roads of National Significance programme, we needed to prioritise the roads which would have the greatest economic and safety impact for the country as a whole.

Within the state-highway network there are a small proportion of highways that carry most of the traffic and most of the freight. NZTA identified 700 kilometres of state highway they called 'high-volume highways'. These roads comprise just 6.5 per cent of the state highways and less than 1 per cent of the total roading network but carry nearly 20 per cent of the traffic and 20 per cent of freight across the whole country. We focused on those. My view was that if we could make material improvements to those highways over a 20- to 30-year period, they would bring both significant economic benefits and a material reduction in the road toll.

Not surprisingly, the high-volume highways linked our largest centres with their regional hinterlands. From Auckland up to Wellsford, down to Taupō and across to and east of Tauranga, from Wellington to Levin and to the Hutt Valley, between Napier and Hastings, and the roads north and south of Christchurch. We then reviewed the work that needed to be done in each area, and prioritised an initial programme of seven Roads of National Significance.

THE FIRST CAB OFF THE rank was the Waikato Expressway, the long-talked-about plan to run a four-lane expressway from the end of the Auckland motorway at the Bombay Hills right through to Cambridge, 100 kilometres to the south. I remember first hearing about it when I moved to Hamilton in the early 1990s, around the time the first Bombay to Mercer section was being built. At that stage the expressway was expected to be finished within ten years.

Since then the pace of construction had been painfully slow.

Eighteen kilometres of the road was built during the time of the Clark government, namely a bypass at Ohinewai and a section from Mercer to Hampton Downs. At that rate of progress it would take another 40 years to build the remaining 80-odd kilometres. No wonder it had been such an election issue. Our commitment to complete the expressway within ten years was very well received by voters across the Waikato. It also made absolute sense. The Waikato is the biggest regional hinterland of the Auckland economy, and an economic driver in its own right. It forms part of the golden triangle, along with the Bay of Plenty and Auckland.

The expressway was also hugely important from a safety perspective. The poor quality of the highways through the Waikato, coupled with the huge volume of traffic generated by Auckland, meant the region had long had one of the poorest road-safety records in the country. The expressway would take the pressure off north–south rat runs like the one through Matamata, which people had been taking to avoid the snail-like progress on the main road.

I received an early briefing from the officials. There were seven sections of expressway still to be built: Longswamp, Rangiriri, the Huntly bypass, the Ngāruawāhia bypass, Te Rapa, the Hamilton bypass and the Cambridge bypass. They took me on a helicopter survey up the route from Hamilton to Mercer. The most intriguing bit was the Huntly bypass, which was planned to head up the eastern side of the Taupiri ranges, in a whole new alignment through some pretty rugged country.

To get all seven sections built within a decade would be a huge challenge, particularly given the small amount of work done on some of them to date. A few were designed and consented, but several weren't much more than lines on a map — as it had been anticipated they wouldn't be built for decades. Engineering work needed to be done, consents obtained and properties purchased.

To get things rolling, NZTA and I agreed they would provide

funding for the first two sections immediately, while officials did the work preparing the other five. Construction commenced on the Te Rapa bypass in 2010, while Ngāruawāhia started in 2011. The combined cost was just over $300 million.

There was some debate about the order of the remaining sections. Hamilton City Council and Tainui wanted the Hamilton bypass built first, Tainui because of the big logistics hub they were planning in Ruakura. I knew both the Huntly bypass and the Rangiriri sections would be more contentious, as they affected iwi land around Taupiri mountain and the pā at Rangiriri. I wanted the design and consenting for those sections agreed, including with Tainui, before we went ahead with Hamilton.

NZTA allocated design funding for Huntly in 2010, and for Hamilton in 2011. By then we had a full plan for building the expressway. According to our plan, the Hamilton bypass would open in 2020, one year after our 2019 commitment. Eighty kilometres of Waikato Expressway would be completed in eleven years.

Construction of the road proceeded at pace. The Ngāruawāhia bypass opened in 2013, Cambridge in 2015 and Huntly in 2020. The final Hamilton section was opened in 2022 after the Ardern government closed down roading construction for long periods during the Covid-19 pandemic. Completion of the expressway was one hell of a milestone to achieve, and a real testament to what can be done if a secure line of funding is in place. The Waikato Expressway proved that big infrastructure projects can be built in New Zealand, on budget and (pandemics aside) on time.

WE SETTLED ON THREE ROADS of National Significance in the Auckland region: the Pūhoi to Wellsford project, the Victoria Park tunnel in the middle of the city, and the completion of the Western Ring Route, including the Waterview link.

The Victoria Park tunnel was the shortest of the seven, but its length belied its importance. The old Victoria Park flyover was a notorious chokepoint in the city, and the reason for the traffic backing up over the Harbour Bridge. People often said the bridge was congested, but in fact it was the two-lane-each-way flyover just south of the bridge that caused the snarl-ups.

NZTA had a plan to build a tunnel for north-bound traffic, and use the old flyover solely for south-bound traffic, turning two lanes south into four. We agreed, and funded it through the programme. The Victoria Park tunnel has the distinction of being the first Road of National Significance funded, and the first opened to traffic, late in 2011. It had an instant positive impact on congestion on the Harbour Bridge.

The Western Ring Route was a project initiated by the Clark government to build an alternative south-to-north through-route using Highways 20, 16 and 18, instead of State Highway 1 through the city. They had started work on it, funding the construction of the Hobsonville motorway through Upper Harbour, and the widening of the Māngere Bridge, both of which we opened on completion.

There is an interesting postscript to the Māngere project, which is a good illustration why ministers should always sense-check the work of officials. As the new minister I had been shown over the Māngere Bridge project, and was interested in how it would tie in with the existing State Highway 20 to the south of the bridge. The bridge was being widened to seven lanes, three going north and four going south, quite a step up from the old bridge of two lanes in each direction. However, it looked to me on the plans that the four lanes going south would be narrowed to just two lanes after the bridge, before widening out again a few hundred metres later into two highways of two lanes each, one going to the airport and one going south to Manukau. Surely that couldn't be right?

I asked the obvious question and was told, yes, things were as they appeared. The road will narrow into two lanes, before widening out again just down the road. The reason was the adjacent on-ramp at Walmsley Road. The engineers didn't want people having to cross three or four lanes of traffic to go from the Walmsley on-ramp to the airport. I was aghast. Surely that wasn't the answer? Dropping down to two lanes so soon after the new bridge would create a permanent bottleneck.

I quizzed the engineers further and asked for a sanity check on their plan. Surely there had to be a better solution? And it turned out there was. A few months later NZTA came back and said they had reworked the Walmsley Road on-ramp. Now it would be extended further south so cars entering from there could no longer cross over the other lanes and head to the airport. With that change made they could leave the main road at three lanes rather than two.

I was relieved, and a little worried that it had taken the minister to get this change made. We'd have to do more work on customer (i.e. road-user) focus at NZTA. Every time I go past that point on the network, I still think how horrible that bottleneck would have been.

The big issue with the Western Ring Route was how to fund and build the Waterview Connection, the link between State Highway 20, which finished at Mount Roskill, and the established North-Western motorway. The Clark government had decided to go for an expensive, fully tunnelled option under the suburbs of Ōwairaka, Avondale Heights and Waterview. This was the preferred approach, naturally enough, of the local MP — who also happened to be prime minister at the time.

The total cost was projected to be $2.77 billion for two two-lane tunnels, which was phenomenally expensive for such a short piece of road, and there was no funding set aside for it. It was assumed NZTA would borrow the money to build the project, and the eye-watering total included some allowance for interest on the huge debt.

I decided we had to have another look at the project in order to get it under some sort of control. I announced we would be relooking at all the options for the link, including a shorter cut-and-cover tunnel, and surface options. I was also concerned at the number of lanes proposed for the connection. My strong sense was with two lanes in each direction it would be full from the moment it opened, just like the Auckland Harbour Bridge 60 years previously. I did not want to be the minister that repeated the mistakes of the Harbour Bridge.

I had a number of discussions with officials on the Waterview project, and at one stage they asked me what I thought would be a satisfactory outcome. I said if they could bring it back to me $1 billion cheaper and one lane in each direction wider then we might have a deal. In the meantime I did a bit of quiet exploration on my own, driving around Avondale and Waterview to get a sense of the level of disruption and acceptability of different options. I wanted it to work for the local communities but also not be gold-plated.

NZTA came back with a new option in September 2009 which looked like it might meet my requirements. They could build Waterview using tunnels for 60 per cent of its length, and the tunnels could be three lanes in each direction. The price would be $1.4 billion, still expensive but nothing like $2.8 billion. Importantly, at that price it could be funded out of the National Land Transport Fund. I gave the green light, and they set to work.

Waterview was a contentious project with a small but vocal group of protesters, mostly based in the Waterview community. The day of the sod-turning was the first time I came face to face with protesters on a roading project. There was quite a bit of spitting and hissing, but nothing more serious. I could understand their stress; the project had been hanging over their community for a long time. Our job was to come up with an answer that worked best for everyone.

One of the protesters' concerns was the new consenting process. Environment Minister Nick Smith had done an excellent job amending the Resource Management Act (RMA) to allow for Projects of National Significance — a new approach developed with big roading programmes in mind. Under Nick's amendments, large projects like these could be 'called in' to a one-stop Board of Inquiry process, with limited appeal rights only on technical points of law. The idea was to encourage both applicants and opponents to turn up with their best offer, and not allow the process to drag on for years and years to the detriment of both sides.

Waterview was the first big project to be called in in this way, and it worked very well. Both NZTA and the opponents on the other side were incentivised to compromise, as there was only 'one shot' at getting the right answer. NZTA made a number of early concessions around the tunnel design and the impact on Waterview Primary School in order to increase the likelihood of approval. The whole Board of Inquiry consenting process took just ten months from beginning to end, and approval was received in July 2011. Such a complex decision would normally have taken years and years with myriad appeals.

Much later I had the opportunity to meet the leader of the Waterview protest at the road opening. Interestingly she told me that despite opposing the Board of Inquiry process, it had been a good thing for the community. They had benefited from a quick decision and won concessions they otherwise wouldn't have received. It was a real vote of confidence in the process Nick had set up.

There was a huge complementary set of work required to widen the North-Western motorway to make room for the Western Ring Route traffic. Construction started there in 2010 with the new Lincoln Road interchange. The contract for Waterview itself was signed in mid-2011 with an international consortium of Fletcher Construction, Downer and Obayashi Corporation. Construction started at the end of that year and the new tunnels opened in 2017.

The Waterview Connection is one of my favourite infrastructure projects. As well as providing the missing piece of the puzzle for Auckland's Western Ring Route, it finally provides a quality link from Auckland Airport to the inner city. For decades people lamented the only way into the city from the airport was through the back streets of Onehunga and Epsom. Overseas visitors would often look sideways at their taxi drivers as they got off the motorway at Onehunga and zig-zagged across the city.

At the time, the *Herald*'s editorial writer John Roughan publicly doubted Waterview would be used as the main route to the city from the airport, but experience has proven it works well. Most times of the day the trip can be done in 20 to 25 minutes. Surprisingly the Ardern government that followed us didn't seem to realise that the Waterview Connection is a game-changer for both car and bus transport, instead promoting light rail between the city and airport, ostensibly to shorten journey times. In every measurable way, light rail will take longer. Including it seems, in the construction.

Chapter Eleven
The 'Holiday Highway' and other follies

IT WAS FORMER AUCKLAND REGIONAL COUNCIL chair and sometimes Auckland councillor Mike Lee who coined the phrase 'Holiday Highway' to describe our third big Auckland project, the proposed four-lane highway linking Auckland and Northland. The highway was to run between Pūhoi and Wellsford, a distance of 38 kilometres.

Mike and I got on reasonably well despite being from opposite sides of politics. We did a lot of work together on the Auckland commuter rail network, and generally came up with sensible and practical solutions. But I thought he was completely wrong to oppose the Pūhoi to Wellsford highway. In my opinion he and many other critics were guilty of a very 'inner-city Auckland' view.

I have been visiting Northland on and off for all my life, and have always been surprised at how undeveloped it was, particularly the Far North. Northland is an area of beautiful beaches, stunning geography and abundant land. But it seems doomed to remain a region of limitless possibility, with high levels of unemployment and the accompanying issues of social deprivation.

The paradox that is Northland is even harder to understand given its proximity to our biggest city. The challenge for places like Taranaki, where I come from, Tairāwhiti and Southland is their remoteness from our centres of population. Northland literally has a city of 1.7 million people just down the road.

And therein lies a clue to Northland's lack of economic success. The roads between Auckland and Northland have always been poor. The geography is challenging, with natural features like the Dome Valley and Brynderwyn Hills acting as a barrier between the two. Add in slippery soils and heavy subtropical rainfall and you need an unusually high quality of road construction to create a reliable, safe route.

The previous Labour Government had extended Auckland's Northern motorway past Ōrewa as far as a little village called Pūhoi, and that was where they wanted to terminate it. Compact-city advocates like Mike Lee didn't want to extend it any further because it would only encourage people to live further north. He wanted to prevent growth outside the Auckland urban limits. The decision was a disaster from a transport perspective, with six lanes of traffic from two roads reducing to two lanes in a paddock just outside Pūhoi. Traffic would then crawl up a dangerously slow highway to Warkworth, Matakana, Wellsford and eventually into Northland proper.

I saw building a decent road, at least as far as Wellsford, as the first step in a Northland Expressway through to Whangārei, to match the Waikato Expressway to the south. I believed, and still believe, that a decent highway between Auckland and Northland is one of only two significant levers that governments can pull to create a prosperous future for the north. The other would be a comprehensive Ngāpuhi treaty settlement, which would create a permanently anchored local investor to rival Tainui in the Waikato and Ngāi Tahu in the South Island. There are lots of things you can tinker with, but only those two can really create a substantial sea change for the north, and the Ngāpuhi settlement requires the iwi to be ready to settle.

The case for the road is unimpeachable, whatever the Green Party might say to the contrary. It is already used by more than 25,000 vehicles a day so it is no white elephant, unlike the Northland trunk railway line which is barely used. Rail freight is completely impractical at the Auckland end, where commuter rail takes up all the available track space.

There is strong evidence for the economic benefits of building roads adjacent to main centres to encourage development. Motu Research, an economic consultancy, did a comprehensive study following the extension of Auckland's Northern motorway to Albany and Ōrewa, looking at its impact on property prices as a proxy for economic development. The uplift in property values was conclusive, as it has been on the Waikato Expressway and the Kāpiti Expressway and Transmission Gully north of Wellington. There is no doubt that building Pūhoi to Wellsford would unlock a huge amount of growth and employment across the middle of Northland, with a halo effect further north.

The first half of the road, Pūhoi to Warkworth, was slated to be completed in the ten-year window for the first tranche of Roads of National Significance, with the Warkworth to Wellsford section starting construction in 2018 or 2019. Pūhoi to Warkworth was also delayed by the Ardern government's pandemic restrictions, but it is now open and delivering excellent benefits for road users and the lower Northland community. It is an impressive piece of highway.

Unfortunately, Warkworth to Wellsford has been on again and off again since the change of government, and shows no sign of being built at the time of writing, six years after our government left office. Four-laning south of Whangārei has also been on the slow track. We seem to have returned to incrementalism, at a time when appalling weather has shown the importance of prioritising resilience for critical highways, especially in the top half of the country.

Warkworth to Wellsford was never going to be easy. It's a very expensive project as a result of the land it travels through, with a price tag something like a billion dollars for about 20 kilometres. It was also one of two projects (the other being the Levin bypass) which weren't going to easily fit within the ten-year funding envelope for the first round of Roads of National Significance. They were flagged as such at the time.

I regret we didn't get the Wellsford project contracted for construction before leaving office in 2017. The plans are there now, and property along the corridor has been purchased. Hopefully a future government will pick it up and run with it, as well as the whole concept of the Northland Expressway, to boost the economic future of that beautiful region and provide a safe means of travel to and from it.

THE TAURANGA EASTERN LINK WAS a much easier project to get going because it had the united support of the Bay of Plenty's leaders. Often when you start talking with regional stakeholders there is a lack of local agreement about what projects should happen first. The Bay of Plenty has no shortage of big roading projects on their list; Tauranga, in particular, has grown hugely over the past 30 years, moving from being just another provincial city to the fourth-largest in the country, ahead of Dunedin.

The roading network on the approaches to Tauranga has not kept pace with the growth in population and traffic. On all three sides, the roads in and out of town were slow and winding with high volumes of traffic, a recipe which encourages risky behaviour. State Highway 2, which brings traffic from Rotorua and the eastern Bay of Plenty through Te Puke, was rated as having the second-poorest safety record in the country, closely followed by the highway on the other side of Tauranga, from Bethlehem to Katikati and beyond.

The Tauranga Eastern Link project was a 23-kilometre highway from Paengaroa to Mount Maunganui, bypassing Te Puke and providing motorway access to the fast-growing Papamoa area. It would reduce the time taken from Paengaroa to the Mount by ten to fifteen minutes. Even Rotorua, whose notorious competition with Tauranga dates back from when it was the bigger city, supported the Eastern Link. It was an easy candidate for the Roads of National Significance.

The new road was going to cost around $450 million to build. The challenge would be fitting it into the first half of the programme, which prioritised projects that needed to be built in sequence (for example, the Waikato Expressway). Officials agreed we could bring the Eastern Link forward if the locals were prepared to toll the road, as that would provide a funding stream to pay for it.

Not so promisingly, the officials wanted to build the road in their old incremental way, initially building one lane in each direction and the extra lanes later when capacity demanded it. I wasn't having it. In the New Zealand infrastructure context, 'later' is generally 'never', as other projects will always get priority and the partly built one will go to the back of the queue. I was firmly of the view we should build it once and do it properly, and in any event I wasn't prepared to toll a road which didn't provide a greater level of service than a normal highway (i.e. it needed to have passing lanes). Takitimu Drive, which Tauranga City Council had built itself, had always been a poor excuse for a toll road, as anyone stuck behind a truck on it could attest.

I came to an agreement with NZTA (tolling plus four lanes), and we went out to the community with a tolling plan to bring the road forward. Over 90 per cent of those who responded agreed with the tolling proposal, and we were able to start construction in 2010, officially opening the road five years later in 2015.

I'm not sure Bay of Plenty residents would have been quite

as supportive of tolling if they'd known theirs would be the only tolled road in the Roads of National Significance programme. I had intended both Transmission Gully and Pūhoi to Warkworth to also be tolled, partly to further introduce the concept of tolling around the country to fund quality roading infrastructure. Subsequent transport ministers have cancelled all further tolling initiatives on state highways, which is a real loss for infrastructure funding.

THE SOUTH ISLAND PROJECTS SELECTED for the Roads of National Significance were the three Christchurch motorway projects: the Northern Corridor between the city and the Waimakiriri River, the Southern motorway linking the city to Rolleston and beyond, and the Western Corridor, which provides a western bypass for people travelling through the city and to and from Christchurch Airport.

I was a big believer in investing in Christchurch from day one in office. Christchurch is effectively the capital city of the South Island, and it hosts the South Island's biggest air- and seaports. Both suffered from poor landside infrastructure, and the roads north and south of the city were congested death traps where many risks were taken and lives lost.

In our initial exploration, the NZTA officials and I looked at the three projects individually. However, all had equal merits, and at a collective cost of less than a billion dollars it made sense to build all three to support the economic development of Christchurch and the whole South Island. Better linkages between Christchurch and its surrounding regions made sense both economically and for safety.

Christchurch is historically quite a conservative city, and there was initially some pushback at the scale and timing of what we proposed. Christchurch likes a more sedate pace. Even our senior local MP Gerry Brownlee took some convincing on the merits of some of the work. The most striking element of the project would be the overpass bridge across the entrance to Christchurch Airport.

There was much sucking of teeth from both Gerry and new MP Amy Adams when that was first proposed.

On the other side of the aisle, I had inherited the former Labour mayor of Christchurch Garry Moore as a NZTA board member when I became minister, and he turned out to be a real advocate for the Christchurch Roads of National Significance. His support tended to blunt the more strident left-wing opposition to building more roads, which is never far away in Christchurch.

You can't discuss the Christchurch motorway projects without considering the impact of the Canterbury earthquakes. NZTA had commenced construction on the first project, Stage One of the Southern motorway, prior to the first quake, and shortly after the second (February) quake I visited the construction crews on the road. They told me how, with all the aftershocks, they had to resurvey the road at the start of most days to check the land was literally where they had left it when they'd finished work the day before.

They also told me about the sudden change of attitude from those living around the project. Before the earthquakes it was all complaints about noise, dust, or simply the act of construction. Afterwards the locals were much more friendly. The onlookers were happy to see something positive happening and progress being made, which gave then some confidence in those early post-earthquake days.

The earthquakes and the rebuilding thereafter underlined the strategic sense of the new Christchurch motorway projects. With people moving from the city and eastern suburbs to new houses in places like Rolleston and Waimakiriri, the need for new highways became acute. They went from being built slightly ahead of the projected need to just in time. In light of the changing shape of Christchurch, more work now urgently needs to be done to extend the motorways both north and south of the city, to further improve safety and journey times.

PROBABLY THE MOST AUDACIOUS AND controversial of the Roads of National Significance was the Levin to Airport project between Wellington and the wider lower North Island. The economic and safety arguments were similar to the other regional projects, but even more accentuated by the geography.

Whoever made the decision to build the capital city of a small country on the site of a fishing village below an exposed earthquake-prone headland at the bottom of one of the country's two islands deserves some sort of medal for courage. The city is a triumph both of engineering and improbable romanticism, but it does make for challenging transport links. When the safest road in and out of a city is likely to be a new highway through a very deep gully in preference to a coastal road at the bottom of a sheer cliff face, or a windy goat-track over a high set of ranges, you know you are dealing with something special.

The lower North Island regions of Whanganui and Manawatū have struggled economically in recent times, failing to develop at the pace of, say, Canterbury, or the more northerly regions of Waikato and Bay of Plenty. A lack of safe, reliable transport links with the capital and its airport, and in particular the roading system, has obviously been part of that story. For its part, Wellington needs much safer land-based links to and from the city, not least for its response to any natural disasters that may come its way.

The Levin to Airport Road of National Significance therefore made strategic sense. The question was where to build each element of it. North of the city, major work was needed from Porirua through to Levin, and one big project, Transmission Gully, had been talked about forever.

Transmission Gully was the proposed replacement route for the coastal highway, and it ran up behind the coastal mountains. Everybody growing up in and around Wellington had heard stories about its history: how the US Marines had offered to build it during the Second World War (that was probably false; apparently they also offered to fix the Manawatū Gorge); how it would be too steep for trucks (also probably false); and how it would be more dangerous than the current road (definitely false). And everyone knew it was expensive, which is largely why it hadn't been built.

As the new minister I was relentlessly lobbied by Ōhāriu MP Peter Dunne, who had made Transmission Gully a cause célèbre for years, and my colleague and friend Nathan Guy, the new Ōtaki MP, whose electorate was hugely in favour of the new road for the access it would provide from the Kāpiti Coast to the city. I was less convinced, and had the officials and Wellington Regional Council Chair Fran Wilde take me on a tour of both the current road and the proposed new route to understand and evaluate the options.

We flew in a helicopter up the gully route, which looked very remote and wild, and then drove the coastal route afterwards. Building Transmission Gully looked very hard, but improving the old highway looked even harder. When the engineers started talking about stacking one direction of the highway on top of the other along the bottom of the cliff at Pukerua Bay, or wiping out much of Pukerua Bay village and taking the end off the bluff at Plimmerton, I could clearly see the problem.

I took a deep breath and started discussing the options with my Cabinet colleagues. A little to my surprise, they readily agreed to support Transmission Gully. Under any objective analysis it was the only option.

I wasn't happy though with the answers I was getting as to what would happen at the northern end of the gully, where it rejoined the old highway at Paekākāriki. The Transmission Gully highway would cost around a billion dollars on its own, and I couldn't see the point in building it if all the traffic then came to a screeching halt at the traffic lights at Paraparaumu or Waikanae.

A planner with commendable foresight had reserved a designation for a motorway corridor through the Kāpiti Coast around 50 years earlier. It was called the Sandhills motorway designation and many people on the coast knew about it, as it manifested as a stretch of lupin-covered scrub that ran from Raumati up to the Waikanae River and then between Waikanae and Waikanae Beach.

It was the logical place to build the new highway, and it would link well with Transmission Gully to the south and the highway further north. In fact it was the only place it could realistically go. The villages of Raumati, Paraparaumu and Waikanae are all located on a small coastal plain between the Ruahine Range and the sea. Given the housing development that had occurred, the only possible north–south transport corridors were the railway line, the old highway next to it, and the Sandhills designation.

I knew the geography like the back of my hand. Our family had moved from Taranaki to the Kāpiti Coast when I was fourteen, and I had spent my teens riding horses all around the coast, down the Sandhills designation, through Queen Elizabeth Park, up the beaches, across the Waikanae River and up to Reikorangi. There wasn't much of the area I hadn't covered.

The problem with the Sandhills designation was that the previous government had proposed allowing it to be used by the local district council for a new local road to meander through the district. I was aghast. This was one time where the forethought had actually been done, and the carefully planned futureproofing was being given away.

I asked NZTA where they planned to put the north–south highway if the designation was indeed returned. Their first answer was to leave it on the route of the old highway, and improve it by bulldozing houses on either side to widen it and make it safer. That sounded disastrous. As well as the cost and the impact of destroying all those homes, the old road ran through the middle of the main shopping streets of Paraparaumu and Waikanae villages, and alongside the railway line. Commuters getting on and off trains would be forever faced with a wide highway to navigate before going home. The two towns would be permanently split in half. This didn't seem like a sensible answer.

Their second answer didn't sound much better. 'Somewhere else.' Where exactly? There was silence. I decided we had to reverse course, and in mid-2009 I made a public call on NZTA and the Kāpiti Coast District Council to come up with a strategic plan for the future of State Highway 1 through the district.

Things were hotting up. The Kapiti mayor at the time, Jenny Rowan, was a Green Party supporter, and she was wedded to the idea of using the Sandhills designation for a local feeder road, and slowing people down as they travelled through her district. Labour and the Greens lined up behind her. On the other side were Nathan Guy and the majority of his constituents, plus those needing to use the highway to move to and from Wellington. Depending on their perspective, I was either the sensible and pragmatic Transport Minister, or the devil incarnate for even suggesting a new expressway through the district. My sister Diane was caught in the crossfire as the editor at the time of the local newspaper, the *Kapiti Observer*.

The council invited me to a meeting to discuss the options, and stacked it with suitable proponents of the 'local road' argument. It was a tense meeting, but Diane unintentionally broke the ice when her phone alarm went off loudly just as I had been invited to speak, which drew laughter from all sides.

There were community meetings along the coast, some for and some against but mostly mixed. I think I attended four or five, and Nathan would have attended more. NZTA tried to propose two options for the road: either the existing highway, or the existing highway through to the Waikanae River, and the new designation north of there. But by then the public had had enough and the call went up for a third option: a full expressway on the old Sandhills designation.

It was the Sandhills Expressway that won the day, and by the end of 2009 the debate was all over. I was happy because we had a sensible plan for the highway, which had no alternative but to travel through the district. It would link well with Transmission Gully.

We moved quickly to build the new highway, and the Kāpiti Expressway opened as the first section of the Levin to Wellington expressway in 2017, just before our government left office. Transmission Gully went through a Board of Inquiry process and commenced construction in 2014. Delayed by Covid-19 restrictions, it opened in 2022. The Pekapeka to Ōtaki part of the expressway, similarly delayed, also opened in 2022. In a familiar story, the Ōtaki to Levin section was cancelled and then rescheduled by the Ardern government, and still hadn't started construction at the time of writing.

OFTEN FORGOTTEN IN THE STORY of the Levin to Airport Road of National Significance is the Wellington end, which included a plan to place State Highway 1 in a dedicated corridor across the city, between the Terrace tunnel and the Mount Victoria tunnel, and then continuing on in a four-laning of Ruahine Street so it would truly be 'four lanes to the airport'.

Unfortunately, that part has not been a success to date. If I have one major regret in relation to the Roads of National Significance, it was the handling of the proposed Basin Reserve flyover and its failure to achieve consent through the Board of Inquiry process.

The NZTA leadership team were adamant that they wanted to take the flyover plan through a Board of Inquiry as a stand-alone project because it was ready to go for consenting, and was a discrete section of the highway. I wanted them to bundle the flyover with the second Mount Victoria tunnel and the widening of Ruahine Street. To my mind it was more in keeping with the 'national significance' part of the Board of Inquiry process, and as a combined project it would bring more benefit to Wellingtonians and people from around the lower North Island. It would then just leave the piece from the Basin Reserve to the Terrace tunnel and the building of the second tunnel as the final project.

I pushed and the NZTA team pushed back. Against my better judgement, I relented and let them do it their way. I felt I had been given a pretty good run and wanted to preserve the relationship. Sadly, the commissioners at the Board of Inquiry went exactly the way I feared they would. They couldn't see sufficient travel-time benefits from the Basin Reserve flyover on its own to offset the environmental impacts, and turned down the project. It was the only consenting defeat suffered by the Roads of National Significance, but it rather stuffed the Wellington end of the Levin to Wellington programme.

There was some subsequent progress on that part of the route, with our government passing legislation to bypass the RMA and build the Arras tunnel to carry a one-way part of State Highway 1 under the extended Pukeahu National War Memorial Park in central Wellington in time for the one hundredth anniversary of Gallipolli. I argued for the tunnel to be made two-way — as that was the route that would ultimately become the path of State Highway 1 across the city to the airport. I lost that one because it was deemed too much to bite off at once, and we still have a one-way tunnel today, with the traffic travelling to the airport winding through narrow city streets.

There has been no progress since, with the ironically named 'Let's Get Wellington Moving' project doing the exact opposite.

It makes absolute sense to have one safe, efficient roading corridor across Wellington to the airport, both to support the wider region, and to take the through-traffic off the inner-city streets. The Aro Valley and the quays would be much more pleasant and livable if that was the case. Unfortunately, there is a strong left-wing lobby in

Wellington Central which doesn't want any roads built anywhere.

Perhaps the ultimate answer is to turn the whole thing around and shift the airport up to Levin. Then nobody would go to the city who didn't already live there, and Wellingtonians would have a four-lane expressway to a brand-new airport!

Chapter Twelve
Safety first

THE PERPIGNAN AIR CRASH WAS an early reminder that the safety part of the transport portfolio is often a matter of life and death. In that regard, New Zealand's road toll is a constant reminder of the price we pay for personal mobility. While it has steadily improved since its nadir of 843 in 1973, in 2008, 366 people died on our roads.

Road safety was one area where I had virtually no guide rails from our election policies. We announced no significant road-safety policy in the 2008 election apart from a commitment in our police policy to 'ensure road policing concentrates on accident prevention by focusing on blackspots and at-risk drivers'.

I knew that on the one hand we wanted to keep the road toll trending down, while on the other hand National governments prefer light-handed regulation. We have a natural allergy on behalf of more freedom-loving New Zealanders to 'nanny state' initiatives, which work by restricting the freedom of many to correct the behaviour of a few.

I had personal experience of that allergy early on in my ministerial career when I took my first paper to Cabinet. It was a fairly innocuous road-safety proposal to tidy up some of the evidential issues around blood-alcohol testing and I rocked up to Cabinet expecting it to go through. My officials had drafted the paper and given me some fairly anodyne talking points.

I was completely underprepared when I was hit with a wall of questions. Every colleague seemed to have examples of constituents who had been put through the blood-alcohol evidence process and many knew the intricate details of it, which was more than I did. I'd come from a commercial background where the important thing for a CEO was a strategy, not every last detail. I was floundering, and agreed to withdraw the paper.

That experience taught me a valuable lesson. In politics ministers need to operate on two levels, both the big picture and the smallest policy detail. I vowed I would never get caught again not knowing all the details of something I was proposing, whether in front of Cabinet or anywhere else.

Many transport ministers delegate safety to their associate. During Annette King's time it was the role of New Plymouth MP Harry Duynhoven. I had Nathan Guy as my associate, and he was very able. However, I wanted to get a full handle on the portfolio before I made any similar delegations, and I thought transport safety was too important a part of the portfolio to delegate en masse. Nathan took on many of the rail, maritime and aviation responsibilities, and we worked very closely on the land-transport part of the portfolio.

There were two immediate road-safety issues on my plate: drugged driving and cellphone use in cars. Then, early on, a third was added when the Christchurch taxi driver was tragically murdered in his cab, followed by an Auckland taxi driver a year later. Those two murders led to compulsory cameras and panic alarms in taxis.

We inherited the proposed drugged driving law from the previous government. The relevant bill had been introduced in 2007 and had languished on Parliament's to-do list. We wanted to get it into law because it fitted our commitment to focus on high-risk drivers.

The key debate was over the means of detecting impairment, as there is no simple breath test which picks up all drug use the way it does for alcohol. Many in our caucus wanted to use a saliva test as one jurisdiction had tried in Australia. However, there are lots of fish-hooks with saliva testing, particularly as it misses many drugs. We needed to focus on the level of impairment, not a particular drug or drugs.

We settled on a physical impairment test, followed by a blood test if impairment is established, and that model continues to run today. Fourteen years later the current government decided to introduce a saliva test for drug testing and passed a law accordingly, only to be told by police what we knew back in 2009, that saliva testing doesn't do the job. They abandoned the plan.

Banning the use of hand-held cellphones when driving was more controversial, although not with the public. Both the National caucus and Cabinet were leery of the change, fearing that it strayed into the nanny-state 'regulation for all' category that had so recently tripped up Helen Clark's Labour government over its plan to restrict the size of shower heads in people's bathrooms.

I marshalled my arguments carefully, focusing on the harm caused by distracted cellphone users, and the fact that New Zealand was an outlier in Western democracies in not banning the use of hand-held cellphones while driving. I also recommended a fairly low initial infringement fee of $80 and 20 demerit points. After a little prodding, Cabinet signed it off and the new rule came into effect in November 2009.

In the meantime we had picked up another problem: boy racers. They had been getting worse and worse, particularly around the streets of South Auckland, Hamilton and Christchurch. They upset residents with their noise, dangerous driving and, in many cases, intimidating behaviour.

After a particularly bad couple of weekends not long after we came into office, John declared on his breakfast TV round that Police Minister Judith Collins and I would come up with a comprehensive set of measures to get illegal street racing under control. He waved his prime-ministerial wand and gave us four to six weeks to draft the legislation and another six months to get it through Parliament.

That was breakneck speed for law-making outside of emergencies, but we nearly made the timeframe. Most street-racing activity was already illegal; we just needed better penalties that hit the boy racers where it hurt: in their cars.

I put together a transport bill full of nine worthy measures to give police and councils more powers. They included the ability to create bylaws to prevent cruising, greater powers to impound cars, mandatory impoundment for street racing, greater penalties for illegally modified cars, and the ability for police to prohibit the sale of a car before they are able to confiscate it (as often happened). It was a full laundry list of all the tools police said they needed, prepared in record time. The ministry officials did a great job.

Judith, on the other hand, had one initiative. Her bill was the Vehicle Confiscation and Seizure Bill, and it allowed the police to seize and crush cars.

I got a real lesson in politics the day we jointly announced the bills. I went to Judith's office to discuss what we would say, how we would cover off the key points and so on. We then went out together for our stand-up. I went through my worthy announcement, which was likely to do much of the heavy lifting, and Judith just arched an eyebrow and said she was looking forward to crushing cars. Crusher Collins was born. I might as well have not been at the press conference that day. It was all about car crushing from then on in.

Both bills passed into law in October 2009, and together they did good work. Illegal street racing went into something of a hiatus for the next decade or so, before coming back into prominence lately. Judith became fond of protesting that she never liked the Crusher

Collins moniker, and that may be true in hindsight. But on that day she loved it.

Nathan and I then started to work with officials on a new road-safety strategy called 'Safer Journeys'. These strategies are ordained to be refreshed every ten years, and a new one needed to start in 2010. Consistent with that line in our election policy, we focused on high-risk road users, those people in society who were most likely to end up in the death and injury statistics. These include recidivist drink drivers and young drivers and their passengers. The ministry did some research into the road-toll statistics and found these groups together caused about half the deaths on our roads.

The young-driver situation was particularly dire. The road-fatality rate of our young people was 60 per cent higher than for young people in Australia. In 2008 nearly 40 per cent of serious accidents in New Zealand involved young people between the ages of 15 and 24, yet they made up only 15 per cent of the population. I decided we needed to go big to contain the problem and put a sizeable number of initiatives in front of Cabinet, including strengthening driver training and lowering the blood-alcohol limit for under-twenties to zero.

The most controversial move was lifting the driving age from fifteen to sixteen. There was widespread public support for it, but it did not go down well with our rural base or the rural MPs in caucus, because of the constraints it would place on the mobility of young people in rural locations. On the other hand, looking back, it does seem a bit crazy that we used to allow fifteen-year-olds to drive. The same argument about mobility was advanced when I proposed a zero-alcohol limit for drivers under twenty. The argument in favour was that it is harder for teenagers to judge when their peers are over the limit, and harder to dissuade them from driving. A nil limit would make it clearer.

Caucus and Cabinet knew we had to take some serious action

to tackle the problem, and they swallowed hard and supported the moves. I was very grateful. The day after the changes were announced the *New Zealand Herald* editorialised that I should have lifted the driving age to seventeen. In hindsight I perhaps should have, particularly as I now have the perspective of having my own teenage daughter, but it was a big deal at the time just moving it to sixteen. The changes had a positive impact for about five years, but the toll for young people started to creep up again after that, I suspect as a result of increased distraction from using smartphones while driving.

When I became Transport Minister, I was well aware that my own driving record had not been exemplary, with a number of speeding tickets and more than one accident over the years. I had duly reported that fact to John Key and Wayne Eagleson, and they had been happy for me to proceed. However, as we got further into the safety area I became more uncomfortable about one thing in particular: a careless-driving conviction I had been given back in the late 1980s for causing a car accident on the open road.

I spoke to my political staff, and we agreed I would front up and acknowledge my history in my first-reading speech for the bill lifting the driving age. I duly did, and in the meantime my press secretary Anita Ferguson obtained a copy of my record from the Ministry of Justice, in case any journalists wanted confirmation of the story.

I got back to my office after the speech and Anita and Kenny were both looking pale. They waved the piece of paper at me and said, 'You realise there were two convictions, don't you?' I'd completely forgotten. I knew I'd had two accidents over a one-year period, but my memory was that the second one had just gone away because the motorcyclist I had collided with had left the scene. My memory was wrong.

I disappeared into my ministerial bathroom and rang Suzanne in shock. How could I have made such an elementary mistake?

There was nothing for it. I had to go back to the House and make a personal statement to correct the record, which I did. It probably made the story a little bit bigger than it would have otherwise been, but I did get points for front-footing it. No doubt it would have been a different outcome if someone else had thought to ask about my driving history first.

ONE OF THE CONFOUNDING ASPECTS for transport ministers trying to improve road safety is that most fatal road crashes are caused by people who are already breaking the road rules in some way. As these people are already on the wrong side of the law, coming up with new rules is unlikely to moderate their behaviour. The new rules risk just upsetting the vast majority of law-abiding motorists. The only way through is to come up with stronger consequences that make it less likely risky drivers will reoffend.

In 2008, alcohol or drugs contributed to one in three fatal crashes in New Zealand. Recidivist drink drivers became the focus of the second part of the Safer Journeys package. Because they had previously shown poor judgement (often several times), we introduced a zero-alcohol limit for repeat drink drivers, increased the penalty for drink and drugged driving causing injury and death, and introduced compulsory alcohol interlocks for repeat drink drivers. With this last measure, the driver has to blow into a device on their steering wheel and register no alcohol in their breath before the device unlocks, enabling them to drive their car. These policy changes had a much easier path through caucus and were again popular with the public.

Sadly, they were never going to be a complete solution. A determined alcoholic or chronic drug user will always find a way of getting behind the wheel, unless they are physically prevented from doing so. However, alcohol interlocks have proven successful and they need to be used more often.

A trickier problem served up to me by officials was what to do about the adult blood-alcohol limit. The limit had been set at 0.08 grams for a long time, meaning a limit of 80 milligrams of alcohol per 100 millilitres of blood. A series of very effective public education campaigns over the years had convinced the law-abiding public that the 0.08 limit equated to two standard drinks. The only trouble was that the 0.08 limit actually equated to significantly more drinks than that for most people. Back in the mists of time politicians wouldn't lower the limit, so the officials had fudged the amount people could drink in their advertising, to try to limit the carnage. The dirty little secret was that a limit of 0.05 would be much closer to what most people thought the limit actually was.

The safety officials wanted the limit lowered from 0.08 to 0.05 as problem drinkers had worked out what they could get away with. That had led to a high number of impaired drivers on the road. For me, it was a potential communications nightmare. Should I keep quiet and play along, as every transport minister before me had, or should I come clean and make the change? It wouldn't be easy to convince Cabinet and caucus to move on this one. With the initiatives I had already brought forward in road safety, they had started to peg me as a 'Safety Sue'.

I secured agreement from John and the Cabinet to float the change with the public and be clear about what the 0.08 versus 0.05 shift was all about. I positioned it as choosing between two options: either dropping the legal limit as proposed or undertaking more research to understand the direct impact on the road toll of drivers between 0.05 and 0.08 blood-alcohol levels, to inform a later decision.

I also decided to conduct my own demonstration for caucus members. I issued an open invitation to come to my office one evening and see if they could 'blow the bag'. I put on beer and wine, and the police kindly sent along their National Road Safety

Manager and a breathalyser machine so we could see for ourselves what the limit was.

Everyone who came (about 30 people) was shocked at the amount they could drink before they reached the 0.08 limit. And some were decidedly merry by then. All agreed there was no way they should drive a car under that level of influence.

That little experiment swayed many caucus members, but none of the big dogs in Cabinet — notably John, Bill English or Gerry Brownlee — were able to attend. I offered the compromise of making it simply an infringement ticket for a limit between 0.05 and 0.08, but John and Gerry in particular remained doubtful, and when push came to shove I couldn't get them over the line.

We went for the research option, and that would ultimately prove inconclusive. However, when the issue did come back to Cabinet after the research, Gerry had succeeded me as Transport Minister and with the help of his officials he had reversed his position on the change. In fact both he and John were much more gung-ho than they'd been in 2010, and wanted to go the full hog with full penalties from a new 0.05 limit. I found myself, along with others, persuading them both back to an infringement regime from 0.05 to 0.08. It felt like we had entered into a weird parallel universe, but at least the job was done.

All the road-safety work did have a positive impact on the country's road toll. The annual number of deaths on the road dropped from 366 in 2008 to 253 five years later. Sadly, the trend couldn't be maintained and the numbers have steadily risen again since then, probably at least in part as a result of continuing driver distraction, particularly from smartphone use, and a perceived reduction in consequences for poor driving behaviour.

WHEN A LETTER COMES IN for a minister, officials draft a response based on government policy and announcements, and ministers either sign it out or amend it. Transport ministers get a huge amount of correspondence, and are expected to reply to all of it. Unfortunately, I found that officials' drafting often left a huge amount to be desired. The language was obtuse and full of bureaucratese, and the tone was often condescending and cold. I could not sign a lot of the drafts I received.

I sent hundreds of letters back for redrafting, rewrote dozens and dozens myself, and tried to come up with templates to make it easier for officials to write with a more helpful, friendlier tone. I also learnt a lot through the drafting process, which was often a window into the policy views of the person writing the draft. I held many back to discuss them at officials' meetings, to ensure we'd reach agreement on a common view of what the government, through me, wanted to say. In that respect the process was helpful, although hugely time-consuming. The blue transport correspondence folders were the bane of my life.

Two issues came up with clockwork regularity in correspondence: compulsory third-party insurance and New Zealand's absurd 'world-leading' give-way rule, where cars turning left had to give way to cars coming from the opposite direction turning right.

I did some research on compulsory third-party insurance, and it didn't fly because in New Zealand we already had similar or higher rates of car insurance than in countries where third-party insurance was 'compulsory', notably the UK and the US. The give-way rule was nuts, though, confusing many locals as well as copious numbers of people from overseas who drove here as tourists or immigrants. I decided to propose a change, in what turned out to be my final safety initiative in the transport portfolio.

Ironically, this change, of all of them, provoked the most worry from colleagues. Everyone wondered whether drivers would cope or whether we'd end up with thousands of angry motorists running into each other because they did or didn't know the new rule. We took a deep breath and went for it, along with a big public awareness campaign. The change didn't in fact come into effect until 1 April 2012, after I had left the portfolio, but it went through without a hitch. Looking back it is easy to wonder what all the fuss was about.

JUST AS SATISFYING AS SOME of the big roading projects were the smaller projects we were able to advance, many of which stayed out of the eye of the national media. A number of long-standing projects which had been languishing for a long time were brought forward and constructed, some forming part of the Jobs and Growth Plan we put together in response to the GFC and the Job Summit.

The Kopu bridge was a high-profile example. This single-lane bridge across the Waihou River just south of Thames was the main gateway to the Coromandel. The old bridge was severely out of date for the volume of traffic it carried, and it was at risk of damage or collapse in a big flood. On holiday weekends cars and trucks queued for hours to get across the river, and Portaloo toilets and coffee carts sprang up to service those waiting. It was a real thrill and quite the party when I was able to cut the ribbon with the prime minister on a new $40 million replacement bridge in 2011.

One of my absolute favourite projects was the Matahorua Gorge realignment. For the uninitiated, which included me prior to becoming Transport Minister, the Matahorua Gorge lies on State Highway 2 between Napier and Gisborne. It is a very isolated area, 50 kilometres north of Napier and 66 kilometres south of Wairoa.

The old road wound through the gorge for nearly 5 kilometres. It was narrow and dangerous, and there were stories of high-sided trucks scraping past each other if they were in the gorge at the same time. The alignment hadn't changed much since the time of horse-drawn carriages. A viaduct had been built across the gorge for the Napier–Gisborne railway line in 1929, but precious little work had been done on the road.

The Matahorua Gorge project engineers did a great job, forming a new alignment which closely followed the railway track, cutting out 1.4 kilometres from the old route, and removing all the hairpin bends, to create a largely straight, safe highway. The road was blessed and opened in March 2011. I was determined to be there. I felt that it was as important to celebrate transport progress in the small regions as the big ones.

I'll never forget the feeling on that day. It was a beautiful morning, quiet and still. It felt like we were miles from anywhere. The opening of the road was a very big deal in this tiny community and they all turned up, seemingly appearing from nowhere. The local iwi welcomed the official party, and the local farmers told stories about times they'd faced horrific accidents on the old road. One farmer had been forced to give up some land for the new alignment, but he was happy the road would now be safe.

I spoke about my own experiences driving up that road and blowing up the engine of my orange Morris Marina back in university days. I also mused that the new road effectively brought Gisborne and Napier five minutes closer together. It was a wonderful ceremony, and the peace and tranquillity was a lovely contrast with the pressures of Wellington. It was a privilege to deliver a rural roading project which had been needed for decades.

From Matahorua we drove down State Highway 2 to open the Hawke's Bay Expressway extension south of Hastings later that day. I spent some time thinking about how many Matahorua Gorge projects it would take to straighten out all those hairpin bends on the Napier–Gisborne road, bring Gisborne much closer to Hawke's Bay, and turn that part of State Highway 2 into a safe, resilient lifeline. It wasn't a busy road, but it was crucial for the East Coast.

When I got back to Wellington I started talking with officials about next steps on the Napier–Gisborne highway, but I wasn't in the portfolio long enough to keep the focus on it. There are hundreds of Matahorua-type projects which need doing on the state highway network around the country. We managed to get some built, but it will take a concerted effort over 20 to 30 years to tackle them all. They would make a massive difference to productivity and road safety in the smaller remote regions.

A lot of the regional projects we kicked off were centred around replacement bridges, where the old bridge was narrow and outdated for the traffic on the road but had never been replaced because of the high price tag. They all had a story behind them.

There were the twin Kurow bridges across the Waitaki River on State Highway 82. They replaced two very old single-lane bridges and at last provided a safe back-up for State Highway 1 between Canterbury and the south. Another was the replacement of the Taramakau River bridge on the West Coast between Greymouth and Kumara, the last of the combined road-rail bridges in the country.

The Kawarau Falls single-lane bridge carrying the highway south of Queenstown had been slated for replacement for years. I was speaking at a business event in Queenstown as Economic Development Minister in 2013, when I confidently declared the old bridge would be replaced within the next five years. It is fair to say there was some cynicism in the room. They'd heard it all before.

However, the bridge indeed made it off the drawing board, starting construction in 2015 and opening to the public shortly after we left office in 2018. Soon after I received two bottles of fine Central Otago pinot noir on the courier, with a card reminding me of a bet with a gentleman who had been confident we wouldn't get the bridge built. I'd long forgotten that exchange, but he was very happy to have had his faith in politicians restored and a key piece of infrastructure in Queenstown completed.

RAIL WAS ANOTHER IMPORTANT PART of the transport portfolio, and we were left picking up the pieces after the previous government's romantic misadventure with a broken railway system.

Contrary to popular belief, I was and remain a fan of heavy rail. I am as romantic about rail as the next rail buff. I told rail audiences I liked rail so much I called my son Thomas. I have always enjoyed using the fantastic rail services in Europe and the UK when I have travelled there, but am realistic enough to understand we don't have anything like the population densities of those countries, and that makes most passenger rail uneconomic in New Zealand.

I used to take Amelia for trips on the trains on the weekend. She and I would hop on a train at the Wellington Railway Station and travel out to Lower Hutt and walk home to Vogel House when we lived there, or we would take a trip up to Johnsonville or Plimmerton on the new trains. In Auckland we'd travel between Britomart and Newmarket, or out on the Western line to the new station the government helped fund at New Lynn.

It isn't hard to justify investing in Auckland or Wellington commuter rail. In both cities, the challenging geography — be it the two harbours in Auckland or the vertical cliffs in Wellington — means that there are limited transport corridors, and they all must be used as efficiently as possible. It is harder to see the argument in Christchurch, where there are other more convenient options which don't require such gigantic subsidies to get people to travel on them.

One thing I didn't want to do was use the hypothecated petrol taxes and road-user charges to pay for big rail infrastructure projects. To me, that cut across the bargain government struck with motorists who pay their petrol taxes and road-user charges to improve the roading network. I could accept public-transport subsidies to take people off the roads, but not siphoning off huge sums to pay for infrastructure like railway or bus stations. They should be funded from central taxation.

Finance Minister Bill English agreed with my approach, but he wasn't completely convinced about shelling out for the planned

Auckland rail electrification given all the post-GFC pressures on the budget. However, John was convinced. He could see we needed to make a high-profile investment in Auckland public transport, and electrification of the city's rail network was the next logical step. We persuaded Bill to include the necessary half-billion for electrification in Budget 2009, and we loaned another half-billion to the Auckland Regional Council to buy 57 impressive new electric trains. Auckland electrification was underway.

Of course, one billion dollars in funding for the electrification of commuter rail was not going to keep the new Auckland Council happy for long. New supercity mayor Len Brown moved straight on to lobbying the government for an expensive new underground rail tunnel through the city, linking the Britomart station with the existing tracks at Mount Eden, which he saw as his legacy project. However, the initial business cases for the city rail link were very sketchy and the benefits were poor, and we pushed it back for further work in 2010 and again in 2011.

As the decade progressed, we began to gain confidence in the revised numbers, and in 2016 Simon Bridges and I agreed a funding package that would see the government pay 50 per cent of the cost of the project and the city pay the other half. We believed the 50:50 split was important to align the interests of both the government and the council in controlling costs and preventing too much scope creep. A 50 per cent contribution was also fairer for the rest of the country outside of Auckland, who would rightly blanch at putting up the full $3.4 billion cost. The City Rail Link commenced construction in 2017 and, following long closedowns due to Covid-19, is due for completion in 2025. Partly as a result of the construction delays, the final cost is now projected to be $5.5 billion.

In Wellington the commuter rail network was already electrified and had been much more developed than Auckland over a long period of time, but it still needed work. We put in another $90 million to replace a lot of the old overhead gantries and to electrify the track up to Waikanae. The next step is to extend it to Levin.

Late in their term, the previous government had bought the railway freight company back from a delighted Toll Group for $700 million, and it came with a licence to spend taxpayers' money. By the time Labour recapitalised it with another $300 million, they'd already spent a billion dollars so Michael Cullen could have his photo taken with the quickly repainted 'KiwiRail' locomotive at Wellington Railway Station. And it would need billions more to be in any shape to operate successfully.

Both Treasury and yours truly were in favour of the parts of the rail freight network that were able to pay for themselves. Rail corridors all work on only one thing: volume. If there are high levels of freight, it is possible to use the income to pay for the track maintenance and infrastructure investment underneath the trains, just like high-use road highways. That is the model for successful rail corridors the world over. They have big anchor tenants who need to carry a lot of freight, like coal mines, steelworks, big milk factories or forestry processors.

The trouble in New Zealand is that there are very few such rail corridors. Ports are great agglomeraters of tonnage and containers, but often the containers need to be dispersed one or two at a time, to and from company depots around every region. That makes them poorly suited to train transport and much better suited to trucks. Moving from rail to road at, say, a remote depot, just creates double handling and increases transport costs.

Our population is so small and thinly spread, our geography so challenging, and our industrial base now so small, that precious little of the rail network can cover its costs. The Auckland to Hamilton and Tauranga corridors are profitable, and I think you can make a case for Auckland to Wellington and on down to Christchurch. The rest of the network is a story of very few trains, very little freight, and expensive maintenance and replacement costs. In places like Taranaki, Hawke's Bay, Northland, Gisborne and the West Coast we struggle to afford a single decent land-transport network, and yet we persist in trying to cover the cost of two. We end up with a poor roading network and a poor rail network — the worst of both worlds.

We had to find a way to make the best of a bad situation. Ministers worked with Treasury and KiwiRail to put together a $4.2 billion turnaround plan, which included KiwiRail's projected operating surpluses for the next five years, plus another $750 million in taxpayers' money. It was a plan, but an optimistic one, and it relied on committed traffic from big logistics companies like Mainfreight and Toll. They were all in favour of the turnaround plan, and regularly came out publicly in support of greater taxpayer investment in the rail network. However, they never offered to pay the true cost of it with their freight. They wanted to use rail as an overflow for their trucking network at busy times of the year. That way they could run a smaller trucking fleet at full capacity year round, and not have extra trucks sitting idle and waiting for the busy times.

Our turnaround plan was actioned, but in the end it wasn't enough, and the next government has spent billions more trying to 'turn KiwiRail around' and 'make up for decades of underinvestment' again. Fundamental questions about the usefulness of large parts of the network remain.

TOP Me at sixteen with Buffy, the 16.2-hand 'showjumper when it suited him' handed down from my sister Diane.

BOTTOM Hosting the afternoon drive show for Energy FM during the 1984–85 summer broadcast.

TOP The Energy FM team at the end of the 1985–86 summer broadcast.
BOTTOM Broadcasting live from a New Plymouth bed store with breakfast host Jeremy Corbett (left).

TOP One of my favourite Tom Scott cartoons from *The Dominion Post* in 2010, reflecting on the momentum we were getting with transport decisions. Alexander Turnbull Library, DCDL-0013850

BOTTOM LEFT Walking the red carpet with my wife Suzanne at the world premiere of the movie *The Hobbit: An Unexpected Journey* in Wellington, November 2012. Neil Price

BOTTOM RIGHT Introducing Amelia and Tommy to snow at Coronet Peak on a brief family getaway to Queenstown, April 2014.

TOP LEFT With Chancellor of Germany Angela Merkel in November 2014, meeting the University of Auckland leadership team.

TOP RIGHT Standing with *New Zealand Herald* cartoonist Rod Emmerson's three-dimensional take on yours truly. The egg was one of 100 created by New Zealand artists and designers in 2015 for the Whittaker's Big Egg Hunt, a fundraiser for Auckland's Starship children's hospital.

BOTTOM Dad joined me for a tour of the Tauranga Eastern Link, courtesy of NZTA, just before the road opened in 2015.

TOP Being interviewed at the site of the Waterview project in August 2015 by 'Breakfast Sam' (presenter Sam Wallace) for TVNZ 1's *Breakfast* programme.

BOTTOM With ministerial colleagues (from left) Hekia Parata, Jo Goodhew and Nathan Guy at the launch of the Tai Tokerau Northland Economic Action Plan, February 2016.

TOP Meeting local farmers at Central Districts Field Days in Feilding, Manawatū, March 2016.

BOTTOM LEFT With Rocket Lab founder and chief executive Peter Beck in September 2016, opening the launch site on the Māhia Peninsula.

BOTTOM RIGHT Walking the Pouākai Crossing in Taranaki in January 2017, when I was Finance Minister: part of a not-so-subtle bid from local MP Jonathan Young for an investment in upgrading the track.

TOP At the opening of the Waterview Connection with Transport Minister
Simon Bridges (left) and Prime Minister Bill English, June 2017. Stuff Limited

BOTTOM Our bright-eyed and bushy-tailed campaign crew at the daily
7 a.m. meeting during the 2017 election campaign.

TOP My valedictory speech at Parliament, 27 March 2018.
BOTTOM With John Key and Bill English at my valedictory celebration.

Chapter Thirteen
Ultra-fast broadband

WE HAD BEEN TOSSING UP whether to make creating an ultra-fast broadband network a 2008 election pledge. Maurice Williamson was National's ICT spokesperson in Opposition, and he was an evangelist for all things computing. He'd done the preparatory work and was convinced fibre broadband could be rolled out to 75 per cent of New Zealand homes and businesses for around $1.5 billion.

John Key's office and the finance team were a little wary of the proposal. Bill English's understandable view was that if the project was needed, the market would provide. John's team were worried the idea was in the 'too good to be true' category. Those who know Maurice will understand that his forceful and relentless advocacy can sometimes perversely create reservations about his cause. He'd done almost too good a job in promoting ultra-fast broadband.

The policy wasn't a first. Kevin Rudd's successful 2007 election campaign had included a pledge to roll out a fibre broadband network across Australia. Voters around the world were frustrated with broadband speeds as the internet became more ubiquitous in their lives. Incumbent, often monopoly, telcos were seen as sitting on their hands or moving slowly, sweating their existing copper assets for as long as they could and paying out dividends to shareholders rather than improving the experience for consumers. New Zealand was one of the worst offenders, with some of the slowest internet speeds in the developed world.

During one of John's regular weekend calls leading into the campaign, he asked me what I thought of Maurice's broadband proposal. I was caught a bit on the hop but said it would be a great announcement, presuming it was doable and would survive scrutiny. John said he was keen. He liked the ambition in the plan, which was consistent with how he wanted to transform the country. He asked me if I knew anything about telecommunications, and whether I could quietly sense-check whether it would work.

I got off the phone and thought, how the hell am I going to do this? It was a bit above and beyond my remit as the campaign guy. I decided to ring the person I knew best who knows about these sorts of things — my brother, Kevin. Kevin is a software architect for a significant multinational software-as-a-service company. He is not a telco professional, but at least he knew more than I did about how the technology actually works.

Kevin and I sat down around a piece of paper, and worked through the number of premises in the country, some round-number costs of each connection, and our estimate of the costs at each node. It was real back-of-the-envelope stuff and the industry would have been horrified if they'd seen it. But time was of the essence and we couldn't share things too widely.

After a couple of chats, Kevin and I agreed that the plan was very roughly doable for the $1.5 billion proposed by Maurice. I reported back to John, and we agreed that we should proceed with the announcement. I locked the timing in with his team, and we moved on.

Flash-forward to the week after the election when John rang me to offer a role in his ministry. As well as offering transport, he said,

'I know you know a bit about this broadband stuff, so I want you to do that as well.'

Righto. I was charged with delivering on the commitment to roll out ultra-fast broadband to 75 per cent of New Zealand within ten years, literally weeks after first looking at it. Where to begin?

In the absence of a plan, I decided listening might be a good start. I was acutely aware I was wading into a complex network industry with hundreds of linkages, thousands of staff and millions of customer relationships. A minister could blunder about and make a huge mess if they weren't careful. I didn't want to be that minister. Fortunately, during the election campaign we had made it clear that we would spend the first year putting the plan together, which meant we did have some time.

I spent the first three months talking to pretty much everybody I could: telcos, internet service providers, user groups, industry groups and lots of other stakeholders; anyone who could offer a perspective. Within those three months, I had received what I refer to as the full 360 degrees of advice.

One of the first decisions I made was to de-fund the previous government's Digital Development Council, which I saw as an expensive talking shop of industry associations. In my view the minister should be talking with all the key players individually and directly, and certainly shouldn't be paying to meet them as a group.

Also early on, I met with Stephen Conroy, my counterpart in Australia. Australia was a year further into their roll-out than we were, so I was interested to hear what lessons they could offer. I asked the officials to set up the meeting.

We met in Stephen's Melbourne office. Stephen is a likeable chap — I met him a few times over the course of our respective times as minister. He was Tiggerish that day, full of energy and very confident about how he was tackling Telstra, Australia's incumbent telco. He believed he had no alternative than to work with Telstra, and he was confident he would persuade them, using legislation if necessary, to play things his way.

It was a high-stakes game. Conroy had made some bullish statements on the timing of the roll-out and was fast running out of runway, while Telstra sat back and waited for him to come to them. I was taken aback by the limited nature of his plan, which seemed like nothing more than strong-arming Telstra to provide their ducts and pipe network for the build. According to the media at the time, they appeared unlikely to play ball.

As we headed back across the Tasman, the officials and I agreed Stephen's plan was likely a lesson in what not to do. We had to have contestability amongst bidders for the project or we could be held to ransom. And we had to be careful not to run up against political deadlines of our own making, which private-sector players could use against us.

Going to Melbourne proved to be a very useful visit, although not in the way we had envisaged. Subsequent events in Australia, where the Rudd government ended up spending tens of billions buying the infrastructure of a recalcitrant Telstra in order to get started on their programme, meant that one return flight likely helped save New Zealand billions of dollars.

Back home, some industry players were fighting a rearguard action against the initiative. There were those, for example, who maintained that rolling out fibre to the home was wasteful and unnecessary. Some, like Telstra Clear with their coaxial cable network in Wellington and Christchurch, feared being overbuilt. Some believed the future was wireless broadband rather than fibre, or that fibre itself would likely become redundant over time, just like copper wires were becoming now. We listened carefully to those concerns, but they all foundered on the technology.

The great benefit of fibre is that once it is in the ground, its potential speed for each user is almost limitless, depending purely on the electronics added to each end. It's not likely to be overtaken by another technology any time soon. Everything else, including wireless, suffers from what's known as contention: the more people who access the same signal, the slower it gets for each user. Fibre is unaffected by the number of subscribers using it.

Wireless did and does make huge sense in sparsely populated rural areas, where there is little likelihood of network congestion and real advantages in receiving the internet through the air. Most farmers don't just need the internet tethered to the house or the milking shed; they increasingly need a signal all over the farm for the myriad sensors they want to connect to it. But in urban areas, fibre was the answer.

Telecom was very active in fighting our plan. They wanted to be left alone to use up their existing copper assets and move slowly into fibre over time. They weren't getting much truck with me, so they spent a lot of time traipsing into the Finance Minister's office. Bill was a bit more receptive both philosophically but also fiscally, and understandably so. There aren't that many finance ministers who want to spend $1.5 billion in the middle of a Global Financial Crisis if they can avoid it.

To resolve the issue and keep moving forward, we hammered out five principles for the programme, which were agreed between the Ministry of Economic Development and Treasury. These were: the government's investment wouldn't line the pockets of or give advantage to existing providers; the new network would be open access; excessive duplication of the current network would be avoided; everyday Kiwis would get access to affordable broadband; and the public–private partnership would focus on future technology.

You don't have to look too closely at those principles to see some potential contradictions, indicative of the battle playing out between officials. Point three about duplication was definitely Telecom's favourite, no doubt because it could be a lever against the competitive tension we needed to get a sensible roll-out. I chose to apply that one selectively.

The requirement for open access was hugely important. In my view the government couldn't fund one operator into an infrastructure leg-up over other players. The infrastructure had to be available on an equal basis to all wholesale and retail operators, which effectively meant the infrastructure owner couldn't also be a retailer. This would also have the benefit of encouraging more competition at those levels.

We decided on a few other key parameters in that first year, which shaped the success of the project. Firstly, we made it clear that the government's money was only going into last-mile fibre — the distance from the node to the home. Lots of people argued for the government to fund back-haul, or international links, all sorts of things, mostly for their pet projects of course! But we decided to stay resolute on the last mile, as the least likely investment area for the private sector.

We also had people saying we should provide uptake incentives or people mightn't subscribe. We resisted that as well. My view was that if we were right and people were hanging out for faster broadband, uptake should not be an issue provided that prices were reasonable.

We decided the taxpayers' money would be a loan, not a grant, to the partner companies, and that we would expect them to put up at least half the build-out cost in their own money. We'd need that to achieve our roll-out targets. And ultimately we wanted the Crown's contribution back, although we would of course be forsaking interest payments on it for the period the companies used it.

We also decided to break the country into different regions, rather than encourage national bids. We figured we were more likely to get competition for the roll-out by going region by region. We knew some electricity lines companies were interested in investing, for example, but they were unlikely to bid for the whole country, and we remained determined not to be landed with Telecom as Hobson's choice.

Finally, we needed a vehicle to manage the government's investment, coordinate the bidding process, and contract with and manage the successful bidders. This was a pivotal decision. In order to contract with the private sector, we needed a company with the same flexibility to move and with access to the same skill sets as those private-sector parties. If ministers and officials tried to do it, they would just get tied up in knots.

We put together a company called Crown Fibre Holdings to make the calls on behalf of the government. Crown Fibre would be critical to the project's success and I wanted the right skills in that organisation, so it could successfully go toe-to-toe with the Telecoms and Vectors of the world.

My observation from my time in politics is that many ministers don't spend enough time selecting the right people with the right skills for their Crown company boards. Let's face it, it doesn't attract many headlines. Also, the pressure on both sides of politics to appoint party stalwarts, regardless of their skill set, is immense. I spent an inordinate amount of time constructing the Crown Fibre board with my colleagues, and I think it paid off. The two key appointments were Simon Allen as chair and Graham Mitchell as chief executive. They both played a huge part in the subsequent success of the roll-out.

INDICATIVE BIDS FOR THE ULTRA-FAST broadband project were sought around one year after we came into government — almost on schedule. Thirty-six bids were received, and then the hard part began.

The negotiations between Crown Fibre and the bidders were tough and took the best part of a year, not helped by a highly reluctant Telecom. There were a huge range of things to resolve, from pricing to roll-out cost, to timetables and repayment schedules. And while everything looked calm on the surface, behind the scenes Telecom were resisting a key element of the plan — a requirement for funded infrastructure providers to divest their retail businesses.

This was crucial to ensuring open access, and to ensure that government-funded infrastructure was not used unfairly against competitors. I was determined to stick to it. My view was that if Telecom didn't want to structurally separate in order to participate, that was their call. They could happily sail on but they wouldn't be able to participate in the fibre roll-out.

Telecom, for its part, had resisted structural separation as an article of faith for years. It believed, despite some international evidence to the contrary, that a vertically integrated telecommunications provider would provide best value for shareholders. Their recently arrived Scottish CE, Paul Reynolds, was hired with the goal of keeping Telecom together, and he was no fan of splitting the company up. Neither was his board.

Telecom and Crown Fibre locked horns, quietly. At least it wasn't a public spat like it was in Australia, or directly between the minister and the telco.

Meanwhile, another concern was being raised by bidders. What would happen if they agreed contracts with Crown Fibre, and then the Commerce Commission, which is independent, came in over the top of those agreements at some point and regulated down the prices successful bidders could charge? Bidders would be relying on that income to help pay for their part of the build. Such a move could ruin the economics of the roll-out, and potentially even make one or more of the roll-out partners insolvent.

I was unsure why the Commerce Commission would do that, particularly if Crown Fibre had negotiated competitive prices, but agreed it was at least theoretically a problem. We therefore proposed a period of 'regulatory forbearance', when build partners would be regulated by their agreements with Crown Fibre rather than by the Commerce Commission.

It is fair to say that the proposal wasn't popular. Many people objected to the government and its build partners effectively being given a free pass around the Commerce Commission. To me it was a practical answer, but it was proving problematic, so ultimately we changed tack. Instead of regulatory forbearance, Crown Fibre would build regulatory contingencies into each contract. If the Commerce Commission decided to regulate the prices below those that were in the contract, the government would wear the cost by providing more favourable terms on the use of its money.

The prime minister's office was starting to get twitchy. We were fast approaching two years in government and there was no new fibre in the ground. While we hadn't come under much political heat to that point, that would surely change soon. For my part, I remained determined not to name target dates and deadlines, well aware that our prospective private partners would use any announcement against us. They had no financial imperative to start by any particular date and could well afford to run down the clock. Politically we had to get on with it.

While we waited for Crown Fibre, the officials and I got on with the rural broadband initiative, a parallel programme targeting better broadband for the 15 per cent of the population living in rural and remote areas of the country. Given the huge distances and very low density of the population, the model here would be different.

We decided on a plan to get fibre to every school and community health centre around the country, and then use those as nodes to deliver fast wireless broadband to the houses and farms around each district, by subsidising the building of big new remote cell towers. The commitment was to get 5MB speeds to at least 80 per cent of rural households, and at least 1MB to the rest. It would not be as good as fibre, but given many people in these areas were still on dial-up, it was a big step forward. This initiative would cost around $300 million and we adopted a straight subsidy model. Taxpayers tipped in $50 million, and the rest was paid for through a Telecommunications Development Levy which every broadband user paid, to support those at the edge of the network.

The Rural Broadband Initiative was a bit of a sleeper in terms of media coverage, but it was executed successfully, on time and within budget. Now the Starlinks of the world will result in a big leap forward in rural coverage again.

Back in ultra-fast broadband land we finally had some good news. Crown Fibre had been in negotiation with a number of parties besides Telecom, and some were ready to sign a deal that met the government's requirements. In December 2010 Crown Fibre announced deals with two of those parties. It would contract with Northpower to roll out fibre across Whangārei, and with WEL Networks to connect up Hamilton, Tauranga, New Plymouth, Whanganui, Te Awamutu, Cambridge and Hāwera. The roll-outs in these centres would be completed by 2015.

That was a relief for my office and the government, and a wake-up call for Telecom. They'd just missed out on 16 per cent of the roll-out. It was clear this train was prepared to leave the station without them.

A short time later Crown Fibre announced they would enter formal negotiations with Telecom, alongside Enable, as bidders for the Christchurch roll-out. But the road was still rocky. We heard there were fierce internal debates inside Telecom about whether to participate. Negotiations rolled on into 2011, and it wasn't until Crown Fibre announced plans to negotiate with Vector in Auckland and another fibre consortium for the rest of the North Island that Telecom finally got serious.

On 24 May 2011, six months before the 2011 election, Crown Fibre announced an agreement to partner with Enable in Christchurch, and with Telecom in Auckland and elsewhere in the country not already contracted. At the same time Telecom announced it was prepared to structurally separate, a requirement of the deal. Crown Fibre had successfully stared them down.

We were now set up to undertake the fibre roll-out for 75 per cent of New Zealand. Telecom split itself into Spark (the retail and cellphone arm) and Chorus (the infrastructure arm) in October 2011, and it was Chorus that partnered with government to lay the fibre.

Once the roll-out started, it happened pretty quickly. By the middle of 2012, our partners had put fibre past 76,000 homes, schools and businesses, and a year after that the number was up to 300,000. Two years later it reached 724,000 premises. The target was to complete the roll-out by 2019 and we were well on track. Whangārei was the first population centre to be completely fibred in May 2014, followed by Te Awamutu, Ōamaru, Cambridge, Tokoroa and Hāwera. By then I had handed on the portfolio to Amy Adams, and subsequently to Simon Bridges.

There was a hiccup along the way. In 2013 the Commerce Commission did indeed come in and regulate down the wholesale broadband price, effectively risking the success of the roll-out. I'll never know why they picked that moment, but after some public nervousness from all the bid parties, including Chorus, we got through it with the help of the contractual contingencies that had been previously negotiated.

It certainly helped that consumer uptake was much better than budgeted. Our nightmare scenario was that people wouldn't sign up or would sign up only slowly, and that somehow they'd turn out to be happy with the slower speeds of the old copper network. What a highly visible white elephant that would be.

We needn't have worried. By the end of 2014 we had 12 per cent uptake, well ahead of what we had anticipated. By mid-2017, it was 33 per cent, and by 2022 nearly 70 per cent of New Zealand received their internet via a fibre connection, making us one of the top ten most fibre-connected countries in the world. As a country we'd blown all the models out of the water.

With the success of the roll-out, we were able in 2017 to extend it to another 151 small towns around New Zealand, for the $300 million which had been paid back in the meantime by the bid partners. This meant that even tiny villages like Midhurst in Taranaki, Naseby in Central Otago, Fox Glacier on the West Coast and Taipā in the Far North would receive fibre. The final ultra-fast broadband programme was completed in 2022, and fibre has now been laid across 412 cities and towns around the country, reaching 87 per cent of the population, all for the initial outlay of $1.5 billion.

A FAIR BIT HAS BEEN made of the success of the New Zealand ultra-fast broadband programme, particularly when comparing it to the Australian experience. They started at a similar time to us, have spent a whopping AUS$52 billion on it so far, and are not even delivering fibre to homes across much of urban Australia.

My view is the Australians made two major errors. Firstly, they didn't structure their arrangements to give themselves other options to contract with besides Telstra; and secondly, they effectively re-nationalised the network by buying Telstra's pipes and ducts, rather than partnering with the private sector, which is almost always more efficient.

It would be a mistake if people think the success of the ultra-fast broadband programme here means the government should make these sorts of interventions regularly. They are not easy. There are many places where this project could have gone horribly wrong. The private sector always has a big advantage over politicians — the luxury of time. They can afford to wait until the politician's back is against the wall, as we saw in Australia.

It is also not often that a commercial opportunity is left on the table by the private sector such that it needs only a relatively small subsidy from the government to make it happen. Most such 'opportunities' require the government to put up a far larger proportion of the cost, suggesting they are not economically sensible decisions.

In this case, if Telecom as the monopoly network owner had been well regulated in the past, and had chosen to or been required in some way to balance its need for capital reinvestment in a fibre network with paying dividends to shareholders, the government may not have needed to be involved at all. To be fair, though, the experience internationally was that most incumbent telcos dragged the chain on fibre.

As it was, the job needed to be done, and I am proud of the outcome and the team that delivered it. Now New Zealand's knowledge workers can work from almost anywhere around the country, and increasingly many do. That's a boon to regional New Zealand, and a boon to people's lifestyles. And as it turned out, very handy in a pandemic.

Chapter Fourteen
An extra portfolio

SUZANNE AND I DECIDED EARLY on to station the family in Wellington during the year so we would all be together. I had been offered a ministerial house, which was in fact the cottage in the garden at Premier House. It was walking distance to Parliament, which was great, and just a short hop and a skip away from John's apartment in Premier House.

The state of the cottage, however, wasn't so great. The rooms were okay but the kitchen was tiny, and there were signs of a rodent infestation which was kept at bay only with Rentokil boxes strategically placed around the house. Premier House and the cottage both back on to Tinakori Hill, where the wildlife was no doubt abundant. We'd brought our dog Gemma with us and she tried to keep the invaders away, but too sporadically to be effective.

I took to walking to Parliament early every morning and back home for dinner at night, before heading back in again to do more work. During longer recesses we'd go home to Auckland, and try to straighten out our house and garden. I was often away on the road, though, so it was left mostly to Suzanne.

The transfers between Auckland and Wellington must have been hilarious to onlookers. We'd arrive at the airport in the ministerial van and traipse across the terminal with bags, child, trundler, a large animal carrier and a big excitable fluffy dog on a lead trying her hardest to meet and greet every possible person.

We stayed at Premier Cottage for much of that first year in Wellington, but the proverbial hit the fan when it became clear there were rats living in the walls. Apparently Ministerial Services had cancelled the rodent-management programme as a cost-saving measure.

Suzanne put her foot down. We were moving out. I told Wayne Eagleson, who must have passed the news on to John, who was horrified. He immediately invited us to bunk down with him in the apartment at Premier House while we sorted out alternative accommodation. We protested but he insisted, and so it came to be that the Joyce family was briefly ensconced in Premier House as flatmates of the prime minister.

We were only there for a couple of weeks and John was mostly away, so we were hardly ever around at the same time. But there was one night where the practicality of the arrangement was called into question. John was hosting a dinner with education sector leaders in the formal dining room while we were having our family dinner in the flat upstairs. All was good until Gemma spotted an open doorway and tore off downstairs to see what fun was to be had.

She could move pretty fast and I am reliably informed she was quite the surprise arrival to John's security detail who were stationed at the door to the room. She enjoyed her game of tackle rugby with the diplomatic protection squad immensely. I'm not sure whether weapons were actually presented, but she did have a lucky escape. We fortunately moved out to an apartment in Evans Bay a week later.

In the middle of all this, Tommy was born in late November 2009. He was an accommodating little man, and fitted in right away with our busy lifestyle. But he didn't get to see much of his dad in those early years, and neither did his sister.

I was starting to get my two main portfolios under control. While life remained relentlessly busy, I had a strong sense of direction in both transport and ICT, so it was now primarily about delivery. I started taking more of an interest in areas outside my direct portfolios, including as Associate Finance Minister.

In those first couple of years it often seemed like we were bouncing from one drama to another as companies large and small tried to deal with the GFC. We were regularly approached by companies almost on their uppers, often squeezed by being unable to obtain credit. Most managed their way through, but Fisher & Paykel Appliances was one that came back to talk a number of times, before the Chinese firm Haier bought a cornerstone shareholding, and eventually a controlling interest.

The biggest problem child was South Canterbury Finance. It had been included in the Crown Retail Deposit Guarantee Scheme along with most other finance companies back in November 2008, under a delegation to Treasury from then Finance Minister Michael Cullen. He had extended the deposit guarantee scheme from the trading banks to finance companies because otherwise people would move their deposits from uninsured finance companies into insured banks, placing the finance companies at great risk of collapse.

It became apparent soon after we came into office that South Canterbury Finance was not in good shape. Treasury officials worked intensively with it for the next eighteen months, before it collapsed into receivership in mid-2010. It generated the biggest call on the Deposit Guarantee Scheme at around $700 million, but, as Bill said at the time, it represented the premium New Zealand paid to avoid a widespread collapse of its banking system through the GFC.

I knew a little more about another company having difficulty. MediaWorks was made up of my former company, RadioWorks, plus the More FM group and TV3. It was struggling to pay the government the twenty-year renewal fees for its broadcast licences which were due for all broadcasters in 2011.

MediaWorks initially approached me for help in my role as Minister for Information and Communications Technology, but I turned them down. I believed they would find the necessary funds and, in short, it was a bit of a try-on. John, however, was very concerned at the thought that half the private broadcast media could fall into receivership, and he wanted to provide some sort of concession to help them stay afloat.

John pushed hard with Bill and me, and eventually we came up with a scheme which could be offered to all broadcasters. They could pay for their licences over five years instead of in a lump sum, provided they paid 11.5 per cent interest per year on the outstanding balance. It was only a little concessionary; we only wanted companies to take it up if they really needed to.

I duly announced the scheme as the portfolio minister, and immediately copped a lot of flak for it. Critics accused me of doing a favour for my old firm, despite having been out of the industry for a decade. Little did they know, if it had been left to me there would never have been a concession. Eight companies in total, including MediaWorks, took up the offer, and MediaWorks paid up in full after three years rather than five.

Bill's big Budget initiative in 2010 was the great tax switch, which saw GST increase to 15 per cent offset with significant reductions in personal income-tax rates. The tax rate on the first $14,000 individuals earned was cut from 12.5 per cent to 10.5 per cent; the rate on $14,000 to $48,000 from 21 per cent to 17.5 per cent; on $48,000 to $70,000 from 33 per cent to 30 per cent; and above $70,000 from 38 per cent down to 33 per cent. The company tax rate reduced to 28 per cent.

The idea was to provide people with more personal reward for their hard work, which we knew was crucial for building a stronger economy.

I was initially nervous about the lift in GST, particularly given John's commitment not to do so before we were elected. However, Treasury was able to produce an analysis which showed all wage earners would be better off under the package, to the order of around 1 per cent of their incomes, so we were relatively confident that voters would see it as quite a different move to just whacking up GST.

We highlighted the importance of the package as a 'tax switch' to encourage economic growth, and the change went through remarkably smoothly. The lack of pushback meant that even after the biggest realignment of tax rates in more than a decade, the government was often accused of 'not doing anything' in those first three years.

I also had a role riding unofficial shotgun to Local Government Minister Rodney Hide's work to amalgamate the seven Auckland councils. I enjoyed working with Rodney and got to know him better through that process. I also enjoyed working with the late Mark Ford, who was an excellent chief executive and did a great job of bringing the council organisations together, including getting the costs under control. Unfortunately, under the subsequent financial stewardship of firstly Len Brown and then Phil Goff, the council's cost structure blew out again. The amalgamation has of course been blamed.

I think Rodney got the big calls in the amalgamation about 85 per cent right, which is about the most you could hope for in such a complex reform. However, in hindsight I think we should have considered keeping Rodney and Franklin districts separate from the supercity.

I have learnt from experience that having separate councils on the border of large urban areas tends to create healthy competitive tension between them for the provision of housing. Those on the periphery tend to be more active in releasing land to build houses so they can grow their rating base, while the larger city council obsesses over urban form and often tries to constrain growth. The counterweight of the border councils tends to keep overall land prices down.

This happened around the periphery of Christchurch after the earthquakes, where Waimakiriri and Selwyn districts were more than happy to step up and release land for development. It also worked with the Waipa District on the border of Hamilton, the Western Bay of Plenty District around Tauranga, and most dramatically the Waikato District around Auckland, as evidenced by the rapidly expanding township of Pōkeno.

Auckland's long-term problem with land for housing was primarily caused by the truculent Auckland Regional Council (ARC), which refused to countenance residential housing outside its own preferred Metropolitan Urban Limit. The ARC ended up taking Auckland's local councils to court when they tried to release land, and during the decade from 1998 to 2008 the ARC steadily ground down the availability of sections in greenfield areas around Auckland to almost nothing. That created a housing shortage that has plagued the city ever since, and directly led to the Royal Commission being set up by Helen Clark's government in 2007.

Once the councils were amalgamated that problem was gone, but the planners and the council ideologues in the new supercity persisted in closely controlling development in rural areas around the city. It is only in much more recent times they have become more sensible, under the forceful pushing of both National and Labour governments. It would be great to have a council structure that didn't need such heavy-handed central government intervention.

AT THE BEGINNING OF 2010, I was given a third major portfolio to get my teeth into.

Anne Tolley had been doing a great job as a reforming education minister, but by the end of her first year in the role she was fighting fires on many fronts. There were many grumblings across the sector, particularly in the universities, who felt their issues were not being adequately addressed. That was a bit unfair on Anne, but John thought he needed to address their concerns and give Anne more time to focus on flagship policies like National Standards in schools. So on 27 January 2010 I was announced as the new Minister of Tertiary Education, alongside my other responsibilities.

I headed straight into another full immersion programme in a sector I'd had little to do with since I'd left university back in the 1980s. I soon learnt that the tertiary education sector is awash with impenetrable acronyms, and for the first two months I had to carry around a glossary of all the terms the sector used.

The Opposition provided me with their own welcome to the portfolio. They got hold of my university academic record and sought to lampoon it for their own entertainment. It amused them immensely that I started my degree in 1981 and graduated in 2002, leaving out the inconvenient detail that I had completed studying for it in 1983. A further reason to regret not graduating alongside my peers!

Another rich vein of humour was the way my study tailed off at the end of my time at Massey University. By the time I'd reached my final year for my zoology degree, I had discovered economics. I took and passed nine papers that year, including three economics papers. I began another six economics papers in 1984 with the aim of completing a postgraduate diploma in social science, but by then I had also discovered radio. I passed three papers and didn't complete the other three. I enrolled again in both 1985 and 1986, but by then I'd really moved on to starting the radio station so study fell by the wayside. I ended up with seven economics papers and no post-graduate qualification to show for them.

Trevor Mallard moved a motion in Parliament without notice to congratulate me for persisting with my degree and graduating 21 years after I started it. Unfortunately, our whips were distracted and allowed the motion to go through. Parliament then entered an unlimited time debate on the academic prowess of yours truly. I suspect I remain the only person who has been formally congratulated on his academic record by the New Zealand Parliament.

My brief in tertiary education was primarily to extract much better value for the country for the investment we made in the sector. New Zealand had one of the highest public investments in tertiary education relative to the size of our economy, but that wasn't reflected in the results achieved, which were at best about average. We weren't seeking to tip the tertiary sector on its head, but we were wanting better outcomes for students in terms of qualifications achieved for the money we were investing.

We were also trying to repair the government's budget, so once again we had no new money to go around. Bill didn't necessarily want any money back, but he did want me to fund things like tuition subsidy increases or more student places from savings. So off I went on a multi-year hunt for performance improvements and savings to drive better results from tertiary education.

The first problem I had to address was the poor quality of advice from the Ministry of Education. It was very 'once over lightly' and involved presenting a few factoids, followed by a favourite policy recommendation which the selected factoids supported. That approach drove me up the wall. I wanted much more analytical rigour, and conclusions and recommendations drawn from the data, not the other way around. To their credit the ministry caught on reasonably quickly and moved some more analytical staff to the portfolio. After the first six months, the advice from the Ministry of Education was some of the highest-quality I received while a minister.

I also had to resolve an ongoing policy turf war between the Tertiary Education Commission (TEC) and the ministry. The TEC often didn't like the ministry's policy advice and had hired its own group of policy analysts to provide different advice. The ministry in turn wasn't happy about the way the TEC made investments in the tertiary sector. It was exhausting. I directed them both to stay in their respective lanes. The TEC could have input into policy from its experience as funder and monitor of the tertiary sector, but I made them wind up their policy team.

We started by following through on performance-linked funding, an initiative Anne had started. The idea was to incentivise tertiary providers to focus on some key metrics of student performance in return for the funding they received. Tertiary providers are funded primarily on enrolments, which is the only sensible way to do it. The tertiary unions would prefer bulk funding for institutions, but even the left side of politics could see the lack of accountability inherent in that idea.

The trouble with what was called the 'bums on seats' funding system was that the performance of people once they enrolled was not reflected in the funding arrangements. In the worst-case scenario, people could enrol and leave six months later without achieving anything, and the provider would still receive full funding.

We wanted to incentivise performance and achievement. The plan was to hold back a small percentage (5 per cent) of funding, and pay it only if the providers met acceptable standards of qualification achievement, retention of students, and progression of students through the institution.

In a low-margin sector, losing 5 per cent of your funding would hurt, but not so much that you were tempted to trash your reputation by cutting corners. In any event, the polytechs and the private providers had the New Zealand Qualifications Authority (NZQA) breathing down their necks on quality assurance.

I knew we were onto something when I visited UCOL in Palmerston North some time later and an academic winningly told me that performance-linked funding had, to their mind unexpectedly, been helpful. Staff at the institution were now spending more time looking at each student holistically and monitoring their progress. I confess I found it a little surprising that this was a new approach.

One big area where we could save some money was in student support. Student loans and allowances made up nearly 40 per cent of the total amount taxpayers spent annually on tertiary education, which was very high internationally. It meant the government was meeting about 80 per cent of the cost to students of their study, while arguably starving the institutions they were studying at.

We were committed to interest-free student loans, but I believed some things needed to change to ensure all students were studying to achieve a qualification while they were taking out these loans. Small changes to student loans might release quite a lot of money.

Over the course of several Budgets we made some judicious nips and tucks to the scheme to ensure taxpayers were getting more value, and to minimise the number of students ending up with a big student loan and nothing to show for it. We introduced a seven-year lifetime limit for student loans for undergraduate study, and a requirement that students pass half of their papers on average to keep qualifying for student support. We also introduced a new fee of $50 a year to cover the administration costs of the scheme.

In 2011 we restricted student loans to covering tuition fees only for people over the age of 55, and removed loan eligibility for people already late on their repayments. Then in 2012 we lifted the repayment rate for student loans to 12 cents in the dollar of income earned, and removed the voluntary repayment 'bonus' started by a previous government.

It was the same on student allowances, which were originally designed for people who weren't able to take up a student loan. The Clark government had left us a ticking time-bomb of increased allowance entitlements, which would see the cost of the scheme blow out by 70 per cent if left unchecked. Over a few Budgets we reined in the cost by freezing the parental income threshold (below which you qualified for an allowance) and cancelling student allowances for postgraduates, on the grounds their post-study income would enable them to pay back a student loan.

During our work on student allowances we discovered a surprising loophole. Some immigrants over the age of 65 who weren't eligible for New Zealand superannuation were instead signing up for student allowances and 'studying' in order to be paid an income. That was quickly knocked on the head.

All of these new settings were criticised by the Opposition at the time, but almost all survive years later. I think most people see them as very reasonable restrictions on a still-generous scheme by world standards.

The third place we went looking for savings was amongst former students who had disappeared overseas once graduating and made no attempt to pay off their student loans. These people had been left in the too-hard basket by ministers for twenty years, and despite only representing 21 per cent of the student-loan book they made up nearly 90 per cent of the overdue amounts. The IRD hadn't considered it worth their while to chase them, which was astonishing to me. It wasn't fair to everyone else, and it also created a perverse incentive to leave the country!

Arguably Helen Clark's government made it worse by extending a one-year repayment holiday for the traditional OE to three years; after which time contact with the borrower had often been lost. We reversed that and started going after people who were deliberately ignoring their student loan. We resourced the IRD to find overseas borrowers and hired debt-collection agencies to help.

A big breakthrough came when we made agreements with the tax departments of key partner countries like the UK, Canada and Australia to share the addresses of student-loan borrowers living offshore. The Australian Taxation Office alone yielded the current addresses of 57,000 student-loan borrowers living in Australia, two-thirds of whom were in default. That gave the IRD a huge number of people to follow up with.

We also got everyone's attention with a new law to allow people to be arrested at the border if they attempted to come back into the country while in default of their student loan. It was only to be used as a last resort, but it certainly helped develop a conscience amongst those borrowers who liked to travel back occasionally to visit family. When the first person was arrested at the border, hundreds more people got in touch with the IRD the next day.

I was a bit stunned at the sense of entitlement of some of the overseas-based borrowers. Some were no doubt doing it tough and there were hardship mechanisms to help those, but many more were working in first-world countries like Australia or the UK in careers like medicine or law, making six- and even seven-figure sums and thumbing their noses at their responsibilities to their country of birth.

The first six years of the overseas-based borrowers initiative netted $360 million in extra repayments to the student-loan scheme, alongside the hundreds of millions saved more broadly in student support. All of those savings were reinvested in increasing the number of study places and lifting tuition subsidies across the tertiary sector. The universities saw their direct operational funding increase by 30 per cent over our nine years in office, as against inflation of 18 per cent. We also were able to turn around some of the long-term decline of our universities in the international rankings, posting ranking increases in 2016 and 2017.

Of course the vice-chancellors weren't exactly grateful for that level of increased investment. More than once I had cause to recall

David Lange's famous description of university vice-chancellors as 'bikies in suits' in my dealings with them. Ironically, I was told after I left the portfolio I was a much better Tertiary Education Minister in hindsight than I seemed at the time. Universities were put on much tougher rations under the next government.

As well as general funding increases, we placed a specific emphasis in areas where New Zealand had a significant shortage of graduates. This included engineering, where I was surprised to learn that New Zealand trained only about half the number of engineers than was the average across OECD countries. On further investigation, this was because the level of tuition subsidy paid to universities for engineering was low relative to the cost. Engineering is an expensive course requiring lots of labs and expensive infrastructure. It was simply more profitable to train people in the arts, social sciences or commerce, so universities tended to restrict the number of engineering places.

I had officials lift the subsidy for engineering, and then for other capital-intensive courses like science and agriculture, so that providers would be at least neutral between training another commerce student versus an engineer or a scientist. Then in 2013 we allocated another thousand places specifically for engineering training. The aim was to double the annual number of engineering graduates by 2017, a target I am proud to say we achieved.

I am only sorry we didn't get to do the same for medicine, another discipline where as a country we train many fewer than we need. Unfortunately, two universities currently have a stranglehold on doctor training, and any increase in medical places must be signed off by the Minister of Health as well as the Minister of Tertiary Education, due to the impact training more doctors has on the health budget. I believed, and still believe, it is ludicrous that a country of our size doesn't have a third medical school, but I was unable to get either of my Minister of Health colleagues over the line.

EARLY ON IN MY TENURE in tertiary education, I happened to be talking with the local owner of my favourite coffee shop in Albany, down the road from home. He'd heard news of my appointment and had a particular gripe he wanted to air. Could I stop the industry training organisations (ITOs) from harassing his staff? I pricked up my ears and asked him to tell me more.

It turned out the ITO responsible for the hospitality sector was going around trying to sign up anyone who moved, right down to the most casual staff member. They were usually enrolled in courses like basic hygiene, because every enrolment meant the ITO received additional funding, whether the student actually achieved any credits or not. He told me it was a joke, and he was horrified to think how much taxpayer funding was being wasted. I decided to have a closer look.

Industry training is training that occurs in the workplace instead of at a university or polytechnic. It includes apprenticeships, traineeships and short courses, and it is very politically popular. Unfortunately, popular initiatives are often measured by how much money politicians pour into them rather than what they achieve. Politicians get kudos for spending an extra $50 million a year on apprenticeships, whether or not any additional apprenticeships are completed.

During the years of the Clark government, government funding for industry training almost trebled, but there were no decent systems in place to drive accountability. I had the TEC conduct compliance reviews, and they found millions of dollars ostensibly spent on training people who had left the employer, had never worked for the employer, or hadn't realised they were signing up. In some memorable cases people had died but were still listed as being in training.

But it gets worse. In 2008 and 2009 more than half the 100,000 trainees on the books at ITOs weren't achieving any credits, despite the money the government was paying for their training. It was industry training in name only, and it was time for a cleanout.

Over the next few years I pushed the TEC to straighten the sector out and focus on delivering actual training which generated meaningful qualifications. I also pushed for ITO consolidation. When I started in the ministerial role we had 39 different ITOs across different industries in New Zealand. Many were very small and unable to do a good job. By the time we were finished there were just ten well-funded ITOs, all of them supervising high-quality training.

We then set about boosting the number of true apprenticeships, with a programme known as the apprenticeship reboot, and another programme for Māori and Pasifika trade training. These helped increase the number of apprentices in training by 20 per cent from 2012 to 2017.

We also encouraged some mergers in the polytech sector, taking smaller polytechs under the wing of larger entities. Thus EIT in Hawke's Bay took over Gisborne's stand-alone polytech, CPIT and Aoraki Polytechnic merged into Ara, and the separate polytechs in Tauranga and Rotorua became Toi Ohomai. What I didn't do was merge all the polytechs and ITOs into one monopoly mega-polytech. That has been tried in Australia and generally led to massive cost and educational failure. We will see how New Zealand's version unfolds.

Monopolies are often touted as 'more efficient' but they generally lead to poor customer service and a lack of innovation. This applies in education as much as anywhere else. At the time of writing there is increased talk of consolidation in the university sector to 'remove unnecessary duplication'. That would be a mistake. New Zealand universities (and the vocational sector) need more innovation and responsiveness to new ways of thinking and new careers, not less.

THE TERTIARY EDUCATION MINISTER IS also the minister responsible for international education, and that became one of my favourite assignments as a minister.

Bringing international students to study in New Zealand provides so many benefits for our country. Yes, they bring export revenue to our trade balance and that helps us pay our way in the world. They also bring income to the institutions they study at, which helps those institutions to be bigger and better funded than they otherwise would be. But most importantly they provide a valuable network of people-to-people linkages between New Zealand and countries all over the world.

International students study here during their formative years. As well as their study, they have experiences and create friendships that last their whole lives. They almost universally form a positive impression of our country, which they take with them wherever they go. We have armies of graduates in China, Malaysia, Vietnam, India, Colombia, Brazil, Korea, the US and all over the world, all with fond memories of their time here, and all positively disposed to New Zealand. As they go through their lives and some form businesses of their own or take up leadership positions at home, they form a network of friends that will repay us many-fold in the future.

I am a passionate convert to the international education cause. As a country, our future prosperity will largely be determined by the strength of our interpersonal relationships in the Asia-Pacific region, and our education relationships are at the forefront of those ties.

During my time in international education, I made three significant changes to foster the development of the sector. Firstly, we created a marketing agency for New Zealand education which would be the equivalent of Tourism New Zealand for its industry. International education had been something of a Cinderella sector, with the Ministry of Education, New Zealand Trade and Enterprise

(NZTE) and a very subscale Education New Zealand Trust all dabbling in it.

We successfully combined the staff and resources of all three together in a new Crown agent called Education New Zealand, and then doubled its budget so it could truly compete with other countries promoting themselves to international students. Education New Zealand started operations in 2011, and under the leadership of inaugural chair and former diplomat Charles Finny it has done a great job creating and marketing the 'New Zealand Educated' brand, which has been very successful offshore.

The second challenge was to get the regulatory settings right. We had to offer an appealing package to prospective students, including things like post-study work rights and short visa processing times, to be a competitive option for quality English-language education against the likes of Canada, Australia, the US and the UK. While most students don't go on to stay and work in the country they study in, they'd like the opportunity to do so if they choose, and that forms a key part of their consideration of where to study. The quid pro quo was to provide NZQA and Immigration New Zealand greater powers to police the sector, so they could root out those who treated the student pathway as an opportunity purely for immigration rather than for study.

Finally, we needed an aspirational goal for the sector, and practical help to achieve that goal. International education was worth around $2.2 billion in annual foreign exchange to New Zealand when I became minister, and we set a target to grow that to $5 billion by 2018. The practical help came in the form of regular ministerial visits to key student markets. In most of our target countries, particularly in Asia and South America, ministerial visits are a key tool to market the sector to students and to the governments that encourage their students to travel.

I made many visits to offshore markets in support of international education, and had many wonderful experiences as a result. From alumni functions in Japan, Korea and China, to guest lecturing in a Vietnamese university, being the keynote speaker at the International Education Conference in Brazil, judging a fashion show in Kuala Lumpur for New Zealand and Malaysian design students, and feeling like an extra in a Bond movie in Saudi Arabia and Oman, I helped Education New Zealand wave the flag for New Zealand education. In doing so I met many people who demonstrated in practical terms the benefit of those people-to-people links. One of my favourite examples was a long-standing chief minister in Sarawak, Malaysia, who had studied at Lincoln University through the Colombo Plan of the 1960s, and who did all he could to help New Zealand in a part of the world to which we don't give enough attention.

We also wanted to foster outward study and research to key countries around the Asia-Pacific. The government set up Prime Minister's Scholarships for New Zealand students to study in Asia and Latin America, and one of my last acts as minister was to set up three Centres of Asia-Pacific Excellence in universities around New Zealand, to strengthen our research, language and study linkages in North Asia, South-East Asia and Latin America. Unfortunately the current government has decided to let the Centres of Asia-Pacific Excellence lapse, which will damage language training at our universities.

The international education plan worked. By 2016, international education was worth $4.28 billion in export receipts to New Zealand, and was our fourth-largest export sector ahead of wood. It went on to crack the $5 billion target in 2018, before a more sceptical government lost interest in it, and then Covid-19 stopped it in its tracks.

Chapter Fifteen
Driven by events

I TOOK THE FAMILY TO Port Douglas in Queensland for a few days in the first week of September 2010. It was our first attempt to have a mid-year break since I'd been in Parliament and since Tommy was born. The weather was lovely and it looked like it would be a great opportunity to relax and unwind.

Then came the shock. I woke up on Saturday morning to the news there'd been a massive magnitude 7.1 earthquake in Christchurch. It sounded appalling, but the early news on casualties wasn't as bad as that seven number suggested. While there had been widespread damage, it had struck very early in the morning and nearly everyone in Christchurch was at home at the time.

I had an instant urge to return to New Zealand and help. I spoke with both John and Wayne, and they persuaded me to stay and finish my break. Hardly had I made that call when more bad news came. This time it was a horrific plane crash on the other side of the South Island. Nine people had died instantly when a skydiving plane crashed on take-off in clear blue skies at Fox Glacier just after 1 p.m. As Minister of Transport, this disaster was clearly in my bailiwick. We dropped everything and came back.

I headed to Wellington and made a statement to Parliament on the crash at the start of Tuesday's session. I then flew down to Fox Glacier to meet the first responders and visit the crash site. By then the accident investigators had moved the wreckage to a warehouse, and there was just the oily mark on the ground where the crash had happened. It was a drizzly, dark day, and a sad and bleak scene.

Amongst those nine people were some who had come from all over the world for an adventure at the southern end of New Zealand's West Coast. They were Australian, English, Irish, and of course there were Kiwis as well. It was a senseless loss of life and New Zealand's worst air accident for seventeen years. We would have to wait for the air accident report, but we were determined to make any regulatory changes we could to prevent such tragedies from happening again.

From Fox Glacier I flew to Christchurch to survey the earthquake damage and check in on the transport and tertiary education sectors. The transport engineers took me on a quick tour of the highway network around Christchurch, highlighting how well the various bridge structures had stood up to the huge forces of the quake. There was one new bridge over the Northern motorway of which the engineers were particularly proud. It struck me that this was because most structural engineers design for these sorts of events in theory and never get to see their work tested in practice. I did find the excited gleam in their eyes slightly disconcerting.

It was a more sobering experience at the University of Canterbury. Vice-Chancellor Rod Carr took me on a tour of the university library, where massive bookshelves heavy with texts had toppled forward, landing in many cases on work areas normally occupied by students. Rod noted that at Victoria University in Wellington such bookshelves were fixed to the wall because of Wellington's acknowledged high earthquake risk, but nobody had thought to do the same at Canterbury.

The mistaken belief was that 'Christchurch doesn't have earthquakes.'

Rod repeated the thoughts of many when he told me that the university was lucky the quake happened at a time when all the students were at home and the library closed. Throughout the city there was a sense that a bullet had been dodged.

It was becoming a year of tragic events. Just two months later, late on a Friday afternoon, news started to break about an explosion and fire at the Pike River mine, north-east of Greymouth. It sounded terrible, and it was. We all watched in horror as the situation unfolded.

The explosion had trapped 29 men deep underground. Over the next few days the police and the Mines Rescue Service tried to find a way to rescue the men or recover their bodies. But it was too unsafe to enter the mine, and three further explosions resulted in the mine being sealed and the men entombed. Despite initial hopes the men may have survived the initial explosion, both the coroner's report and the eventual Royal Commission on the Pike River Coal Mine Tragedy found that all 29 men either died in that first explosion or very shortly thereafter.

Pike River dominated the government's activity throughout the second half of November and into December. John Key visited the West Coast twice, firstly to comfort the families, and then to lead a memorial service at Greymouth Racecourse on 3 December 2010. He spoke movingly and memorably at both his press conference after the second explosion, and at the memorial service. At times like these, prime ministers must embody the best instincts of their people, mourn those lost and comfort those left behind. He did a sterling job at a difficult time.

BY THE END OF THE YEAR, we were all needing a break. And like it or not, thoughts had to turn towards the next election in just eleven months. It's about this time that MPs start to think whether they want to commit to another three years. You wouldn't expect many ministers to retire after just three years in the ministry of a new government, so it was a surprise when North Shore MP Wayne Mapp decided to leave Parliament.

Wayne had done fifteen years in Wellington, which is a decent stint. He'd enjoyed being Minister of Defence along with the Research, Science and Technology portfolio, and treasured his role as North Shore MP in one of the strongest National electorates in the country. Wayne is a great observer of people, with a very dry sense of humour which often didn't quite translate in the media. He is one of a small number of colleagues I regularly keep up with post-politics.

Wayne's departure created a bit of a dilemma for me. Immediately after he announced his resignation, I was approached by a number of senior people from the North Shore electorate, asking if I would seek the nomination for the seat. I was very flattered and admit that my head was turned a little. Seeking an electorate seat wasn't in the life plan, but if there was ever a seat I would love to represent, it would be my old stomping ground of Takapuna, Bayswater and Devonport.

A number of people saw it as a good idea for me to stand, particularly if I had aspirations beyond being a minister. List MPs were still a bit frowned on within the party for leadership positions, and Don Brash's example, while successful on some levels, hadn't changed that. It was a lot to think about in a short space of time.

I sought the advice of Wayne Eagleson and John, and John was quite blunt that he thought it was a dumb idea. 'Why would you want to audition for a job you've already got?' His view was that if I wanted higher honours at any point in the future, whether or not I held a seat would not be the determining factor. He was always encouraging his senior people to consider future leadership aspirations, so I didn't get the sense he was seeking to protect his patch. Anyway, I wasn't that ambitious. It is entirely possible however that he did not want his campaign manager to be distracted in an election year.

As much as I liked the idea of being the MP for North Shore, I realised there was no way I could devote the time to winning the nomination, and then winning and holding a seat. No electorate deserves an MP who phones it in before they've even begun. With three big ministerial portfolios, and the Associate Finance role and campaign chair responsibilities, I had more than enough to do. I rang my friends in the North Shore electorate and politely turned them down.

Mappy wasn't the only minister to retire in 2011. An even bigger surprise was the departure of my friend and close colleague Simon Power, who announced he was pulling up stumps in early March. This was a bigger deal. Simon was one of the tight five in the Kitchen Cabinet, a close group of senior ministers who met regularly and informally as a sounding board for the PM and each other. Simon was ranked at number four in the ministry, with a big future in front of him. His departure was a bolt from the blue.

I was working in my office one evening when Simon and Murray McCully arrived together without warning. 'I have something to tell you. I'm leaving,' Simon said bluntly. He gave some reasons which didn't sound too convincing, but later we had a private discussion and I think I got to the bottom of what was going on. Simon had come into Parliament as a young person, without a commercial career behind him. He was very aware of what people like John and I had done pre-politics, and he told me he wanted to try his hand commercially, and see what he could achieve. His mountain to climb was the mirror image of mine.

I really enjoyed working with Simon and knew I would miss him. We were both clearly workaholics and perfectionists, and we realised early on that, notwithstanding the prodigious work ethics of people like John and Bill, we would often be the last to leave the building. We were both determined to knock over as much work as we could each night so we could start the next day up with the play. We each read everything, and took our roles as Cabinet 'sweepers' seriously, delving into every complex Cabinet paper trying to find the fish-hooks in every policy proposal.

We got into a habit of picking up the phone and calling each other for chats about 11 or 11.30 p.m., and used to joke about refusing to leave before the other guy left, or making meeting appointments for each other for 1 a.m. Sometimes when I wanted to go home at an indecently early time like 10.30 p.m., I'd leave my office lights on so when Simon left he'd look up and think I was still beavering away.

John fired the first public shot for the election year by announcing in February that 26 November would be the election date. This decision was partly pragmatism and partly principle. New Zealand was hosting the Rugby World Cup in September and October, and John wanted there to be no conjecture about election dates leading into the celebrations.

He liked the idea of a set election date anyway, so the government could get on with governing during the year and everyone else could get on with life until the campaign period arrived. As his campaign chair, I quite liked retaining an element of surprise as to when the election would be, to help keep the other side off balance, but as a minister and a New Zealander I liked the settled date, and I hope it continues to be a New Zealand tradition.

WE WERE JUST GETTING INTO campaign planning when all hell broke loose once more. At 12.51 p.m. on 22 February, round two of the Canterbury earthquakes struck. This second beast was much more devastating; 185 people died, including 115 people in the collapse of just one building, the CTV building on Madras Street, near Latimer Square.

It was Tuesday lunchtime, so we were all in the Beehive. It was a big shake even in Wellington, and everybody stopped to comment on it. Then the news everyone dreaded — it was Christchurch.

As word started to filter out about the extent of the devastation, John called an emergency Cabinet meeting. Information was trickling in, but all of it was sketchy. John flew to Christchurch with Gerry Brownlee, while Bill and Civil Defence Minister John Carter fronted an initial press briefing. John, Gerry and local mayor Bob Parker briefed the media from Latimer Square. There was carnage all around.

Back in Wellington we were working on ways to help Christchurch. Much of those first 48 hours is a blur, but one thing sticks in my memory. Murray McCully came to see me to say that as Foreign Minister he was being inundated with offers of assistance from urban search and rescue (USAR) teams from around the world, but Civil Defence didn't want to accept the help. They thought they had it all in hand, although a glance at a television would show they didn't.

Murray, Simon Power and I held a late-night meeting with Civil Defence National Controller John Hamilton, exhorting him to take up the offers of support. We wanted to leave no stone unturned. I could see that John was under real pressure and feeling defensive. He felt that it would be too late by the time the other USAR teams arrived. We agreed that was possible but wanted to try. We remonstrated with him to accept the offers. After a 40-minute discussion he relented and agreed. Some teams arrived in time to help, and others were indeed too late. But we needed to know we'd done everything we could.

John Key appointed Gerry as Earthquake Recovery Minister within three days of the quake, and the first business and job-loss support packages were announced within a week. John was born in and grew up in Christchurch, and felt the disaster very keenly. He made the city's recovery a personal mission, visiting nearly every day for weeks, then almost every other week for the rest of his premiership.

Gerry, too, made it his mission to help the city heal and recover, and I feel he has not been given sufficient credit for Christchurch's recovery. They were very tough times, with big, unprecedented decisions needing to be made initially every week, and then every month or so for years. Nobody was going to get them all right, but he managed most of them correctly. Both John and Gerry can be very proud of their legacy in that city. It is now bigger and stronger than it was before the quakes. In those early days there was no guarantee that would be so.

My personal link to the earthquakes came through my role as minister responsible for international education. It rapidly became clear that one of the greatest losses of life would be in the collapse of the CTV building, and on the fourth floor of that building there had been a private English-language school, King's Education. I spoke initially by phone to the school's director, John Ryder, and he was distraught. We quietly talked through how we would obtain a copy of the school's records and get them to the Ministry of Education so they could make a list of the missing, and we agreed to keep in touch.

Nearly all of the missing people were international students, from China, Japan, the Philippines, Thailand, Korea and the Czech Republic. I worked with Murray to ensure the embassies were able to support the families. Five days after the quake I went to Christchurch myself, to meet with the remaining leaders of the school, and the families who were assembling there.

The Japanese embassy had leased a motel not far from the central city, and the conference room was full of embassy staff and the families of missing students. I talked with the families, gave my condolences and offered all the help we could provide. By then they knew their children were probably gone. They were very reserved and respectful, but there were many muffled tears. It was one of the saddest moments of my time in Parliament.

Nearby the Chinese families had assembled in a school hall for a similar meeting. There the mood of the meeting was one of anger. They were demanding explanations for what had happened to their children. I had no satisfactory answers, but promised there would be a full and thorough investigation.

It was a very sombre day. I was taken to see some parts of the damaged city, and the sights of buckled roads and broken houses along the riverbanks were hard to comprehend. The earthquake had unleashed colossal forces. I knew we would have a huge task ahead.

I attended a memorial service in mid-March at Burnside High School for those who had lost their lives at King's Education. It was led by Peter Beck, the dean of ChristChurch Cathedral, and Mayor Bob Parker. It was another immensely sad occasion. I met and talked with some of the families. In total, 81 King's Education students and staff lost their lives in the CTV building collapse.

It transpired later that the design of the CTV building was deficient and a building permit for it should not have been issued. Police sought to bring prosecutions against those responsible, but legal technicalities meant that was not possible. The collapse of this building to my mind remains one of the absolute travesties of New Zealand's construction history.

CABINET WENT INTO OVERDRIVE WORKING out how to rebuild our second-largest city. We were very conscious that decisions needed to be made swiftly or there was a risk the city would hollow out, with much of its population moving permanently elsewhere. The city's CBD looked like a war zone, and a huge percentage of housing, particularly in the east of Christchurch, was uninhabitable. The whole country had discovered new terms like 'liquefaction', where soil liquefies and swallows up cars and even parts of houses.

There was much debate internally and amongst the public about how to approach the rebuild. John set up a Cabinet Committee on Earthquake Recovery chaired by Gerry, and experts in various areas came to talk with us about aspects of the recovery. One session in particular stands out. We were worried about the risk of setting a precedent by writing off huge areas of land as 'red-zoned' and unsuitable for development. A very senior geotechnical engineer was asked by John what he would do in our position. 'Prime Minister,' he said, 'I'd just roll it all flat and start again.'

He went on to explain that New Zealand was a very geologically young country and much of it was prone to slips, floods and earthquakes. 'If you rule out too many areas for building platforms, pretty soon you are ruling out much of the country.' While we didn't take his advice verbatim, it was a reminder that very few places in this country are completely 'safe' from disaster. It also underlined for me that the country should always have a financial buffer to help deal with whatever comes along.

I personally spent a lot of time on the rebuilding of tertiary facilities in the city, and I arranged the creation of fast-tracked training courses for building trades and the like. On the transport side, I took Gerry a proposal early on to set up an alliance of NZTA, Christchurch City Council and the major civil contractors to rebuild the city's broken horizontal infrastructure. The idea was they would coordinate their plans and do what needed to be done, with set margins. The government would pick up the tab to a set amount. Gerry took a little convincing, but we ended up announcing it in May 2011. While it wasn't perfect, it did a great job of rebuilding the city's roads and water pipes much faster than would otherwise have happened.

During the development of the Christchurch motorway projects, I had come to know Christchurch's Urban Development Strategy, a plan for urban growth for the next 30 years agreed between the local councils and Environment Canterbury. The strategy determined what greenfield land was to be developed in what order, so amenities like water services and transport could be rolled out accordingly. It helped control infrastructure costs for the participating councils, but at the expense of high land prices for home buyers as only the favoured tracts of land would be available for building on at any one time.

Gerry came and asked me about the strategy. I explained what I knew, and he said he would need to release some of the land ahead of schedule, to ensure land prices in Christchurch didn't go crazy following the loss of the red-zoned areas. I agreed with him.

He went away and came back to say that his officials wanted some of the land released but he was planning to release all 30 years' worth, to ensure competition amongst developers. I gulped a bit at the audacity of the idea, but agreed it made sense.

That one decision kept Christchurch section prices reasonable right through the rebuild period, and the city's house prices remained some of the most affordable in the country for years afterwards. It should be seen as a compelling case study for the benefit that expanding land supply can have in ensuring house prices remain affordable.

Chapter Sixteen
Squeezing in an election

WHILE THE EARTHQUAKE RESPONSE CONTINUED, both the Rugby World Cup and the 2011 election were roaring towards us. I had precious little bandwidth spare for campaign planning, so I was lucky I had Jo de Joux back for her third campaign as operations manager. Jo, her team and our advertising contractors were now a well-oiled machine and they used my time sparingly, mostly around the strategic marketing and advertising calls.

We had some new personnel on the core campaign team. Judy Kirk had decided to retire as party president in 2009 once she had safely seen a National-led government installed, and her replacement was the very able Peter Goodfellow. Peter had different strengths to Judy, but one thing they had in common was their fundraising ability. Campaign fundraising didn't miss a beat. Peter attended so many fundraising dinners he used to describe his role as 'eating for his country'. On the administration side, Greg Hamilton joined as general manager. Greg was a very safe pair of hands who ran a very tidy ship at Party HQ and took his party secretary responsibilities very seriously. Both became key contributors over an extended period.

The campaign team agreed we would try to draw together the threads of the past three years into a coherent narrative. A lot had happened, especially recently, and that risked obscuring some of the bigger longer-term calls like the tax switch, the changes we'd made to speed up the Resource Management Act, and investment in things like transport and ultra-fast broadband. We settled on the slogan 'Building a Brighter Future' as a logical flow-on from 2008's 'Choose a Brighter Future.'

As a party National had been polling around 20 per cent ahead of Labour for the whole three-year term. On one level that was great for us, but on another it created risks, particularly that our voters might become complacent. There were also problems in our support parties. Through much of 2011, the Māori Party was going through a very public divorce with its firebrand Te Tai Tokerau MP Hone Harawira, and the ACT party's backers were agitating for a change of leader from Rodney Hide. In April, former National leader Don Brash challenged Hide for the leadership of ACT and won. Hide then announced he was retiring at the election, and another former National MP, John Banks, was nominated to replace Rodney in the Epsom seat. None of this was helping the ACT vote.

We set our party vote target at 47–48 per cent to allow for the fact we would be unlikely to have many potential coalition partners of any size. We would of course have loved to achieve a party vote of 50 per cent, but we believed this was both highly unlikely under MMP and political poison to our chances if anyone verbalised such a goal.

We were helped all the way by Labour's negative tactics. They had been led by Phil Goff since Helen Clark stood down on election night 2008. Phil seemed content much of the time to oppose pretty much everything the Key government did with a vehemence that suggested he was relitigating the 2008 election result. It's never struck me as a smart strategy to spend your time telling the voters they got it wrong last time. We amplified Labour's approach in a series of ads with road workers using Stop / Go signs. Labour were 'Stop' and we were 'Go' — the clear inference being we needed to keep the country moving forward.

One area where Labour was getting some traction was in arguing we didn't have a plan. The sheer speed of events through the previous eighteen months had obscured our economic narrative, and they were taking advantage of that. The traditional counter to such an attack would be to release a heavyweight manifesto and, given no one much would read it, rely on its existence and point to it as evidence of the plan. I wasn't sure that would do the job in this case, and given how thinly spread we were I doubted one could be produced in time. Anyway, we had a coherent plan of sorts. I just needed a visual way to illustrate the plan to the general public.

I decided to borrow an old marketing technique I had used in radio. We had thousands of hoardings printed, each with one numbered element of our six-point 'Brighter Future' plan on it, such as '1. Balancing the Books Sooner' or '3. Rebuilding Christchurch'. By placing different-numbered placards all over town, people would see a different-numbered part of the plan each time they noticed a hoarding. We backed those up with policy papers and ads which spelled out each part of the plan in more detail, and pretty soon the 'doesn't have a plan' narrative was neutralised.

THE RUGBY WORLD CUP LANDED in the middle of the pre-campaign period, starting on 9 September and running through until Labour weekend. Many people opined that hosting the World Cup would be a huge boon for the incumbent government, but as campaign chair I wasn't convinced. Sure, if we won the World Cup on home soil there would be a feel-good factor. But I didn't like the feeling of hanging an election result on the outcome of a rugby game or two. Also, the hosting of the event needed to be seamless, or that might reflect badly on the government.

As it turned out, there was a big issue in the first week. I was coming back from speaking at a function at Formosa Golf Resort in south-east Auckland on Friday afternoon, and noticed unusually large amounts of traffic heading into rather than out of the city. We flicked the radio on and Mayor Len Brown was exhorting the whole city to come to the waterfront for a wonderful opening-night celebration. From what I could see, Aucklanders were responding. I was uneasy. Could the city handle this volume of people?

Some 200,000 people jammed into the waterfront. It seemed to cope for a while, and then the inevitable happened. The city's rickety train system collapsed under the strain of thousands of people trying to use it to move from the waterfront to Eden Park in time for the opening game.

It was a bad, high-profile own goal for the city. Fortunately, we weren't in the immediate firing line as the council controlled the trains, but we were under no illusion that a repeat would be a problem for the whole hosting of the World Cup. John read the riot act to Mayor Brown, and I did the same for his executives, including supercity supremos Doug McKay and Mark Ford. For good measure, Murray McCully, who was Minister for the Rugby World Cup, took over the running of the downtown fan zone. The city had to do much better.

After that false start, things did run a lot better, largely I think because of the wake-up call of the opening weekend. Auckland had been suddenly catapulted into the big leagues and it had to adapt quickly.

From there on it was up to the All Blacks. They duly progressed through the draw to the final at Eden Park, against the enigmatic French team. I eschewed any official duties that day, and bought my own tickets so I could take my dad to the game. He had been taking me to rugby games since I was a little kid, especially to watch his beloved Taranaki. He had been an All Blacks fan throughout his life, but I'd discovered a few months previously he'd never seen the All Blacks play live. I was determined to get him to this game.

We sat in the crowd and watched anxiously along with 60,000 others as the tense arm-wrestle unfolded in front of us. I received several increasingly nervous texts from John. When it got to 8–7 he asked, tongue in cheek I think, whether we were confident about this. I went back reminding him that Murray was the Rugby World Cup Minister, not me. I thought it was important to get that on the record.

In the end, of course, it all turned out well.

I HAD ANOTHER PROBLEM ANYWAY. On 5 October, the idiot captain of a container vessel known as the MV *Rena* had decided to take a short cut to Tauranga Harbour to ensure he would make the tidal window for the shipping channel around the Mount. In doing so he ploughed straight into the Astrolabe Reef, right opposite Mount Maunganui's main beach.

I was in Auckland that day for an electric-train announcement with Len Brown, but I headed to Tauranga when news came through. I arrived around 24 hours after the ship had struck the reef, but already the atmosphere was feral.

The response to the grounding was being led by Maritime New Zealand, which is a tiny agency unused to much public attention. At the early briefings they were like possums in the headlights, as worried locals demanded to know what they were doing to prevent tonnes of oil leaking from the vessel and coating their pristine local beaches.

I had no choice but to step into the middle of it all. I took over the briefings and started loading up the media with as much information as I could. The problem was that the salvors had to come from Singapore, as there were none closer. And a storm was approaching.

We scaled up the salvage and recovery operation, setting up a base in a disused local supermarket. With John's support, I called in the navy to help, and they brought two vessels to Tauranga to operate as a staging platform for the oil salvage operation. The salvage operators chartered a barge, and after several days of frustration the salvage operation started.

We were starting to get the public messaging under control when my good friend Environment Minister Nick Smith arrived in town. Despite my exhortations to keep his tone measured, he unfortunately went out to the media and declared the *Rena* was the worst environmental disaster New Zealand had ever seen. And off they went again.

We ground it out. I was counting the tonnes of oil safely removed from the ship on a daily basis. Some days went well, and other days the operation had to stop because of bad weather, a pump breakdown or something else. Each day I texted John, Bill and local MPs Tony Ryall and Simon Bridges with the tally of the oil removed that day. Some oil did make it onto the beaches; it was simply impossible to prevent all of it escaping, although we did catch most of it.

I'd spent so much time in Tauranga by then that Suzanne recounts a telling episode one evening when she had a friend round while the television news was on. The by now familiar sight of the *Rena* and its precarious stack of shipping containers filled the screen. Four-year-old Amelia walked up to the screen, pointing and saying, 'That's where my daddy lives.'

In the last month before the election, the *Rena* position had stabilised sufficiently for me to return to the election campaign. And by 14 November, all the heavy oil had safely been removed from the wreck.

WITH THE RUGBY WORLD CUP duly won, there was now just under five weeks to the election and the televised debates were fast approaching. Phil Goff was seen as a diligent-enough bloke, but he certainly hadn't set the world on fire in his time as Labour leader. On top of that, his policy mix was inexplicably out of tune with the electorate. He had made several big spending promises at a time when the public knew we were faced with both a multi-billion-dollar bill from the Canterbury earthquakes and the ongoing hangover from the GFC. By way of contrast, Bill had set a target for the government books to be back in surplus by 2014–15, so we could be ready for whatever crisis came along next.

To underline the point, we put together an attack website called Owe Our Future, which helpfully added up all of Labour's commitments. Over several weeks, as the promises mounted up, I made a number of press releases as campaign spokesperson highlighting Labour's mounting pile of spending promises. The releases didn't get a huge uptake from media, but by the time of debate season those in the press gallery were all primed on Labour's weakness.

For the first time, the big debate moment came not on broadcast television but during a streamed debate. Following the earthquakes, the party leaders had agreed to do a debate with *The Press* in Christchurch. It was during this debate, while Phil was detailing one of his spending promises, that John called out, 'Show me the money!' It was one of those priceless moments that crystallised the issue everyone was thinking about. Labour never came back from that.

Two weeks out and we were travelling very well. Everything seemed to be running smoothly, indeed almost too smoothly. I was, as always, worried about what would happen next.

We were heading into what is sometimes called 'small party week', where the small parties have their debate, and the public and the media's thoughts turn to potential coalitions. We had decided John would have a symbolic cup of tea with ACT's Epsom candidate John Banks, so National voters in Epsom knew to vote for Banks, in the way they had previously voted for Rodney Hide.

After the event I received a call from then press secretary Paula Oliver, who was with John on the road. 'How did it go?' I asked. 'Weelllll …' said Paula, 'the event was fine. Everyone got their pictures so everyone's happy.' She paused. 'But there's just one thing. One of the journos left a microphone on the table, and we think it taped their conversation.'

Okay. Maybe this wasn't as bad as it sounded. I spoke with John and asked him what he had said to Banksie and whether there was anything to worry about. He said no, but he sounded worried and angry. He believed the taping was deliberate and he was angry at himself for not seeing the microphone, which was concealed in its carry pouch on the table.

Without knowing fully what was on the tape, we had to do our best to shut it down and get the campaign back on track. John laid a complaint over the taping, and the police advised media outlets not to publish it. TV3 and the *Herald on Sunday* had both been given copies of the tape, but declined to run it.

Meanwhile, Winston Peters smelled an opportunity. After three years out of Parliament, New Zealand First had been languishing below the 5 per cent MMP threshold for the whole election campaign. It had been looking likely they wouldn't return. The 'teapot tapes' scandal was manna from heaven. Somebody, probably from the media, tipped off Winston that John had said something disparaging on the tape about New Zealand First voters 'dying off'. He was away.

Winston thrives on oxygen, and he finally had some. Say what you like about him, he is a consummate campaigner and he didn't need inviting twice to make himself centre-stage in the last week of the campaign. We will never know whether it was Labour's weakness that caused him to get the votes he needed, or the teapot tapes and their aftermath, but on election night he was back over 5 per cent and back in Parliament.

With the campaign all but over, I joined John on a two-day bus trip up the North Island from Wellington to Auckland. We stopped in as many places as possible to exhort voters to turn out. The polls still had us 20 per cent ahead of Labour and we were worried people would think the election was a fait accompli. We finally arrived in John's electorate on Friday night believing we'd done all we could.

The next day John and Bronagh invited Suzanne and I to a cafe in Kumeū for lunch after we had voted. We took Amelia along and she was the star of the show, with John picking her up and chatting with her. Thank goodness she was there. I'm never good on election day, as there is nothing to do but feel nervous. John is a little the same. I think he'd hoped our lunch would settle him, but I fear the reverse was true. We built on each other's nerves and both ended up more anxious at the end of lunch than at the start. Needless to say, the invite wasn't repeated in 2014.

We needn't have worried too much. National achieved 47.3 per cent of the party vote in the election, compared to Labour's 27.5 per cent and the Greens' 11 per cent. That gave us 59 seats in a 121-seat Parliament, one more than in 2008. Labour had lost eight seats and were down to just 34. ACT was duly decimated as a reward for its revolving leadership door, winning only one seat, that of new / old MP John Banks in Epsom. However, with that one vote, and Peter Dunne's single United Future seat, we had a majority, just. We also completed a confidence and supply agreement with the Māori Party again, and that took us to 64 seats.

On the back of all the drama of the teapot tapes, Winston Peters made it back into Parliament with 6.6 per cent of the vote and eight MPs. In a sign of how much people still don't understand MMP, I met a number of people over the next three years who admitted they'd voted for Winston, but didn't realise he'd 'bring all those other MPs with him'!

After a roller-coaster year it was a pleasing result, and the highest party vote achieved yet by any party under MMP. But there was no time to waste. We all had huge to-do lists, from the Christchurch earthquakes to lifting economic growth and much else besides. We celebrated briefly and then it was back to work.

Chapter Seventeen
New challenges

WE'D DONE A GOOD JOB of promoting the 'Brighter Future' plan, but the truth was there was a sizeable bit missing.

The big picture was good. Bill had a great handle on restoring the government finances, and he was doing it without sacrificing public services. According to Treasury, we had inherited a projected 'decade of deficits' as a result of the GFC and the previous government's big increases in spending. The Christchurch earthquakes dealt the country another big fiscal blow, but Bill again patiently charted a course back to surplus, projected for the 2014–15 year. However, it was a grind, and both the world economy and our own were recovering modestly from the GFC in the meantime.

The problem child was the microeconomic side: the myriad policy settings and incentives that apply to different sectors which can either encourage businesses to invest and grow, or not. We'd had lots of disparate ideas over the past three years in various microeconomic policy areas, and some of them were good ones. But they hadn't been drawn into a coherent narrative for the business sector to latch onto and be encouraged by. Too often one of the economic agencies would be doing its best to encourage business investment while at the same time another agency would be doing things that ran completely counter to that goal.

Many people argue we already do better than many countries in enabling businesses to invest and grow. And it's true. Lots of large countries are very bureaucratic. But our small size and relative isolation means we have to work harder to attract businesses and entrepreneurs to set up here than they do in, say, Texas, Tokyo or even Sydney. The reality is that it is easier to make money in a bigger population than a smaller one.

I always remember a simple but stark illustration of that truism from my early radio days. We had a client in New Plymouth called the Egmont Steam Flour Mill, which was a really good pub and live dance venue. They were one of our biggest clients, but man did they have to work hard for their turnover in a small city like New Plymouth. They advertised different theme nights every night, had a stunning light show, excellent food, and a lovely historic venue all done up with panelled wood. It was impressive, and still they struggled to get enough business to make it all worthwhile. Often on a Tuesday or Wednesday the bars and restaurant would be almost empty, largely because not many people in New Plymouth are willing to go out on a weeknight.

I remember going to a pub on Sydney's North Shore around that time and marvelling at the contrast. That Manly pub's only concession to marketing their business was a chalkboard outside and a lonely string of coloured lights across one corner of the huge barn of a bar, above the DJ. Despite their lack of effort, the pub was packed every night of the week.

As it is in hospitality, it is everywhere else. New Zealand firms are faced with a tiny home market, which means they have to be born global to be successful. If we don't create a competitive platform from which they can take on the world, then the only businesses located here will be the ones whose business is dependent on our resources: our land, water and scenery. Like farming, or tourism.

Our government understood that. The problem was organising ourselves to have a concerted positive impact on all the myriad microeconomic policies that affected businesses trying to grow.

We inherited any number of small economic agencies and not one of them had the mandate to take the lead on economic growth. Between MED, DOL, MSI, Customs, MPI, NZTE, MBH, the TEC, MOT, NZTA, MFE, LINZ and MFAT, we had agencies with acronyms up the wazoo but no cross-sector leadership. Theoretically the Ministry of Economic Development had the right name on the tin, but it was a tiny agency which mostly contained odds and ends, like the Major Events Fund or NZTE. It was in no way an economic powerhouse. Treasury could have possibly taken on the role but it has an important job critiquing all the initiatives from other agencies, a job it does with relish. My collective noun for a group of Treasury officials became 'a refusal'. It is hard to promote your own initiatives while refusing everyone else's. And as an agency it is very thinly spread. My general view was that Treasury was a mile wide and an inch deep.

It was the same with ministers. Bill had enough on his plate, and no one else had the mana or mandate to make things happen. Leading up to 2011 we used to have late-night meetings around the big round table in John's meeting room with all the heads of the aforementioned acronym agencies and their respective ministers. John would ask how the economic plan was coming together, and we'd all debate who was up to what and how it might be shaped. Nothing was getting out of the starting blocks. I took to advising John and Wayne Eagleson that they needed to mandate someone to put a plan together and get on with it, or a big part of our economic policy would continue to drift. They seemed to be listening, but I wasn't sure there'd be any change.

After the election we were all called in turn to John's office to discuss portfolios. When I went in, it was just him and Wayne. John said he wanted me to keep Tertiary Education and add Skills and Employment to it, and take on Economic Development and Science and Innovation, while losing Transport and ICT. This would come with a promotion to number four in Cabinet. There would indeed be change.

I had mixed feelings. On the one hand, taking up those three portfolios was a huge opportunity, but on the other hand, I'd be losing my beloved transport portfolio. I was less worried about losing ICT because the path was now well set in the broadband space. With transport, I felt there was much more still to do, like seeing through the KiwiRail turnaround plan and setting up a second round of Roads of National Significance once the current round was bedded in.

I asked if there was any way to hang onto transport, and John said, 'Sure, but it's a package deal. Have a think about it.' It didn't take long. You have to go forward in life, and this was a whole new challenge. I accepted his offer. Gerry took over the transport portfolio alongside his Canterbury earthquake recovery responsibilities. And Gerry and I became bench mates in the House.

I did a quick stocktake of my new agencies and their opportunities and challenges. I also chatted with Bill and the other economic ministers to see what they were planning. I quickly ended up back where I was before the election. We needed a more joined-up, consolidated approach, and we needed a clear microeconomic plan.

I went back to John seeking a mandate to merge three of the small economic agencies together to create one agency with more horsepower to lead a proper growth agenda, and also his endorsement for me to lead the development of that agenda, alongside Bill.

It was a little ironic that I, of all people, ended up pitching for the biggest public-sector merger of our time in government. We were rightly quite wary of them, and I was more wary than most. Mergers can take a long time and suck up a lot of the officials' focus. You can spend all your time rearranging the deckchairs rather than delivering results. But in this case I was prepared to make an exception as I believed the case for change was strong.

The three agencies I proposed to merge were all underpowered for the role they were performing, and we didn't have any money to grow them. To a greater or lesser extent, they were orphans of previous restructures. The old Department of Labour had lost focus since Steve Maharey had broken away the Employment Office (now WINZ) and made it part of his Ministry of Social Development. The remnants of DOL spent much of its time shadowing MSD and the Tertiary Education Commission (on skills training).

The fledgling Ministry of Science and Innovation (MSI) was an amalgam of the old science twins MoRST and FoRST (research policy and research funding respectively). Frankly, we had made a mistake creating MSI a couple of years previously, and should have merged it into the Ministry of Economic Development in the first place. MED was itself Jim Anderton's old so-called job machine, made up of a hodge podge of stuff, from tourism policy to the America's Cup to various pots of government subsidies. I figured we could combine the three into an entity that focused on three of the key ingredients for economic growth: skills, investment and innovation. And we could likely save some money along the way.

Some of my colleagues were sceptical, notably new State Services Minister Jonathan Coleman. But I had an ally in State Services Commissioner Iain Rennie. He believed we had too many subscale government departments and he was all for simplifying the organisational spaghetti.

However, for his own reasons, he wanted to include a fourth ministry, the Department of Building and Housing, in the merger. I wasn't sure how much synergy there was between housing and the other three. I think housing and urban development are both more closely associated with an agency like transport, but I reluctantly agreed to include DBH at his behest.

Cabinet finally signed it all off and MBIE, the Ministry of Business, Innovation and Employment, was born, under the leadership of MED Chief Executive David Smol. It had a mandate to both save money and drive the government's Business Growth Agenda (BGA). And it delivered on both. We saved $12 million in operating costs through the immediate change, and ultimately another $40 million when the organisation was brought together under one roof in Stout Street. It did take a while for the agency to gel together, but it became the core engine room of the government's growth agenda.

There were of course dramas on the way through, as there are with all mergers. Once you create it, how it behaves is your responsibility. When MBIE moved buildings, those responsible for the fit-out spent $140,000 on a curved television screen above its reception desk, unbeknown to either CE David Smol or to me as minister — at least until it was helpfully pointed out to us by the Opposition.

After that it was open season on MBIE. The Opposition criticised the spending of $400 on hair-straighteners in the women's toilets, and $745 repairing two inflatable sheep that were mysteriously damaged at the staff Christmas function. However, the issues were sufficiently small beer that they mostly amused the public rather than anything else.

More seriously, MBIE was criticised as an unwieldy mega-ministry. In fact it was dwarfed in size by some of the big social ministries. With 3200 staff while I was minister, it was about the same size of the Ministry of Justice. Eleven years on, there has been no serious talk about relitigating the merger.

WITH MBIE UNDERWAY, THE NEXT big challenge was to get the Business Growth Agenda going. But how to structure it? It needed to be focused on businesses rather than government agencies. It also needed to fill the information gap between government and business so that businesses could see at a glance what the government was up to, and respond to it.

Too often businesses had no idea what the government was doing. I lost count of how many times senior businesspeople had told me 'you guys should be doing this', where 'this' turned out to be already underway. Business owners tended to have a meerkat approach to government. They'd be flat out growing their businesses, and every now and then they'd pop their heads up to see what the government was up to and how it might affect them. I used to do it myself at RadioWorks. We all wasted a lot of time getting everyone up to speed at those moments, time which I believed would be better spent working on new challenges and opportunities. Government agencies needed to do a much better job of communicating our agenda in a straightforward, easy-to-digest way.

After talking with Peter Chrisp at NZTE, I landed on the idea of grouping all our microeconomic initiatives under six key inputs that international businesses need to succeed from a New Zealand base. These were capital, export markets, skilled people, natural resources, innovation, and the necessary infrastructure to support their businesses. Not all businesses needed all six, but most needed most of them.

By bringing all of the government's activities in these areas together under a common group of ministers and agencies, we could align what we were doing, and present it to businesses as a coherent plan which they could respond to and build on. That was the theory anyway.

The key organising principle was six informal groups of ministers and public-sector CEs, one for each theme. We got them together once a month or so for an hour, normally in an evening, to compare notes on what they were doing, and what one another could build on. That way the level of alignment or non-alignment would emerge.

Each group's secretariat would keep a record of all the initiatives, and that would form the basis of public reports to the business sector.

I was conscious this cut across the normal hierarchical approach of the Westminster system. Normally a minister beavers away in their own silo with their own officials, and brings a proposal to Cabinet committee and then Cabinet, which is either supported or shot down by colleagues. I was asking ministers to socialise their ideas and those of their officials early with relevant colleagues, and work on them together, before bringing them through to Cabinet. Done well, it should ease the path of some initiatives through Cabinet, as ministers in related portfolios would understand the initiative ahead of time, and hopefully be supportive of it.

It was important that the groups be informal, or some colleagues wouldn't have been happy to participate. To my mind anyway, the strength of the groups was their informality. The fact that everybody knew any minister could reserve the right to do their own thing meant the meetings were not too 'high stakes', and that allowed for more open discussions.

I asked Bill to chair two of the groups, on capital and infrastructure — which were most aligned to his and Treasury's interests. I chaired the other four, most of which touched on at least one of my portfolios.

We had some fascinating discussions. Getting all the key agency CEs and their ministers in a room to chat for an hour turned out to be extremely valuable in its own right. Some of the BGA meetings were so popular to attend you could almost sell tickets. Even the lobby catch-ups were constructive.

Some great ideas came through the BGA process. My favourite example was the Predator Free 2050 programme. Predator Free was originally a simple funding proposal from the Department of Conservation and its minister Maggie Barry. If Maggie had brought it through Cabinet in the normal way I doubt it would have flown.

It was panel-beaten at the BGA natural resources meeting where the idea of involving philanthropists and community groups was added. By the time it got to Cabinet it was fully supported by all of the natural resources ministers and myself as chair. John was a bit sceptical but we talked him around, and it has been a great programme. It is a 'moonshot', but I for one am very passionate about it. With a lot of collective endeavour and some judicious use of new technology like the gene-editing of pest species, I believe we can make New Zealand predator-free by 2050, which would be amazing for our native birdlife.

The BGA meetings were particularly helpful in socialising complex issues like RMA reform, and resolving thorny issues where one agency and its minister was supportive of something, and another was implacably opposed. This regularly happened at the natural resources meeting, where the Ministry for the Environment and the Department of Conservation often started on the opposite side of the table from Primary Industries or Trade. Some of the discussions amongst skills ministers also surfaced strong and divergent points of view.

Generally we were able to hammer out compromises which kept things moving forward, an immeasurably better outcome than the trench warfare that can ensue if a proposal takes a direct route to Cabinet and is implacably opposed by other ministers.

We released six reports on the Business Growth Agenda, one on each theme, over the course of 2012 and into 2013. Each contained 40–50 initiatives the government was working on and their status. The commitment was to continue completing them and adding new initiatives, and to keep updating the thinking. We maintained that through to 2017.

The Business Growth Agenda received broadly, although not unanimously, positive reviews. Some senior journalists commented that it was a more serious and successful attempt to run a consistent positive economic agenda than they'd seen for many years. It was compared favourably with the Knowledge Wave of the Clark years, although I would have considered that a reasonably low bar.

Others lamented there were too many initiatives, and not enough big ones. That didn't worry me. I'd learnt enough about business to know that single Big Bang initiatives seldom if ever deliver what they are supposed to when you are dealing with thousands of individual firms.

A few consultants derided the BGA, largely I think from a personal welfare perspective. Consulting businesses generally make huge fees helping governments organise and re-organise themselves around the economic theme du jour, and having a steady framework of initiatives is not good for their businesses.

Internally the BGA was mostly successful. The ninth-floor press office would amuse themselves from time to time suggesting how many times 'Business Growth Agenda' could be added to an economic press release. And there were one or two old-style ministers who really didn't want to join in, and were nearly always mysteriously busy when the relevant ministerial group got together. But even Murray McCully turned up to the export markets group once or twice.

Politically it did the job. The Labour Opposition spent six years from 2011 trying to discredit the government's economic agenda by, for example, suggesting there was a manufacturing 'crisis' and various other crises, but in the face of the full-court press of the Business Growth Agenda they largely failed to stick.

The most important test was whether the BGA helped our economic performance. By 2017, New Zealand was the fourth-fastest-growing economy in the OECD. That is of course down to a number of things, including our macroeconomic and fiscal policies, plus a bunch of things outside of the direct control of government. But the Business Growth Agenda played its part, and more recently we have experienced the counterfactual, where bad microeconomic policy can distinctly slow down an economy. Nobody is seriously suggesting that happened in the period between 2011 and 2017.

IN THE SCIENCE AND INNOVATION portfolio my first challenge was to build a 'high-tech HQ for Kiwi businesses'. During the 2011 election campaign we made a pledge to grow one of the Crown Research Institutes, Industrial Research Ltd (IRL), into a more all-encompassing Advanced Technology Institute catering to a wide range of new technology businesses. It was a great concept, but nobody quite knew what it would look like. John had envisaged hundreds of researchers in white coats doing research and development (R&D) for different businesses, but there were some challenges with that vision.

The eight Crown Research Institutes, including IRL, grew out of the old Department of Scientific and Industrial Research (DSIR) in 1992. They have been more successful at producing industry-relevant research than the old government department monolith they replaced, although some have performed better than others. AgResearch, Plant & Food Research, and Scion (forestry research) are closely associated with their respective industries and generally seen as doing a good job. They are effectively the shared labs for farmers, horticulturalists and foresters. Landcare Research also has positive relationships, particularly with environmental and conservation organisations. NIWA, GNS Science and ESR have had more nuanced reviews. The odd one out was IRL. While it did some good work, a lot of it wasn't particularly close to businesses, and they had a few core specialities which didn't and couldn't cover the breadth of our growing high-tech sector. For much of New Zealand's high-tech sector, IRL was irrelevant.

The more I looked at it, the more I didn't think any organisation could cover that breadth. It was a real head-scratcher. We didn't want to just create a bigger IRL. There was already no shortage of organisations, both public and private, that carried pieces of New Zealand's research DNA. It took ages just to map out all the existing research entities. We couldn't afford to duplicate all that in one organisation, and why would we?

We started asking high-tech companies what they wanted in their 'High-tech HQ'. They were pretty much unanimous. They wanted practical assistance with their research and development, particularly in terms of advice about who they could go to, and they wanted financial help to grow their own R&D capabilities. Unlike the farming or horticultural industries, they didn't want to contract out their research as a common good that the whole sector could use. Their intellectual property was their secret sauce and they needed to develop it mostly in-house, perhaps with the assistance of one or two specialist scientists at, say, a university, either in New Zealand or overseas.

I went back to John and mapped out what I believed we needed to do. It wasn't his original vision, but to his credit he went along with it.

The Advance Technology Institute would do some of its own research, but primarily it would provide a nationwide network of advisers to work with high-tech companies in all fields. They would help those companies grow their own R&D by matching them with relevant researchers elsewhere, and guide them to public subsidies that would help them get more bang for their research buck.

That last bit was important. New Zealand urgently needed (and still does need) a lot more knowledge-based firms in order to become more prosperous. One way to do that is to stretch each firm's R&D budget with some sort of taxpayer grant, with the idea of growing the whole R&D pie. This acknowledges that increased R&D activity brings wider benefits that are not all captured by the firm making the investment. There are many examples around the world of big research-intensive companies and industries spinning off more start-ups and growing the high-tech ecosystem to the benefit of the host country. We wanted to catalyse the same thing, and we were prepared to put some government funding towards that, as most OECD countries do.

Putting this money through the Advanced Technology Institute would solve another problem for me. When I inherited the portfolio we had a discretionary programme called the Technology Development Grant, and there I found individual account managers within the ministry making very large bespoke payments to individual companies because they had been sold on their R&D plans. That made me very uncomfortable. It was picking winners in a very overt way, and I was at a loss to understand how two or three account managers in the Ministry of Science and Innovation had accumulated such huge wisdom to know where to place the taxpayers' bets.

I wanted a much less discretionary, much more objective criteria for R&D grant support. We changed the system so that firms which were sufficiently R&D-intensive and spent sufficient sums on R&D conducted in New Zealand, would simply receive 20 per cent of their spend back over a five-year period. This was the R&D growth grant system, where I was slammed for 'picking winners'. The irony is I did nothing of the sort, and in fact stopped a process where winners were being picked. But as they say in politics, explaining is losing.

Some countries, rather than using a grant system, use R&D tax incentives instead, and Labour has now introduced such a system here in lieu of growth grants. We investigated such an approach and concluded it was less effective, for two reasons. Firstly, R&D tax incentives are deducted from tax paid, which is hardly helpful if you are an early-stage company with little income and no tax liability. Tax incentives don't encourage the research-intensive companies that need the most help.

Secondly, overseas examples show tax-rebate schemes encourage companies to engage clever accountants to exploit loopholes and reclassify expenditure from operating costs to research and development. That's why in places like Australia much of the money in their R&D tax-incentive scheme is being claimed by the likes of banks and mining companies, rather than true high-tech start-ups.

It is happening here, too. Soon after Labour's new scheme was introduced, I ran into a Kiwi restaurateur I knew on the streets of Melbourne. When I asked what he was up to, he grinned and said he was with a few of his senior staff 'on a research trip' which he would be claiming off his taxes.

We wanted to know taxpayers' money was going on R&D not on tax dodges, which is why only the Advanced Technology Institute could confirm eligibility for our grant scheme. Only they were close enough to the companies to see the actual quality of the research and development being done.

I approached the family of the late Sir Paul Callaghan to see if we could use his name for the Institute. It was Sir Paul who'd first articulated the concept of New Zealand being good at the 'weird stuff', the narrow, deep, niche businesses that bigger companies in bigger countries either overlooked or didn't think laterally enough to discover.

From my travels around the country and my experience with hospital-bed manufacturer Howard Wright, I knew he was for the most part right. New Zealand is full of companies which started out as general engineering firms back in the day and had to reinvent themselves or die when the border was deregulated and trade able to flow freely. So you have a freeze-dried food equipment maker in Marlborough, a liquid fertiliser trailer manufacturer in Dannevirke, world-leading retail refrigerated-display makers in Hawke's Bay and Christchurch, and so on.

Similarly, on the IT front, it seems any number of companies were spawned from the great Post Office carve-up and the privatisation of Telecom. Smart people who found themselves made redundant started their own IT companies specialising in weird niches like the GPS mapping of underground mines in South America.

This Advanced Technology Institute was to be the partner for all these clever tinkerers and entrepreneurs, so it was right to call it Callaghan Innovation.

The organisation took a while to hit its straps, but over its first decade it has done a great job of stretching companies' R&D budgets further. Unfortunately, it had the wind taken out of its sails when control of the tax subsidies was passed to the IRD, but at this stage the private sector's R&D investment continues to grow. We are also now seeing a second round of start-ups being spawned from the likes of Rocket Lab, F&P Healthcare and Xero. It is exciting to see.

THERE ARE BROADLY THREE CATEGORIES of science funding around the world, and most science systems dedicate funding to all three. Callaghan Innovation leads the business-led R&D programme for New Zealand. At the other end of the scale is investigator-led research, which is often called fundamental or 'blue skies' research. That is where the scientist pitches what they want to research.

In New Zealand, investigator-led research mechanisms include the Marsden Fund, the Health Research Fund and university research funding. All three were in reasonable shape and we only tweaked them around the edges. Our main job was to increase the size of each fund so that more of the great proposals were funded, and we did that regularly over our time in office.

The middle area is what is known as mission-led funding, where scientists from different disciplines and organisations get together and seek to solve a stated problem through a mission-funding mechanism. That was a real gap in New Zealand when I took over the portfolio, and we sought to solve it with two new initiatives.

The first was the Endeavour Fund, which grew out of various

contestable funding processes inherited by MBIE. The Endeavour Fund is now one of the biggest sources of funding for mission-led research in New Zealand, and Endeavour Grants are highly sought-after. The second was the National Science Challenges, which were promoted by our highly active ideas factory, John's Chief Science Advisor Peter Gluckman. Peter had seen National Science Challenges developed internationally and was eager to try them here.

We set up a public process to determine the ten biggest science-based challenges facing New Zealand over the next decade. Once they were identified, consortia of science organisations were recruited to oversee each challenge and allocated a pot of funding of $50 million–$100 million for research projects targeted at solving that challenge. We settled on eleven challenges in the end, including topics like High-Value Nutrition, which aimed to identify high-value foods with validated health benefits; the Deep South Challenge, which sought to better understand how the Southern Ocean influences New Zealand's climate; and Resilience to Nature's Challenges, which sought to enhance our resilience to natural disasters.

We wanted to have the best scientists from different disciplines all over the country working together to solve these major macro problems. It was surprising how difficult that was to achieve. The three health challenges in particular exposed existing fault lines between the public-health people, who wanted to focus on prevention and community measures to solve health problems, and the biological-health specialists, who wanted to focus on understanding diseases and designing better interventions. It proved very difficult to get the two groups to truly appreciate each other's contributions, and each of the three health challenges took time to get going.

A decade on, and it will be very interesting to evaluate what the challenges have achieved. Unfortunately, the current government has taken to describing the National Science Challenges as a 'rushed, stopgap measure', and all indications are they have been neglected. It would be pleasant to see party politics removed from something as long-term as national science projects.

We sought to be good custodians of the science sector. I even persuaded John and Bill to theme the 2016 Budget as an investment in 'Innovative New Zealand', although John was disappointed at the level of media coverage it received. That is sadly often the fate of something that everyone agrees with.

According to Treasury, during our time in office we lifted total government science investment from $0.85 billion in 2007/08 to $1.66 billion just over a decade later, nearly double, despite the challenge of restoring the government's books after the Global Financial Crisis. I believe it should grow further. It is one area where a government can successfully pay it forward to help create prosperity for the next generation.

Chapter Eighteen
From Paymaster General to Minister for Yachting

A NEW PAYROLL SYSTEM FOR 110,000 New Zealand school teachers and support staff had gone live in August 2012. Known as Novopay, it made its first pay run on 5 September, and problems with the new system were immediately apparent. In that first run some 5000 teachers were underpaid, and at least fifteen weren't paid at all. The errors were initially dismissed as teething troubles, but the problems with the payroll system snowballed. Every fortnight when the pay was made, a growing avalanche of issues was reported.

The media was having a field day. The nightly *Campbell Live* ran example after example of teachers not being paid enough, being paid too much or not being paid at all. And it wasn't getting any better. Associate Education Minister Craig Foss was in charge of the roll-out, and Fossy was initially slow to publicly acknowledge the size of the problem.

At the end of November, he announced an independent review

of the new system to start early in 2013, but it was unclear whether this was anything more than a normal post-implementation review. Meanwhile, the issues kept coming and the new system was heading into the most challenging time of the year: the end-of-year / start-of-year changeover.

Education Minister Hekia Parata was being drawn into the fray. Novopay was threatening to take over the news cycle, and all around the Beehive concern was being raised that the teachers' payroll could become a political litmus test for the competence of the government.

One of those most stridently concerned was Jo de Joux, who was at that stage working in my office as my senior political adviser. 'If we are not careful this thing will cart us out,' she said, more than once. Jo encouraged me to make an offer to John to sort Novopay out. 'If we don't, everything else is a waste of time,' she said. 'It needs to be you. If we don't fix it there won't be a campaign worth running at the next election.'

I wasn't overly convinced this was a great idea, and I certainly didn't need the extra work. But with Jo's assurance she would help, I went up to the ninth floor early in the New Year, and made the offer to John. If he'd like, I'd take on the headache that was Novopay and get it sorted.

It's fair to say he jumped on the idea with some speed. 'Excellent,' he said. 'Let's do it.' Shortly after that, Jo and her husband Phil moved to Christchurch. So much for the help!

John was making a Cabinet reshuffle announcement near the end of January. Lockwood Smith was retiring as Speaker and heading to London, and David Carter was taking his place. Phil Heatley and Kate Wilkinson were both moving on, with Nikki Kaye and Michael Woodhouse from my year becoming ministers and Simon Bridges moving inside the Cabinet. My new role as 'Minister Responsible for Novopay' was tacked on to the end of the announcement. Novopay was now my problem.

I had to move fast, but also manage expectations. I held my first press conference a few days later and told everyone there would be no quick fixes and the problems were likely to continue for some time. I then instituted a technical review of the software, tipped in an initial $5 million to a new remediation plan, and started the investigation of a contingency plan to roll the whole thing back to the previous payroll supplier Datacom. That was followed by the announcement of a Ministerial Inquiry to investigate what the hell went wrong.

The Secretary of Education, Lesley Longstone, had been struggling in her role for a range of reasons, and resigned around the same time. Peter Hughes, formerly of the Ministry of Social Development, was drafted in to replace her. He co-opted the ministry's call centre to provide more support to the dedicated Novopay call centre, and we stood up an extra 30 or 40 people into data processing.

Meanwhile, I went out on the road to meet some school principals and hear first-hand about their problems. TV3 followed me to the first meeting in Karori and asked me whether Novopay was a dog. I described it as a dog with fleas, and they ran it with a shot of me walking alongside a friendly neighbourhood dachshund who happened to be passing by.

A problem shared is a problem halved, so I made the call to get all the information on Novopay into the public domain as quickly as possible, warts and all. I figured there was no point holding any of it back. There was no such thing as waiting for Official Information Act requests on Novopay. People had to see the size and scope of the problem so they could see what we were dealing with. We released hundreds of documents, and pretty soon the journalists stopped asking questions. They had everything we did.

We started with no objective statistics about how the system was performing in each pay period. We needed some reliable metrics to transparently show whether we were moving forward or backwards.

Without those, the only public test was whether *Campbell Live* could find another teacher who had a problem and was willing to go on TV, and there were hundreds of those every pay period. We hired one of the big four accounting firms to publish every payday how many staff were paid, how much money was paid, how many staff weren't paid, how many were underpaid or overpaid, and from how many schools.

We set up a new Backlog Clearance Unit, and slowly, very slowly, things started to get better. It was a grind but the stats started to improve, before getting worse again for the changeover to the new financial year. Each time we tried to anticipate what would happen and publicly preview it for better or worse, so we could start to build trust that we now knew what we were doing.

In May the situation had stabilised sufficiently that nobody was greatly surprised when we made the call to stay the distance with Novopay, rather than put everyone through the difficulty of a roll-back to the previous system. Then in June we released the Ministerial Inquiry, conducted by former Department of the Prime Minister and Cabinet head Maarten Wevers and Deloitte New Zealand head Murray Jack.

The report identified problems with the project going right back to when the previous government started the process in 2003. The Ministry of Education had promised the vendor they would simplify the pay arrangements for teachers, and then failed to do so. There were still 19 separate collective agreements when the system went live, and all the complexities of the old system were still in place. Swathes of the project were signed up to on an 'agree to agree' basis, development ran late, and when the pressure went on, both PwC and the State Services Commission, who were supposed to provide independent quality assurance to ministers, were drawn into the process and lost their objectivity.

Anybody who is undertaking a big public-sector IT project

should read that report as a cautionary tale of what not to do.

While the focus was naturally on fixing the immediate issue, I came to realise the longer-term problem is the way we try to pay our teachers. We want every teacher to earn the same according to their experience, but then we set up thousands of little standardised variations to cater to the particular skills of individual teachers, without trusting their employing school to make those pay judgements themselves. We wanted the union's mantra of 'everyone is equal' along with flexibility on the quiet so the system worked for individuals.

We also standardise how many teachers are funded at each school, but then we set up elaborate systems to allow schools to 'bank staffing' for when they want to get around the standard ratios.

We insist on a single payslip for every teacher whether they work for one school or across several. Everywhere you look, we make it as complex as possible, and then smack the payroll system if it fails to cater to our contradictions.

That's not to excuse in any way the contractors, Talent2, who created the Novopay mess. As I became fond of saying, there was plenty of blame to go around for everyone. It's just that, to borrow the old Irish joke, if I was trying to get there I wouldn't be starting from here.

The whole system eventually settled down, and by September the error rate was at or near industry standards for payroll systems of that size. Backlogs were cleared and schools were coached extensively through the end-of-year and start-of-year process. By the middle of 2014 the crisis was over, and we arranged a new government-owned payroll company to take over from Talent2. I remained Minister Responsible for Novopay for another two years, but the job was largely done.

Sorting out Novopay was one of the most challenging things I led in government. It was like trying to change a tyre as you drove down the motorway, conducted in the full glare of the public and of course the affected teachers. It was a constant and exhausting drumbeat every fortnight for two years, but quietly rewarding in the end. Big credit should go to Peter Hughes, Murray Jack, Patsy Reddy, the late Cathy Magiannis and their teams for their tireless efforts and quiet determination to resolve what was a serious crisis in public administration.

I was called on to help with another serious issue while all the Novopay stuff was continuing. In early August 2013, Nikki Kaye, as Food Safety Minister, raised the alarm internally over a recall notice that the Ministry of Primary Industries was about to make for some WPC80, a whey protein concentrate manufactured by Fonterra. WPC80 is an ingredient in infant formula. John held a call on the Saturday and asked me to lead a group of five ministers — myself, Tony Ryall (Health), Tim Groser (Trade), Nathan Guy (Primary Industries) and Nikki — to coordinate the response to the news. It was a very big deal, involving our largest company and the world's largest dairy exporter, our largest trading partner and several other countries, and the most sensitive foodstuff of all: infant formula fed to young babies.

Tim Groser and I hightailed it to Auckland on Sunday to meet with the Fonterra leadership team at NZTE's offices on the waterfront. Then-CEO Theo Spierings was returning from offshore, so it was their chair John Wilson, their head of production Gary Romano, and their government relations head — one Todd Muller — who walked down from Fonterra HQ and ran the gauntlet of waiting media to meet us.

I'll never forget Gary Romano explaining to me and Tim that they had sent the offending powder off to be tested, expecting it to be fine, but then 'the bloody mouse died'. The death of that mouse set in chain a course of events that played out publicly in subsequent weeks and months.

There were further tense meetings with Fonterra in Wellington for me and Nathan Guy the following week. A big focus was the initial difficulty of tracing the errant product from source to Fonterra customers. Thankfully that was resolved, and subsequent tests showed there was no botulism, but the damage in reputational terms to Fonterra and the country was significant. After at least three separate inquiries and at least one court case, my assessment was that Fonterra had been taught a difficult lesson in the step up from being a general milk processor to manufacturing something as sensitive as infant formula, with the stringent and necessary safety disciplines that required.

One thing I wasn't able to help fix was Jasons Travel Media. The news came that it had collapsed into receivership in November 2013, five years after I departed the company. When I went into politics I had placed my shares in Jasons and other companies into a blind trust, so I only knew what I read in the newspapers about the company's demise. It was clear, though, that it had lost momentum at some stage after my departure, and subsequently lost the race to digitise. I thought it was unlikely that my trustees had been able to quit such a significant shareholding in the meantime, and my investment had probably gone down with the ship. It was a heavy entry price for going into politics but there was nothing I could do about it, so I banished it to the back of my mind.

THE ECONOMIC DEVELOPMENT PORTFOLIO COVERS a grab bag of responsibilities besides the core one of fostering the growth of New Zealand businesses. For example, it oversees the Major Events Fund, which doles out money to support major events being staged in New Zealand. The idea was based around the success of Melbourne as an events city, with the Australian Open tennis tournament, the Australian Grand Prix and so on.

I wasn't a big fan of the responsibility. To my mind, it was all a bit mercenary and transactional, and not likely to be a big game-changer for the country. It is also hard to know which events would have occurred without government funding, and which, generally in hindsight, didn't need to occur. It can be debated how much value the country really derives from hosting some of these events. There was constant tension between events that were truly national in scale and capable of gaining attention for the country, and making sure the money went around the regions.

Some of the decisions, which were made by a group of 'worthies' but defended by the minister, seemed, well, inconsistent. For example, the Major Events Fund supported the New Zealand Winter Games and the New Zealand Open golf tournament, both in Queenstown, but didn't support the ASB Classic in Auckland, which is the closest we get to the Australian Open in Melbourne. We sometimes supported events which would be great if they caught on, but were difficult flops to defend if they didn't. You ended up just doing the best you could.

Another thankless task was overseeing the support New Zealand gives to the screen sector for movies like the *Hobbit* trilogy. Film subsidies have been a great lark for the international movie business, effectively auctioning off the location for filming a movie and the jobs and work that goes with it to the country willing to cross the studios' palms with the most silver. Film companies can have up to 20 or 30 per cent of a film's production cost met by the host country, so naturally that's very important to them.

The studios are quick to say that they wouldn't be making movies in New Zealand if the talent base wasn't exceptional, which is undoubtedly true. However, it's also clear the movies wouldn't be made in New Zealand if the incentives weren't competitive, regardless of the talent base. Even Peter Jackson wouldn't be able to insist his movies be made in Miramar if there was no financial subsidy to the film studios.

I've never been a fan of industry subsidies. If you have to subsidise an industry to make it happen in a location, then is it really an industry? It feels more like a Potemkin village. And if you do it for one industry, why not others? Car manufacturing, for example, or silicon-chip manufacturing? None of these industries are economic in New Zealand, but maybe they could happen here (for a second time, in the case of cars) if we paid them enough taxpayers' money. New Zealand has a long and chequered history of almost bankrupting itself to subsidise selected industries. In the early 1980s we were even subsidising farming!

Where the film industry does have a point is where there are benefits to the country of having a film made here beyond the direct benefits of actually making it. This was the case for the *Lord of the Rings* franchise and the *Hobbit* movies. New Zealand found fame as Middle Earth, which brought us a much higher profile on the world stage than would otherwise have been the case. The movies boosted the visibility of the country and brought increased tourism to New Zealand. I don't think there is any doubt the country benefited by at least the cost of those film subsidies, and probably much more.

The challenge is to get the soufflé to rise twice. While there have been successful movies made in New Zealand since the *Hobbit* movies, I can't recall any that profiled the country or told a New Zealand story in a way that would provide the country a higher profile or more tourists.

I tried to wind back the level of subsidy on my watch and tie the grant more closely to the telling of unique New Zealand stories, but, as is often the way, the competitive international environment meant we ended up lifting rather than reducing the subsidy, adding 'New Zealand' elements in return for a further uplift. Thus under my watch the *Avatar* trilogy deal was signed, and a one-off movie called *Pete's Dragon*. I'm sure they are great movies, but they haven't exactly placed New Zealand on the map like the hobbits did.

I was more enthusiastic about the development of a new International Convention Centre for Auckland. A world-class convention centre has huge potential to bring large international conferences to New Zealand and entice delegates to stay on for a look around the country. Every major city has a high-quality convention centre, and Auckland was going to keep missing out on a lucrative revenue stream if it didn't come up with something a bit more impressive than the showgrounds at Alexandra Park.

The process to build a centre had been excruciatingly slow. The previous government had started talking about it in 2006, and we weren't doing much better. Three years in and we had only just decided to negotiate a deal with SkyCity, who were the obvious partner given we clearly didn't have any money in the budget for building one ourselves. Every other potential partner needed government funding; only SkyCity could leverage their casino business and hotels to pay for the centre itself.

On being appointed Minister of Economic Development I decided to try and move things along faster, but no sooner had I got underway than the Auditor-General threw a spanner in the works. With the encouragement of the Labour Party and the Greens, he'd decided to investigate the process to date, and whether SkyCity had been given an inappropriate inside track.

I was frustrated. At first I thought we could continue in parallel with the Office of the Auditor-General (OAG) inquiry, but Wayne Eagleson quickly disabused me of that idea. I'd just have to cool my jets until the Auditor-General had done his work. Another eight months passed before the OAG reported back. While they didn't find the officials' process perfect, they didn't believe it would have changed the outcome. We were cleared to go ahead.

With the help of some key commercial advisers, we finalised a Heads of Agreement three months after the OAG report, in May 2013. SkyCity would build and operate a $400 million International

Convention Centre catering to up to 3500 delegates at a time for 35 years, in return for an additional 230 pokie machines and 40 gaming tables, and a commensurate extension to their gaming licence, which was otherwise due to expire in eight years.

Labour and the Greens, along with a few sympathetic journalists, duly hit the roof, calling the deal absolutely outrageous. They went completely bananas, which was very hypocritical as Helen Clark's government had done a similar deal back in 2001 for the existing, much smaller, SkyCity Convention Centre, also exchanging the convention centre for 230 more pokie machines. Ours was a far better arrangement, resulting in a far superior facility for Auckland.

One wrinkle in our arrangement was that after Labour had done that previous deal, they had changed the law to prevent something similar happening again. We would have to pass a new law to allow the deal to proceed.

Two months later the final agreement was signed, and we had the legislation before the House. I didn't want to muck around in case any of our coalition partners had a change of heart. The Māori Party wasn't voting for it, so I needed both United Future's Peter Dunne and ACT's John Banks. In the end, both were rock solid, and the bill passed in November 2013.

With designing and consenting it took another two years before construction started, but when it did the project had grown to a $700 million investment for SkyCity, including a third international hotel, a laneway and parking, and an additional $70 million investment in the convention centre.

Construction began in 2016, and I had a look through the partly completed facility in 2018. I can confirm it will be an amazing building when it's finished. Sadly, a fire occurred during construction late in 2019, and at the time of writing the centre is still not finished. The opposition to the project died out as soon as the government changed in 2017, and I have no doubt that the politicians who were so against the project at the time will happily come to the eventual opening if they are invited.

IT IS A LITTLE-KNOWN FACT that the Minister for Economic Development is also the minister in charge of the government's involvement with the America's Cup. So it came to be that I headed to San Francisco in September 2013 to see the final days of the 2013 America's Cup race. As Foreign Minister and Sports Minister, Murray McCully had been New Zealand's Johnny-on-the-spot in San Francisco, but he needed to head off to meetings in South America so I was drafted to take his place.

I wasn't that enthusiastic. I'd just come back from a trip promoting international education in Japan and Korea and wasn't dying in a ditch to travel again about a week later. I was also reasonably ambivalent about yachting, but in the end I didn't mind spending a few days in San Francisco, a city I had previously enjoyed.

It didn't look like I'd be there long anyway. On the day I arrived, Team New Zealand was effectively up seven to one over Oracle Team USA, as Oracle had been penalised two of its three victories. I travelled straight from the airport to San Francisco Bay and arrived in time to watch Dean Barker chalk up his eighth victory. It was match point to Team New Zealand; I thought I'd be hardly unpacking my bags before it would be time to go home again.

Although perhaps not. On the next day, day nine, I was invited out on one of the Team New Zealand chase boats alongside Labour MP Trevor Mallard, who was so passionate about Team New Zealand he was almost the team mascot. It was fantastic to see the boats up close on the amazing San Francisco harbour. Less fantastic was the result, with Team New Zealand losing to Oracle to take the score to 8–2. Still, it could only be a matter of time.

Day ten and I was on the chase boat a second time, alongside Team New Zealand sponsor Stephen Tindall, and director Gary

Paykel. It was another magnificent race and it looked like the victory was finally Team New Zealand's. They were nearly two minutes ahead approaching the finish line, but they were racing the clock. The rules said the race had to be completed inside 40 minutes. The winds were the lightest they'd been, and when the 40-minute mark arrived our guys still had 10 per cent of the course to cover, so the race was cancelled. The second race that day did go ahead and was won by Jimmy Spithill and Oracle. It was 8–3.

The next day the wind didn't play ball and there was no racing. That was okay for me. I had lots of work to catch up with, and a range of events set up by New Zealand Trade and Enterprise, who were using the America's Cup to promote New Zealand technology and innovation to investors from San Francisco and Silicon Valley. There was no hint of panic in the team.

September 22 took the regatta into its third week. It was now officially the longest America's Cup match in history, and I was getting twitchy. I had work piling up at home and I needed to get back. But I also knew it would be a bad look if the minister went home after the team lost a few races, having turned up at nearly match point. I asked my office whether I could be relieved, but there was no one else who could come up at short notice. Anyway, we were only one race away from victory. By the time whoever they were got off the plane it would likely be all over. I arranged for some more work to be sent up instead.

That day was a very bad day at the office for Team New Zealand. They lost two races in a row and suddenly it was 8–5. Even to a novice onlooker like me they were starting to look a little fried. Jimmy Spithill had been sledging them at the post-race press conferences all the way through, which showed amazing chutzpah when you are six or seven points behind. As his team got closer, the banter was starting to bite.

The next day was yet another win to Oracle. It was now 8–6 and

Oracle had won five on the trot. I was close enough that I could see it was all going wrong. The New Zealand team was dejected, and both Grant Dalton and Barker looked isolated. There was an air of inevitability developing about what would happen next.

I was sufficiently worried that I asked Stephen Tindall whether he thought anything could be done. It wasn't my place as a government minister to intervene, but I sensed someone needed to. I was surprised there didn't appear to be a strong team off the water who could call a lay day and get the sailors back in the right head space. He didn't seem to have an answer either.

I suspect my observation was accurate. Grant Dalton had made himself a grinder on the boat, which many people thought was a mistake, but no one could move him off as he was running the show. They had lost one other director during the regatta, and were left with just one onshore. For whatever reason, there was no one who could do anything to change the team's fortunes.

It felt like Groundhog Day. Each day the Kiwi supporters faithfully got up and hoped for something different. But it didn't happen. I could certainly not go home now — I would be the rat leaving the sinking ship.

On 25 September it was mercifully all over. I felt keenly for Dean Barker in particular. He is undoubtedly a great sailor, but he just couldn't change the fortunes of his team when he needed to. Having said that, I don't think he had enough help.

Back home, Claire Trevett from the *Herald* decided I was the unlucky charm and labelled me 'Jinxy Joyce'. I pointed out the team had won the first race after I arrived as evidence against the curse, but she was unconvinced. When Team New Zealand won the Cup back in Bermuda four years later and I was nowhere near the Atlantic Ocean at the time, she took that as confirmation of her theory.

Chapter Nineteen
Grinding it out

AFTER THE MISADVENTURES AT Premier Cottage, and then time at Evans Bay, in 2011 the family inherited the use of Vogel House in Lower Hutt as our Wellington base. Vogel House was the former home of Rob Muldoon, and of Jim Anderton during the Clark government. Governor-General Sir Anand Satyanand had been in residence while Government House was being refurbished, and once he returned to the city we were able to move in.

The house is huge, with large formal rooms downstairs and an apartment upstairs, a bit like Premier House in town. It is a wonderful property, with large established gardens which I enjoyed taking Amelia and Tommy for little walks around in on the weekend.

I got to know the perimeter fence at Vogel very well. Gemma the dog loved having the run of the gardens, but she also loved the Hutt more generally. She fully exploited the weaknesses in what had initially seemed like quite a sturdy fence. I spent many (sort of) happy hours in the early days at Vogel House crawling along the fenceline, stuffing bits of concrete and branches into holes Gemma had found. Even then Gemma became a frequent flier at the Hutt City pound, much to the amusement of Mayor Ray Wallace. I lived in trepidation of an unfriendly headline in the *Hutt News* about the minister's marauding mutt.

We enjoyed our time in the Hutt, but it didn't change the fact that the family still wasn't seeing much of me. If anything they saw less, as it wasn't really practical to get home for dinner during the parliamentary tea break. I'd leave early each morning, get back late each night, and spend much of Saturday and Sunday afternoons shovelling paper in my office at the Beehive. As the time approached for Amelia to go to school, we made the call to base ourselves back home in Auckland. At least then the kids would have access to all the things we had there, and would get used to seeing our house as their home.

I had been an absolute workaholic during my time in radio, sacrificing every other aspect of life to make the most of RadioWorks and ensure its success. When I left radio I rebalanced my life and swore I'd never work so hard again. Then I went into politics, only to discover the commitment required is on another level entirely.

Once based in Auckland I adopted a new weekly schedule. I'd get up on Monday around 5 a.m., aiming to be at the airport by 6.30 for the 7 a.m. plane to Wellington. On the way to the airport I'd talk with John from the Crown car at around 6 a.m. ahead of his Monday-morning media round, a ritual we kept up weekly for his entire time as PM, and daily during election campaigns.

We'd go through all the topics he'd been pre-warned about and any others that might come up. He'd have briefing notes from his staff but he liked to test them out, plus any other lines he might have thought of overnight. I'd quietly dissuade him of any 4 a.m. brainwaves that would take us off-message, and help focus him back on the key ideas we wanted to get across.

The VIP drivers were very discreet. Nothing said, whether on the phone or otherwise, made it outside the cars. The cars were effectively mobile offices, and they greatly added to my productivity.

I got on well with nearly all the drivers, but it is fair to say they didn't always get on with our long limestone driveway at Dairy Flat. Every time someone picked me up or dropped me off they would head back to their base afterwards to clean off the limestone splashes. The rumour was that the driver rostered on to negotiate my driveway each week considered they had drawn the short straw. It was quite the celebration when the final part of the Joyce driveway was concreted.

When I landed in Wellington I'd head into the office and go straight into a round of pre-Cabinet meetings, starting with my own officials, then Bill and the Treasury officials, and then pre-Cabinet with the kitchen cabinet of senior ministers and Chief of Staff Wayne Eagleson. After Cabinet it would be straight into another round of meetings. If Cabinet finished early, I might get to leave the building to buy a coffee somewhere. More often it would run late, and subsequent meetings would be backed up like a doctor's waiting room.

Tuesday through Thursday it would be a 6.30 or 7 a.m. start, and a 10.30 or 11 p.m. finish. Each meeting would last half an hour or an hour, and then go straight into the next one. I generally wouldn't get any time to order my thoughts between meetings, instead relying on advisers picking up the threads and the agreed actions so the machine could keep going. A one-pager was thrust under my nose to help me change gear for the next meeting, and on we would go, with the odd break to go down to Parliament. I learnt how to mentally spin on a dime, from discussing one complex issue to another, and then on to a third.

We'd have caucus every Tuesday morning, and once every parliamentary session I would make a presentation on our internal polling, plus the insights from any focus groups we may have completed, and report on how that all fed into our overall strategy. I performed that role almost continuously from when I first became general manager in 2003 until I retired in 2018. The presentations were always the unvarnished facts, good, bad or indifferent. It was crucial to me and the leadership that caucus knew where we were at.

I attended what was called the 'eight o'clock meeting' every morning on House sitting days, where we would discuss the day's tactics. On Wednesdays I was only able to be there for the first six minutes, before heading back to my office for my long-running Newstalk ZB slot with Mike Hosking and Annette King. Both Annette and I really enjoyed those on-air chats, and we did them almost continuously for the full nine years National was in government. Annette and I got to know each other during the ad breaks between each segment when the producers left our mikes on so we could talk. She was easily the Labour person I knew and liked best. Sometimes we'd just chat about family, other times there might be some good-natured needling, and every now and then there'd be a message to be passed back or forth.

Cabinet committees were generally held on a Wednesday, and I was a member of four or five of them, chairing two or three most weeks in the latter half of my time. Economic Growth and Infrastructure was an obvious one for my participation, and Finance and Expenditure Control. I was also an active participant in the Social Policy and Treaty of Waitangi committees. Chris Finlayson and I had many good discussions about various proposals in Treaty settlement papers, with me always keeping an eye on the likely political calculus.

Done well, Cabinet committees are a great drafting gate, where straightforward papers can be waved through and simply reported to Cabinet, while the more complex or controversial ones are discussed more fully and either referred for discussion at Cabinet the following Monday or pushed back for more work. One advantage at committee time is that senior officials are also present, and they can be grilled on the proposals. I made a habit of seeking to understand fully every paper that made it to Cabinet. The ones to particularly watch were the complex ones and those that went direct to Cabinet because of time pressure. I used to regularly call colleagues on a Sunday afternoon in a bid to understand where they were headed with their paper, or more likely a particular recommendation.

One committee I was, shall we say, less diligent in attending was Appointments and Honours. I was happy participating in the government appointments side, but I couldn't get excited about the lengthy honours discussions on Monday evenings leading up to honours announcements. I was happy to leave that to others.

Lunch was always at my desk, and sometimes dinner too, although usually by then I'd be desperate for a break. I was never particularly institutionalised, and I struggled with the idea of staying in one building all day every day. Many of my colleagues would head to Copperfield's Cafe in the Beehive for dinner, often taking a table together to talk about their day. I'd prefer to take a magazine and have a quick meal on my own in a restaurant or cafe outside the precinct. That would give me some quiet time to help process the day's events and prepare for the night ahead. Maria Pia's Trattoria (now MariLuca Ristoro) was a regular haunt.

On Tuesday nights at nine I would host a glass of wine for John, Wayne and senior ministers in my office. That was a great opportunity to catch up informally and discuss the thorny issues of the week, of which there were always a number. It was a chance for all of us to provide some support and advice to the PM, which is important, because it is often a lonely job. More often than not we'd stay and wait for the polling to come in at around 10.30 p.m., and review that before we headed off.

As a minister your time is almost never your own. There are always hundreds of people backed up to call, meet or chat with. When I was in radio, I used to try to keep some control of my diary, much to the frustration of my EA. In politics I just had to give up and go with the flow. Every minute was planned. Calls were even scheduled for when I travelled from place to place.

A minister's diary is truly a production line, and I had three people managing mine. When a meeting request came in, the portfolio secretaries would be asked to give their department's view on a meeting, followed by the political staff. The senior private secretary would hold a weekly diary meeting and decide on a recommendation about each meeting, and only then the request and the relevant form would show up in my diary folder in my weekend bag, along with about 30 or 40 other requests. I'd circle my preferred answer (meet, decline, or the dreaded 'discuss'), and the fruits of those decisions would then turn up in my actual diary at some point over the next couple of months. By then the rationale was long forgotten, and when I read the next day's diary entries I'd often react with 'Why did I agree to that?'

On Thursday afternoon the core campaign team, including party staff, would meet for what we called a continuous campaign meeting, to keep us focused on the next election at all times. On Thursday nights I'd mostly take a late plane back to Auckland, so I would at least wake up at home on Friday morning. As I wasn't an electorate MP, Fridays would often involve trips around the country, or at least the city. Sometimes I'd also head home briefly during the week for a function in Auckland in the evening. They seemed to always run late and I'd arrive home at Dairy Flat around 11.30 p.m. before leaving again in the morning about 5.30.

I spent a lot of time reading papers on planes. It was the only time for reading during the week, aside from late at night. I'd regularly clock up six to eight or even ten flights in the course of a week, shuttling around the country or even offshore. I liked to get out and meet people so I was my own worst enemy, but it was the only way to stay in touch. Wellington is a vortex where your political compass can get scrambled with all the plausible, earnest advice you receive from policy analysts, lobbyists and colleagues. Getting out whenever possible was an opportunity to listen to real people living real lives, and reset that compass again.

On the weekends ministers would be sent a large briefcase of papers to work on while they were at home, or out around the country. I would shut myself in my home office after lunch on Saturdays and Sunday afternoons, working through the papers till about 5.30. Some of my hardest times as a minister would be when Amelia wanted to play with her dad, and I'd have to keep going. I'd chat with her briefly, and then her mum would come and take her away while I continued on.

The weekend bag would be delivered by ministerial car each Saturday morning, normally about 7.30 or 8.00. There were two sizes of bags, the normal large solid briefcase and then the double-sized one, which was used when there was too much paper for the normal one. My heart would sink if the double-sized bag turned up. Kathleen tried to use it sparingly, because she knew how demoralising it could be. She would literally jump up and down on the normal bag trying to close it, in preference to using the bigger one.

In the later years, we started using what I called a 'digital bag', where portfolio secretaries could send me an email on Friday afternoon with everything I needed to read for that portfolio, and I'd send back long emails of notes with my comments. Eventually Cabinet papers were also delivered on a secure digital system and the use of the physical bag died out. Of course the trouble with a digital bag is there is no physical limit as to what can be included, so the weekend's reading tended to grow rather than shrink.

The only active relaxation I had during the year was my vege garden at home. I figured out that as long as I found a day or so around Labour weekend and then devoted two or three hours in the garden most weekends after that, I could nurse a reasonable vegetable garden through to the summer break. I used to make many of my weekend phone calls from the garden while I was weeding or planting out, and John and other colleagues became used to hearing birds and cicadas in the background of our weekend chats. The garden was also a great source of 'vege garden tweets' to lighten my social-media feed.

It was about this time we learnt Tommy had autism. He'd been struggling to learn to talk for a long time. He seemed to pick up a word, like 'Dadda', and then lose it again. Doctors had counselled patience, but we were getting worried. When he was diagnosed, we kept it to ourselves, and hoped his development would catch up. It never did. As his paediatrician said, autistic children do develop, but at a slower rate than those without autism. As Tommy got older, he was slipping further and further behind. We had no answers and there were no obvious actions we could take. Like a lot of worried parents whose children have autism, we just boxed on.

THERE WERE TWO BIG CROSS-GOVERNMENT initiatives in our second term, and I had a hand in both. The first was selling a minority stake in four government-owned enterprises: the three power companies (Meridian, Mighty River Power and Genesis) and Air New Zealand. This was known as the mixed-ownership model. That idea had taken shape in our first term, when Simon Power was the relevant minister.

The government owns an eclectic range of companies, often for no discernible reason beyond an accident of history. Not many people will realise, for example, that their government owns one of New Zealand's largest property valuers, or a telecommunications company called Kordia. The government also tends to end up as what I call the shareholder of last resort. The politics of selling shares in anything is contentious, so taxpayers own a post office in the days of the internet and a broadcast television company in the age of streaming.

There is a major challenge achieving accountability of these government-owned companies. Ministers are rightly required not to interfere in the running of them, but that means there is little shareholder discipline to ensure they run well. Without specific and robust shareholder attention, the directors and management often follow their own flights of investing fancy, all the while having arguments with monitors in the Treasury about whether Treasury is using the right yardstick to measure their performance.

The mixed-ownership model was conceived as much as an idea to provide discipline to some of the largest Crown companies as it was to raise money for the government, although that was important too, given the state of the books following the GFC. I was a big fan of the model. As Minister of Transport I had studied the relative performance of the Port of Tauranga and the Ports of Auckland. The Tauranga port had the regional council as its cornerstone shareholder, was listed on the NZX, and had been a huge financial success while staying under practical council control. The Auckland port was 100 per cent council-owned, subject to constant political interference and managerial whim, and a financial basket-case in terms of returns to its shareholders.

The mixed-ownership model took a long time to happen, largely because of the attempts of various parties (political and otherwise) to frustrate it. It was a clear policy of ours at the 2011 election, which National clearly won, and yet we were also forced by the left to put the question to a referendum. The Waitangi Tribunal wanted a clear extra benefit to Māori, and that had to be negotiated carefully. On top of that the Labour Party, in what I thought was a disgraceful episode, attempted to economically sabotage the share floats by threatening to renationalise the industry and to exempt government-owned power companies from company tax.

As Associate Finance Minister, I worked alongside Bill and Tony Ryall (who replaced Simon) to get the floats of the three power companies and Air New Zealand successfully away. The process took a huge amount of time but was ultimately very successful, raising billions of dollars for taxpayers, revitalising the NZX, and dramatically lifting the performance and value of the participant companies.

The second major initiative was the Better Public Services targets, and these turned out to be instrumental in getting a major lift in performance and accountability out of some of the core parts of the public service. They were born out of the success Tony had in our first term getting the health services to meet some clear, measurable targets for things like emergency department wait times and cancer treatment.

Initially the public service was tasked with coming up with targets, but both they and their ministers were often wary of targets they might not achieve, and the ensuing likely public embarrassment. Some of the draft targets were woolly and unambitious at best. Wearing my campaign hat I argued vociferously for stronger and clearer targets, but with a reasonable timeline within which to achieve them. With a fair amount of pushing and pulling on all sides, they eventually came together and were announced by Bill and the PM in June 2012.

The Better Public Services targets were to run initially for five years. They included goals for reducing the number of long-term beneficiaries, reducing the number of assaults on children, increasing infant immunisation rates, reducing criminal reoffending, and increasing participation in early childhood education. I was directly responsible for three targets, including two I shared with Education Minister Hekia Parata: achieving 85 per cent of 18-year-olds with at least NCEA Level 2 or equivalent by 2017, and 55 per cent of 25–34-year-olds with a qualification at Level 4 or above by the same date.

It was heartening to watch the public servants galvanise them-selves around achieving the desired result and thinking longer term, rather than just being subject to the whims of the vested interests in each sector as they often otherwise were. It's fair to say the Better Public Services programme was much more powerful in achieving results in the public service than anyone anticipated.

In our case we reached 57 per cent of 25–34-year-olds with the targeted qualifications by the end of 2016, up from 52 per cent in 2012. We also reached 85.2 per cent of 18-year-olds with the NCEA Level 2 standard by 2017, up from 74 per cent in 2011. New programmes like youth guarantee, trades academies, the apprenticeship reboot, and Māori and Pasifika trades training all helped achieve those goals. Looking back, those new initiatives had one thing in common: they were about meeting the learner in their preferred environment and providing them with the skills they needed, rather than the old 'one size fits all' education system. The education system clearly needs more innovation and variety in delivery, not less.

Sadly the Better Public Services targets came to a sticky end in 2018, along with Tony's health targets. The combined forces of public-sector unions and Labour's tribal politics meant they were unceremoniously scrapped. Since that time public-service performance and accountability have dropped away, in some cases precipitously.

Chapter Twenty
Moments of truth

BY 2013 THE NEW ZEALAND economy was strengthening, and comparing well with our peers across the developed world. Through a combination of good luck and good management we had not suffered as badly as many countries as a result of the GFC, and the Reserve Bank had not resorted to quantitative easing, or money printing, as had happened in many countries, including the US. Our economic policies were much more orthodox than many, and the results showed it was the right approach.

We took soundings on the public's attitude leading into the 2014 election campaign, due in twelve months' time. The research and more anecdotal feedback both showed that the government was being seen to manage the country for the most part competently and well, and had a strong plan for the future. There was broad recognition of the relative strength of New Zealand's economic performance.

That contrasted well with the Opposition. When Phil Goff resigned after the 2011 defeat, Labour initially elected David Shearer to the leadership, and then replaced him with David Cunliffe in the middle of 2013. The change to Cunliffe took place under their new voting system, which allowed party members and unions to vote alongside the caucus. It was clear the caucus hadn't voted for Cunliffe, giving his leadership a shaky foundation from the start.

However, an overconfident David Cunliffe was unperturbed. Under his leadership, Labour adopted a much more radical policy prescription than that of the recent Clark government. They promoted big changes in tax policy, including a capital gains tax, a broader departure from orthodox economic policy, and a huge role for government in house building and several other areas of economic activity.

Their problem was that the public wasn't demanding such wholesale changes. In order to justify the radical surgery they proposed, Labour first had to convince voters that, notwithstanding their personal experience to the contrary, New Zealand was heading to hell in a handbasket. The public wasn't buying it. Over the first nine months of Cunliffe's leadership Labour's poll numbers dropped further, from the low thirties to the mid-twenties.

Our problem was the reverse. National's polling was very high, and if anything we were more dominant over Labour than in 2011. Our biggest fears were complacency amongst our voters, and the perennial problem of the weakness of our potential coalition partners.

We started discussing how to state our coalition preferences at the end of 2013. Nobody was keen to repeat the 2011 cup-of-tea moment, so there was broad agreement when John proposed to get it out of the way as early as possible. We decided we'd indicate our preference to work with our current coalition partners (ACT, United Future, and the Māori Party), and to continue the electoral accommodations with ACT in Epsom, and Peter Dunne in Ōhāriu. That part was relatively easy, apart from the unfortunate issue of Peter Dunne's recent misadventure in 2013, when he had to resign his ministerial post following a purported leak from his office. John decided to rehabilitate him as a minister at the same time as he announced the electoral accommodation.

The more difficult part was deciding what to say about New Zealand First, and the new Conservative Party headed up by a quirky religious chap called Colin Craig. There were plenty of party members wanting us to reach an electoral accommodation with Craig. They believed he could be a reliable coalition partner, particularly as both United Future and ACT seemed to be winding down. The problem was the party's policy platform and his own public comments. We knew a seat deal with the Conservatives would tie John to defending Craig's every utterance between then and election day and, from what we'd seen so far, that could be an arduous task. It could also scare off more centrist voters, and encourage some to vote New Zealand First as an alternative. Such a dynamic could only erode National's party vote, as it did Helen Clark's in 2002 when some Labour voters used their party vote to try to choose New Zealand First, United Future or the Greens as their preferred coalition partner for Labour, rather than voting for Labour itself.

We settled on leaving the door open for a post-election accommodation with either the Conservatives or New Zealand First, but no seat deal with either. John announced all of those calls in late January 2014, and followed that with the election-date announcement in early March, once we'd arrived back from a joint Cabinet meeting with Tony Abbott and his crew in Australia.

Both John and Wayne Eagleson wanted an early date so the new prime minister would get to attend the big round of end-of-year multilateral events like APEC and the East Asia Summit. There was a big G20 summit in Brisbane in mid-November, and there was every likelihood the New Zealand Prime Minister would be invited to attend. Jo de Joux and I on the other hand were worried about securing the voter turnout we were looking for in an early spring election.

John of course prevailed, and he announced 20 September 2014 as the election date.

He also prevailed with his plan to hold a referendum for a new New Zealand flag. He'd first floated the idea internally after the 2011 election, planning for it to be one of the first announcements on forming the new government. However, a number of us were against it, and I particularly argued him back from the brink. While I wasn't against a new flag, I felt the timing was completely wrong. We'd just been re-elected on a platform to fix the country after the GFC and the Canterbury earthquakes, and I felt it would be jarring to the public if we embarked on something which could easily be depicted as trivial in such serious times.

Fast-forward to 2014 and I still wasn't convinced John should waste his political capital on a new design for the country's flag, but he was very enthusiastic, and at least it was more in keeping with the more positive mood of the times. The country was looking forward and outwards, and a more independent flag would perhaps capture that confident mood. I folded my tent.

BY APRIL THE ELECTION CAMPAIGN preparations were coming together nicely. Again we had some new members of the core campaign team, which helped freshen us all up. Kelly Boxall, Craig Howie and Cam Burrows were excellent additions from the Leader's and Bill's offices, and Sean Topham, who went on to co-found Topham Guerin, was a great addition to our social-media game. Anna Lillis from my office had become very involved on the campaign comms side, and she had an innate understanding of public sentiment. My colleague Nathan Guy took over from Murray McCully as my direct sounding board as Murray disappeared further and further into the world of foreign affairs.

Our advertising creatives had come up with an excellent campaign concept, using a sleek rowing boat to represent New

Zealand's progress under National, contrasted with a leaky lifeboat full of bickering Labour and Greens MPs that was turning in circles, which we dubbed 'the Laboureens'. We felt it was a great metaphor for the current state of the country and the political choices voters faced, and we knew it would resonate well. The campaign slogan we adopted was 'Working for New Zealand', and that tested well with floating voters.

Meanwhile, Labour and its mates were cranking up what I called their 'John Key is the devil beast campaign'. This was predicated on the theory that the friendly, personable and positive prime minister with the high levels of public support was all a front, and behind that friendly facade he was a nasty individual doing horrible things to New Zealand. The message was: you shouldn't have voted for him in 2008, or in 2011, and you definitely shouldn't vote for him this time. Leaving aside the obvious factual issues with this characterisation and that it didn't in any way reflect the voters' experience of John, Labour was effectively now telling voters they made the wrong decision twice, which is a helluva way to get them onside.

Labour had a new ally in this cause, the German would-be immigrant Kim Dotcom, who was caught up in an extradition fight over the purportedly illegal actions of his file-sharing company, Megaupload. Dotcom, a colourful but hardly mainstream character, decided to enter the political fray and teamed up with MP Hone Harawira in an electoral coalition called the Internet MANA party, with the stated aim of ridding the country of John Key.

Somehow Labour did not see the perils of being associated with this ragtag lot, and couldn't quite make up their minds to distance themselves. It was therefore easy to tie Internet MANA to the putative Labour–Greens coalition. We'd already recorded all our TV and billboard commercials, but we went to work with the colour key, changing one of the green figures in the Laboureen boat to purple, the colours of the Internet MANA party. In a case of life imitating art, the longer the campaign went on, the more the image of the Laboureens boat resonated.

At our election-year conference at the end of June the polls had National at 50 per cent to Labour's 27 per cent, and our major concern was voter turnout. The election was looking too much like a fait accompli, and elections were never that. At the conference we put a major emphasis on our Get Out the Vote campaign, or ground game, and in a departure from normal practice the campaign team agreed I would also go out on the road visiting electorates over the last six weeks of the election campaign, highlighting the importance of getting the votes out and avoiding any complacency.

NO ELECTION COMES WITHOUT TWISTS and turns, and in 2014 the big curveball came in the form of Nicky Hager's book *Dirty Politics*, which was released in mid-August, five weeks before election day. It was based on a trove of hacked emails belonging to perennial party hanger-on and self-proclaimed specialist in the dark arts of politics Cameron Slater, who is the son of former party president John Slater. Slater junior and his mate Simon Lusk had been around the edges of the National Party for a long time, often seeking to influence candidate selections by telling stories and spreading rumours online about people standing against their preferred candidate. They were proponents of the maxim 'the end justifies the means', and Hager's book detailed a selection of these.

The book had to be responded to, and the press gallery were in a big lather over it. I was sent out to do media interviews as campaign spokesperson over that first news cycle, seeking to place the book into context and answer some of the broader questions. That gave John time for the temperature to drop a little before he responded. The main emphases of the media's probing were on John's relationship with Slater, the actions of two people in his office delegated to work with bloggers alongside more traditional media, and the relationship between Judith Collins and Slater.

I personally have always kept well away from Slater and Lusk. I didn't like their style of politics. National would, in my view, have been well advised to keep clear of them and one or two others with similar attitudes, notably Jami-Lee Ross. Sadly, these sorts of people hang around on both sides of the aisle, and their no-holds-barred style can always find someone willing to use their services. The trick is not to give them legitimacy. My strong advice to John was to stay well clear, but he didn't think that was always possible given the influence Slater's Whaleoil blog had on the opinions of some party members in its early days.

Judith was ultimately the biggest political casualty of the book, although not directly. Shortly after it was released, and with questions swirling about her relationship with Slater, John's office was sent an email purportedly from Slater which alleged Judith was 'gunning for' Serious Fraud Office Chief Executive Adam Feeley. Judith was the minister in charge of the SFO at the time. She was already by then on her second final warning from the PM after being pulled up for endorsing a milk firm of which her husband was a director on a China trip earlier that year, and for material contained in the Hager book in relation to a staff member at the Department of Internal Affairs. A number of us counselled Judith to resign her roles. I myself had a long call with her while standing at Amelia's birthday party at Kelly Tarlton's Sea Life Aquarium in Auckland. After a discussion with John she did that, seeking an inquiry in order to clear her name.

The *Dirty Politics* book dominated the media for ten days, throwing the election campaign completely off track. But the public were also getting frustrated with the media, feeling their election campaign was being taken away from them. I witnessed a couple of events where members of the press gallery were being given robust feedback from voters that they had had enough. Once Judith resigned, journalists finally started to tear themselves away from what one had called a scandal 'equivalent to Watergate' and back to the election at hand.

But there was more to come. Kim Dotcom and his Internet MANA party began touting an event called 'The Moment of Truth', to be beamed around the country from the Auckland Town Hall on the Monday night before the election. It would 'end John Key's political career'. The event would include international whistleblower Edward Snowden and famed left-wing journalist Glenn Greenwald. They would apparently provide evidence that John Key was intervening at the behest of Warner Bros to get Kim Dotcom deported, and that the New Zealand Government was undertaking mass surveillance of New Zealanders.

We weren't too worried about the so-called facts to be revealed at the event, as we knew that nothing of the sort existed. But from a campaign perspective we were worried our polling had been declining as a result of all the mud being thrown. We went into that final week with our internal polls telling us we were at 44 per cent, rather than the 47 per cent we would need to safely form a government. Talk started to again turn towards giving a late nod to the Conservatives.

I watched some of the 'Moment of Truth' event from my motel in Napier, where I had been campaigning that day. I realised within about twenty minutes that it would rebound badly on Internet MANA and the Opposition generally. The event billed as telling New Zealanders 'what's really going on' had nothing of substance to say, and rested on a bunch of foreign speakers telling New Zealanders they shouldn't vote for the governing party. I don't think voters in any country would like outsiders telling them how to vote on the eve of an election, and I very much doubted New Zealanders would. I decided to stop worrying.

The public were indeed completely fed up. The 'Moment of Truth' was cathartic, their moment to rebel against all the scandals, and confirm their own decisions on who they wanted to be their government. Their country had been going along just fine until this weird election campaign had come along, and they were ready to reject what they had heard over the past few weeks and make their own call. We had a significant poll bounce in those last few days.

THERE WAS ONE FINAL TWIST in the tale that was the 2014 election. We'd had a complaint early on about our television advertising, with US performing artist Eminem, a.k.a. Marshall Mathers, complaining that our original backing track sounded too like his song 'Lose Yourself'. We were confident we'd licensed the music we were using correctly through established publishers, and the track at issue, while called 'Eminemesque', had been used commercially before in both the US and Australia without issue. But nevertheless we agreed to quickly change it at the artist's request.

That wasn't enough for Mr Mathers, and he filed papers to sue the party. At one point it looked like we'd get to the election without the issue hitting the public domain, but on the Tuesday of election week word started to get around that the National Party was being sued by Eminem.

I was in Christchurch that day with John, turning the sod on a new Faculty of Engineering building and Science Centre the government was funding for the earthquake-ravaged University of Canterbury. The journalists attending the event were unusually showing more interest in doing a stand-up with me rather than John, and Anna Lillis came over and confirmed the Eminem story had indeed dropped.

I told the media what we knew of the case, and that we believed we'd done everything properly in licensing the track. I deliberately played it all very low-key, because I didn't want it to blow up into a major story four days before election day. I didn't want to assert it was completely legal, and set up a distraction for the rest of the week as the armchair legal boffins tried to pull my position to bits. So I settled on what I thought was a handy enough semi-ambiguous position with sufficient wriggle room for everyone. I decided to assert our approach was 'pretty legal'.

And it sort of did the job — although I did have to take it on the chin for inventing a new legal test, and 'pretty legal' lives on as one of the top quotes from 2014. Subsequently the National Party defended its position before the courts, and I was relieved that after a protracted process it ended in a reasonable outcome which in turn was ameliorated by the other parties to our defence. Importantly, 'pretty legal' got us through to election day without any polling damage.

Our final message to voters was that if they wanted a National-led government they needed to vote for it. And in the end they largely did. On election day we posted almost exactly 47 per cent of the vote to Labour's 25 per cent, the Greens' 10.7 per cent, and New Zealand First's 8.7 per cent.

With the help of wasted votes for the Conservatives in particular (who scored just under 4 per cent) and Internet MANA, we received 60 seats in the 121-seat Parliament, one more than in 2011 and the most any party had achieved to date in a New Zealand MMP election. We would be able to form a government with either of the two MPs we had provided an electoral accommodation to, Peter Dunne in Ōhāriu, or the newly installed solitary ACT MP, David Seymour in Epsom. It was another excellent result.

Kim Dotcom and Hone Harawira, on the other hand, blew up spectacularly. Labour's Kelvin Davis beat Harawira for the Te Tai Tokerau seat, which meant the marriage of convenience which was Internet MANA received no seats. Dotcom reportedly spent $4 million of his own money on the campaign and had nothing to show for it.

Chapter Twenty-one
Post-election speed bump

WE WERE STRAIGHT BACK INTO it after the election, and international affairs had a big focus through the rest of 2014. Through the good work of Murray McCully in particular, New Zealand had obtained a two-year spot as a member of the United Nations Security Council. Meanwhile, the PM travelled to APEC in Beijing and the East Asia Summit in Myanmar, before coming back to host a number of heads of state on their way to and from Brisbane for the G20 meeting.

There were so many leaders coming and going that on one day we ended up with a bottleneck, and that gave yours truly an opportunity to spend some time with one of the key world leaders of the period, Chancellor of Germany Angela Merkel. Merkel was spending the day in New Zealand, and Canadian Prime Minister Stephen Harper was also coming in that afternoon, so John gave the morning to Merkel and the afternoon to Harper. I was recruited to host the chancellor for the afternoon and evening before she flew on to Brisbane.

It was fascinating to spend a bit of time with Merkel who, while obviously very intelligent and right across her brief, was also a very down-to-earth, pragmatic sort. During our time together she gave a lecture at the University of Auckland, had an afternoon tea with some German students living in Auckland, and then we walked down to the Auckland Art Gallery for a well-attended function of German and New Zealand businesses.

At the lecture there was a bit of a game on with some of the student union attendees wanting to ask Merkel about Germany's policy of free tuition fees for university students. They hoped to use the event to embarrass our government about not doing the same. I was sitting in the audience as the inevitable question came and was a bit concerned the chancellor would not realise its loaded nature. I needn't have worried. Merkel shared that she didn't like her own country's policy and wished it had never been implemented, because they were spending so much money directly supporting students that they had less to spend on strengthening the quality of education at the universities. It wasn't quite the answer the activists were looking for.

It was quite a surreal moment for me as the two of us walked down through Albert Park to the art gallery, with a helicopter watching overhead and diplomatic protection officers stationed around the park at discreet distances. Merkel was very relaxed and curious. She wanted to know what I thought of the Scottish independence referendum, which had been held a month previously. In a prescient moment, she offered the thought that David Cameron was reckless and a risk-taker for agreeing to a vote that could dissolve the United Kingdom.

'Imagine doing that,' she said, shaking her head. Of course a short time later he rolled the dice again on Brexit.

I didn't meet many world leaders, who of course tend to meet leader to leader. I did however meet China's President Xi Jinping and Premier Li Keqiang while accompanying the prime minister.

Both were very friendly and avuncular in person, and both very warm towards New Zealand.

We inherited the stewardship of the China relationship just after the Clark government had signed the New Zealand–China Free Trade Agreement. John unapologetically embraced the FTA, seeing it as a huge opportunity for New Zealand. He used to say that we could never be sure what might happen in the future between China and the rest of the world, but that we should absolutely make the most of the opportunities the FTA gave us in the meantime. He encouraged ministers to visit China and build trade between the two countries. I myself made seven trips there in my nine years as a minister, primarily promoting international education but also our broader economic relationship.

I did have the misfortune of being the first senior New Zealand minister to visit after the 2013 Fonterra botulism scare, and my reward was an understandably tense meeting with the Chinese Minister of Commerce. I don't speak any Mandarin, but I had no doubt of the minister's views based on both the length and tone of his remarks. The Chinese clearly felt let down by their friends in New Zealand. At one point our ambassador Carl Worker leaned into me and said, 'I don't think I need to translate this all verbatim, Minister. There are a few choice phrases here that I might leave out. I think you get the gist of it.'

I did see quite a lot of the various Australian prime ministers who were in office while we were in government, of which there were five (Rudd, Gillard, Rudd again, Abbott and Turnbull). This was by virtue of the joint Cabinet meetings which were held regularly while John was prime minister.

I found the first joint Cabinet meeting the most memorable. It happened in Sydney soon after we were first elected. Each country was represented by their prime minister and about eight other ministers. We sat either side of a long meeting table at the Royal

Australian Navy fleet base in East Sydney. It was quite structured, with the PMs making opening comments, and then inviting relevant ministers to comment on their portfolios.

The contrast in styles between John Key and Kevin Rudd was readily apparent. John would let his ministers say their piece without interruption. Rudd, on the other hand, would let each minister run for about two or three minutes, before invariably interrupting and taking over. He spoke at length, during which some of his ministers fidgeted like restless school students. I sat opposite my counterpart Minister for Transport Anthony Albanese and Senator Penny Wong, and the body language from the two of them was not positive towards Rudd. I could see why.

The Gillard meeting was much more informal, and included lunch in a relatively casual Melbourne restaurant and watching the tennis at the Australian Open. I was seated next to Julia Gillard at lunch while John was seated opposite, and I had an enjoyable conversation with her about family and time outside politics. She was very personable and not at all like the more formal and scripted version of her we saw on TV.

We met Tony Abbott at Kirribilli House in Sydney. That included a formal joint Cabinet meeting, and an informal dinner involving John, Wayne Eagleson and myself, along with Tony, his chief of staff Peta Credlin and his polling strategist Mark Textor, who had also advised us. The relationship between the National Party and the Liberals is very fraternal, and I've always enjoyed it. Tony, however, never let his guard completely down, always choosing his words very carefully.

The two Australian politicians I got on best with ended up competing with each other to be the country's prime minister in the 2022 Australian federal election. I had continued to keep in touch with Scott Morrison over the years, and we ended up Finance Minister and Treasurer respectively under Bill English and Malcolm

Turnbull. I met and got to know Anthony Albanese when we were both transport ministers.

Australia ran a regular series of ministerial council meetings where the federal and state ministers for a particular portfolio would get together and try to find a way to pull in the same direction, or at least hammer out their differences. New Zealand has a standing invitation to attend these meetings, and when I was Transport Minister officials suggested I attend the upcoming meeting to be held in Perth. I wasn't sure I could spare the time, so I asked then Ministry of Transport CEO Martin Matthews what I would learn from going. He stuck his tongue firmly in his cheek and said, 'You will learn, Minister, that it was a very good decision for New Zealand not to join the Commonwealth of Australia.'

It was considered good for the Australian relationship for us to attend at least one such meeting a term, and I ended up attending two, both chaired by the aforementioned Mr Albanese. Albo is a garrulous, informal type, given to pragmatism, and he welcomed me much as the sorcerer might welcome a new apprentice.

Given that New Zealand doesn't have much skin in the game in these meetings, it was an opportunity for me to observe federal–state politics up close, and Albo was a great tutor. He'd tell me what was likely to happen and how he was planning to navigate the issues of the day, and sure enough he'd mostly achieve it, either through ruthlessly managing the day's agenda or at the informal session over a red wine or two the night before.

Martin Matthews was right. The raw interstate politics was something to see. The tribal differences between Victoria and New South Wales seemed to run much deeper than the left–right divide. One of the issues du jour was where to locate the new national regulator for the railways, and when I left the debate South Australia had the inside running, as neither New South Wales nor Victoria could abide the other hosting it.

OUR 2014 ELECTION WAS IN many ways a 'steady as she goes' result, with the new Parliament reconvening in late October and the government continuing to roll out the agenda of the previous term.

With the strength of the overall economy, the economic team had started to move our focus to improving the performance of individual regions that were struggling to keep up with the likes of the big five: Auckland, Waikato, Wellington, Canterbury and Otago. This was real micro stuff, analysing the opportunities for growth in each area and looking at what the government could do to catalyse more private investment in those regions.

I used to love my regional days, where I would check in with some of the fast-growing businesses, and ensure that agencies like NZTE and Callaghan Innovation were being helpful and adding value. There is nothing I liked better than spending a day, say, up the East Coast and visiting outfits as diverse as Pultron Composites, a wonderful company selling composite materials all over the world, the horticulturalists at LeaderBrand, the school-furniture exporters Furnware in Hastings, or Connect Global, who used the ultra-fast broadband network to open a call centre in Ruatōria. New Zealand is full of companies doing Sir Paul Callaghan's 'weird stuff', and my job was to help each region develop more of those companies.

We started in 2013 by setting up 'regional growth studies' for the East Coast and Northland, to identify how the government could help more private companies invest in those regions. With the East Coast the challenge was remoteness and weak transport links, while in Northland it was persistently high unemployment.

We followed those up with Manawatū-Whanganui, Bay of Plenty (particularly the eastern Bay), Southland and the West Coast. On the basis that 'if you can't measure it, you can't manage it', we also rolled out regional GDP statistics for the first time. While there were various private-sector proxies for regional activity, there had been no Stats NZ series, and that had allowed previous governments to downplay the relative performance of individual regions.

There was also one broader policy area where we were particularly keen to restart significant reform after being stalled by the make-up of the previous Parliament. That was the Resource Management Act. The RMA had been world-leading legislation when it was passed in the early 1990s. Unfortunately, it is another of those situations where the rest of the world didn't get the memo, or chose not to follow.

It was based around the seemingly simple concept of putting planning and consenting decisions for development projects like subdivisions or new factories together with the consideration of the environmental effects of these developments in a one-stop legal shop — the RMA. While it was supposed to streamline the process, it in fact made things much more complex. The RMA has been widely acknowledged as a big drag on economic development in New Zealand, but without being effective at managing environmental impacts either. It has been a particular handbrake on economic development in regional areas.

Environment Minister Nick Smith completed some urgent changes to the RMA in 2009, including creating the Board of Inquiry process for major projects, which was so helpful for the Roads of National Significance, and stopping vexatious objections to projects by competitors looking to delay or halt competition. That change led to an explosion of new supermarkets and DIY stores around the country.

He'd then embarked on a slower, more major reform process, but that stalled following the 2011 election. Whereas previously we had been able to make changes with just the support of the ACT party, after 2011 we needed the support of either United Future or the Māori Party as well, and neither were keen. The Māori Party wanted a significantly greater say for Māori in any amended Act, and Peter Dunne had worked alongside his former colleagues in the Labour

Party back when the RMA had been introduced, and was fond of it the way it was.

After the 2014 election we at last had the numbers again. With the pro-reform David Seymour from ACT and our own 60 seats, Resource Management Act reform was back on the table. We could finally make some positive change that would help boost the country's development, especially in regional New Zealand.

Not so fast. In mid-December we received news that one of our MPs was in some sort of personal trouble. One-term Northland MP and former police officer Mike Sabin was reportedly being investigated by police on an assault allegation. The news broke in the week before Christmas, and Sabin went to ground, refusing all comment. The police also refused to confirm they were investigating him.

That position could stand over the summer break, but by mid-January Mike needed to be answering questions, and he was either unwilling or unable to.

I didn't know much about it. It appeared to be part of a complicated family matter but the details were sketchy. Politically it was untenable because no one either knew or could say what was going on. It became increasingly inevitable he would stand down from Parliament, and he announced his resignation at the end of January, citing 'personal issues which were best dealt with outside Parliament'. Eventually his name would be cleared, but much too late for his political career.

We had a political headache. We'd just been returned with a slightly larger caucus, but already one electorate would have to go back to the polls, and we were unable to offer a satisfactory explanation as to why. But there was nothing for it. John announced the by-election for the end of March, and we set about getting ready for the campaign.

We came into the Northland by-election with a solid majority of more than 9000 votes, but we knew we couldn't be complacent. By-elections are often used by voters to send a message to incumbent governments, so we needed everything to go our way. It didn't.

For a start, it took too long to get a candidate. Northland is a huge electorate and National had a very big party membership there of over a thousand. That made the candidate selection process very complicated. Branches all over the region needed to run their own meet-the-candidate meetings and so on. And it's parochial. People in the Far North want someone from their area, while those around Dargaville and the Kaipara district want a candidate from their end.

As campaign chair I wanted the party to come up with a candidate quickly so we could have as much time as possible to get them known around the electorate. However, the quickest the party thought they could do while keeping the members happy was a month, so we had to cool our heels. It was the end of February before we had our candidate, Mark Osborne, an executive at the Far North District Council.

Meanwhile the old crocodile was on manoeuvres. Northland is an old stomping ground of Winston Peters. Although he lives in Auckland, his family is all up that way and he had a bach on the family farm at Whananaki. Standing in the by-election was not without risk for him. It would have been a telling blow if he stood and then lost, so in early February Winston teased a possible run before using much of that month to evaluate whether to take a shot at it. He announced his candidacy just before we announced Mark, standing in front of a big bus emblazoned with 'The Force for the North'.

While a loss in Northland wouldn't cause problems for the government's majority, we really wanted to hold the seat, partly because it had always been a National stronghold, and partly because we needed it to advance the RMA reforms. Without it we'd be back to the stalemate we'd had since 2011. We vowed to fight hard, and we poured all the party's resources into it. We were not going to die wondering.

Unfortunately, we read the dynamic wrong, and Winston read it right. We hadn't done much independent research in the electorate, relying instead on the views of local members, and they underestimated the sense of neglect the region felt, going back decades. We'd started to focus on accelerating the growth of the region in the previous twelve months, but that work was just beginning. Winston's line was that Northland had been taken for granted, and it seemed there were plenty of people who agreed.

The irony was that the harder we tried, the more we played into Winston's hands. We'd send up more MPs and extra volunteers to campaign in the seat, and that just made it look more like we weren't trying previously. John was particularly exercised. He wanted the electorate carpeted with signage, but any extra attention just rebounded on us. Winston kept saying we were only showing an interest in Northland because he was standing. John slammed Winston's chances of winning early on, and that rebounded as well.

And then there was the ten bridges. It became clear out on the hustings that a long-standing failure to upgrade at least some of the ten one-lane bridges on the main highways around the region was a key bugbear for locals. It was head-shaking material as to why this hadn't been on our collective radars previously. The party had held the Northland seat since it had been created twenty years earlier.

Perhaps former long-standing MP John Carter had simply been too accommodating to his Wellington colleagues. Or perhaps there was so much focus on Pūhoi to Wellsford, a crucial project for the whole region, that John felt unable to push further. The ridiculous thing was that it was estimated that the cost of building all ten bridges was around $70 million, although in hindsight that proved to be too light.

We knew we should promise to upgrade some of the bridges; the debate was over how many. The rumour was that Winston would be announcing a similar pledge, so we didn't want to be trumped. Two of the ten, the Darby and Joan bridges in Waipoua Forest, were actually ramps over the roots of some ancient kauri trees. I queried those with Simon Bridges, who by then was Minister of Transport. Simon was pretty gung-ho on announcing all ten, and he assured me the road could be routed around the forest. Ultimately it couldn't. John too was in a damn-the-torpedoes mood, so away we went. Again, all it did was make it look like we were scrambling, and reinforcing Winston's narrative that we hadn't cared enough before. We were damned either way.

Labour had sensed a chance to give the government a bloody nose, and new leader Andrew Little got out the semaphore flag, telling Labour voters 'to think very carefully about how to vote' if they wanted to 'send a message' to the government. That duly collapsed Labour's vote, and boosted Winston's by twenty points.

The writing was on the wall, and in the end we lost the by-election by 4500 votes. Mark ran a solid, workmanlike campaign, but he was a novice and ultimately it showed against Winston the old showman. For my part, it was the first time I'd seen Winston operate up close, and I went away with more respect for his campaigning skills. I don't like a lot of what he stands for or his propensity for looking after number one ahead of everyone else, but he certainly knows how to turn a campaign to his advantage, given half a chance.

Of course it's an ill wind that blows no good. We had committed to proceeding with the Northland bridge programme regardless of the by-election result, and as a direct result of that pledge four of the ten bridges are now either built or in the process of being built. The twin Matakohe bridges opened in July 2019, and the Taipā bridge opened in October that same year. The Kāeo bridge is due to open in early 2024. Sadly, no others have been advanced significantly since we left office in 2017.

Winston's moment in the Northland sun was surprisingly short. He was beaten just two years later by our National candidate, Matt King, who was helped by Labour choosing to campaign properly again in the general election. What the by-election result did do was scupper any chance of positive RMA reform during our remaining time in government. Ironically, that hurts resource-dependent regional economies like Northland the most. But the majority of Northlanders weren't too exercised about that. They just wanted to send their message, and they made sure it was heard loud and clear.

Chapter Twenty-two
Regions, projectiles and another quake

AFTER THE NORTHLAND BY-ELECTION WE redoubled our efforts on the regional-growth programme. Action plans were completed for all the targeted regions, and catalyst projects to encourage more private-sector growth were identified and funded. These included putting $4 million into the new Hundertwasser Art Centre in Whangārei as part of the Northland plan, $25 million into upgrading new port access roads in Hawke's Bay as part of their regional strategy, $3 million into the initial stages of the Ōpōtiki harbour development in the eastern Bay of Plenty to support aquaculture, and funding towards a new Palmerston North ring road in the Manawatū and the revitalisation plan for Whanganui's port.

One of my favourite projects had little to do with taxpayer funding, just a bit of lateral thinking and a couple of ministerial introductions. I'd been talking with NZ Māori Tourism's Pania Tyson-Nathan about the need for a tourism and hospitality college in the Bay of Islands to provide career opportunities for young people in one of Northland's biggest industries. I had a random thought and introduced Pania to Eion Edgar and the team at Queenstown Resort College in the South Island. They hit it off, and the upshot was the new QRC Tai Tokerau Resort College which opened in Paihia at the end of 2015.

Some of the regional work could be quite confounding, especially for the Wellington-based officials. We decided a senior official at deputy chief executive level would be delegated to be the point person for each region's growth programme; someone who, while working in the Wellington bureaucracy, would be accountable for progress on the plans. These people often encountered early cynicism about what 'Wellington' could do in a particular region, but most built enduring partnerships with the region to which they were delegated. All described it as a great way of better understanding what real people in the regions really thought and wanted from the capital.

In Northland the presenting issue was high regional unemployment, so our man on the Northland Growth Programme, MPI's Ben Dalton, started by making contact with all the large regional employers and asking what it would take for them to take on more staff. The surprising answer was that all would take on staff the very next day, if only they could find the people.

This sent Ben off on a path to track down some of the large numbers of recorded unemployed to get them into some of the available jobs. He worked with the Ministry of Social Development to set up a bespoke pilot programme in the Far North to get young unemployed people into work. This programme had a tall ex-netballer called Jo as the chief wrangler, and we had regular updates in Wellington on Jo's progress getting these young people ready for work and into employment. All the big employers lined up to take on some of the young people.

Anne Tolley and I went up to the programme's graduation in Kawakawa. It was a wonderful event, hosted by MSD and the local iwi, with all the businesses and students and Jo present. I had a good chat with some of the students and their employers. The students had all had hard-scrabble lives. Some were young parents, some were from homes where drug addiction was rife, and many just had trouble turning up every day. Jo told stories of going around to houses at ten o'clock in the morning to find the kids and get them back on track.

The employers said the programme had been much harder than they had anticipated, and it would take six months or more before many of the students were actually contributing to the workplace. For the businesses, their involvement had turned out to be much more in the realm of contributing to their community than solving their need for workers, at this early stage anyway, but all said the experience of working with these young people was rewarding.

I've seen other examples in my time in politics where intensive programmes linked to employment can turn young lives around, but it is never easy. Legendary Ōtorohanga mayor Dale Williams used his position to get young people into work by literally walking them into prospective employers, and then keeping tabs on them to make sure they didn't go off the rails. He started the nationwide Mayors Taskforce for Jobs, but it was never as successful elsewhere as it was in Ōtorohanga.

The conclusion I've come to is that politicians and officials in Wellington cycle through all these different employment programmes with fancy names and constantly changing accountabilities, but the key in every case is finding that one passionate individual, the wrangler or coach if you will, who will take the kids on, provide structure in their lives, and follow through with every employment relationship. We could do a lot worse than to simply find those special people in every community wherever they are and whatever their position, and back them with whatever funding they need, to get people who have fallen out of society back on track and making their contribution.

I LOVED MY TIME IN the north and I really enjoyed the pilgrimage to Waitangi for Waitangi Day. I went three or four times as a minister and appreciated the mostly laid-back vibe and the overwhelming friendliness of locals and visitors alike, all set against that wonderfully warm Northland summer.

Even the protests often weren't such a big deal when you were there. They'd look huge and angry on TV, which is the beauty of a narrow camera angle where everything in the picture looks like tumult. If you widened the shot, you'd mostly see people simply looking bemused.

One of my favourite examples of this was in early 2014, when a hīkoi protesting deep-sea oil drilling was timed to arrive at Te Tii marae at the same time as John. It was a lovely sunny day and everyone was waiting for John on the road outside the marae; MPs and ministers, media and protesters all mixed up together. John's car was late. His security detail was waiting for the hīkoi leaders to be welcomed on to the marae ahead of him. We all chatted quietly amongst ourselves, protesters, MPs and journalists, greeting old friends and checking our phones as we waited for the main event.

Then, suddenly, John's car swept up, with two Diplomatic Protection Service (DPS) cars in convoy. The journalists assumed their positions, the protesters theirs, cameras were switched on, and politicians surged forward to take their place on John's flank. There was jostling and shouting mixed with a chant of welcome, but it was all over within minutes. There were no serious incidents, and John and the rest of us were safely on the marae. The cameras were turned off, the day settled down, and serenity resumed.

In 2016 we were all once again assembling in Waitangi. I had arrived on the night of 4 February, and was staying at the Copthorne Hotel over the bridge, below the national marae. The iwi leaders were holding their meeting in the large conference room across from the hotel proper and, just as in previous years, John was leading a team of ministers to meet with the iwi leaders.

The air was slightly more tense than usual. I'd spoken to Wayne Eagleson by phone once or twice and he'd passed on that police were concerned a more significant protest was brewing that year. Their intelligence had picked up a plan to target John explicitly, and they were evaluating how to handle it. I reported back that things seemed to be as relaxed as ever on the ground in Waitangi, but the police presence certainly seemed a bit more beefed up.

It wasn't a complete surprise when I received another call to say John had been advised to cancel his trip. As the senior minister present I was asked to lead the government delegation and deputise for John at his scheduled events, apart from at Te Tii marae, which we'd decided not to attend. I happily acquiesced, but was immediately a little nervous as my first duty would be to lead the ministerial delegation at the iwi leaders' meeting. While I had participated previously, I'd never led the discussion. My te reo certainly wasn't up to the standard of Bill's or even John's, and while my knowledge of protocol had improved over my time as a minister, I certainly wouldn't describe myself as confident.

I needn't have worried. With John's decision to withdraw, the tension dissipated. With the help of my colleagues, we had an enjoyable discussion with the iwi leaders, many of whom I knew personally. After we finished, I went out for the normal stand-up interview along with fellow ministers Nathan Guy, Louise Upston, Amy Adams, Maggie Barry and Jo Goodhew. It was a small group of journalists, including Paddy Gower of TV3, Helen Castles from 1News and Claire Trevett from the Herald. The media too had lost some interest with the PM no longer coming. A couple of uniformed police officers were standing some distance away, with their arms folded, watching on. It was a calm, still day and very quiet.

I was just wrapping up the interview when I felt something hit me in the face. I heard someone shout something, but not what they said. We all — journalists, MPs, cameramen — instinctively looked down to see what had hit me. Whatever it was had rebounded off Helen Castles and hit the ground.

It looked like some sort of . . . plastic dildo. Thoughts raced through my mind. What does one say in these situations? Keep calm, I said to myself. Everything is okay, you are fine, just wrap it up and walk away. What I said was 'Good-oh'. Behind me Nathan said quietly 'We're off', which was a good hint. I said 'Let's go', and we walked calmly off as a group while the police took the person who threw the projectile away.

As we walked away I had a thought. It had all happened so fast, maybe the cameras had missed it. I said under my breath to Nathan, 'Do you think the cameras picked that up?' 'Yes,' he said, 'keep walking'.

Inside the hotel, I started to process what had happened. My immediate reaction was that it wasn't that big a deal. I rang Suzanne and let her know I was okay. My press secretary Serene Ambler came up and said the police were asking for my view on pressing charges. My gut instinct was no. Everyone was okay and the protester would just milk their situation for all it was worth. It was the police's call, but I sent the message back that I wasn't pushing for charges to be laid. There was a moment of thinking 'What if it had been something more serious?', but I pushed it to the back of my mind.

I had to go and officially open the new Museum of Waitangi, so I readied myself for that. I made the speech, cut the ribbon and had a look around inside. It wasn't till I came out again and faced a barrage of media that what had happened earlier started to sink in a little more, including how big the moment was proving to be.

By then I was firmly back to seeing the funny side of it all. I told the media you have new experiences in politics every day and that it was 'all part of the privilege of serving'. I then tweeted for someone to 'send the gif over to John Oliver so we can get this over with', in reference to the American weekly talk-show host who had developed a bit of a fixation with New Zealand politics. Then I had the evening off. We'd all been invited to MP Andrew Bayly's brother's place for a barbecue out on the Waitangi peninsula. It was a great opportunity to relax a little and regroup.

Clearly John Oliver didn't relax. He outdid himself the next weekend with a big(gish) budget production number roasting me, which included choirs, dancing dildos, flying dildos, and Peter Jackson waving a giant new dildo-inspired New Zealand flag. I had to admit I was impressed, and amused.

The next morning, Waitangi Day itself, I was due to speak in John's place at the dawn service. The police had ramped up their security to PM-type levels and I had DPS officers all around me. By then of course the horse had bolted, and the morning was a lovely service which passed without incident. I enjoyed giving the reading on behalf of the prime minister. Afterwards I amused myself quietly as we wandered around the Treaty Grounds by playing a private game of spot the plain-clothes policeman. As I moved in one direction, with our team, the police and DPS moving with me, seemingly random members of the crowd in shorts wearing backpacks moved too. As I moved back the other way, they did the same, always keeping the same distance.

BACK IN WELLINGTON, I HAD a meeting with a guy called Peter Beck. Peter was the chief executive and founder of Rocket Lab, and ministers had been marvelling at what he'd been setting out to achieve since back when Wayne Mapp was Minister of Research, Science and Technology and Peter was test-firing what amounted to advanced skyrockets from Great Mercury Island, off the Coromandel Peninsula.

Economic development ministers and science ministers get used to being approached by people with stories of amazing inventions which are going to change the world. Often it starts by having a large envelope filled with drawings and tightly typed notes thrust at you after you speak at a function. You learn to be quite sceptical. There were initial doubts about Rocket Lab back at the beginning — how could a commercial space company launch rockets out of New Zealand? It was fantastical stuff.

Meeting Peter at his small factory close to Auckland Airport was enough to convince me he was the real deal. He was building and test-firing rockets made from carbon composites and 3D-printed engines. His manner, focus, determination and confidence was infectious. It was science fiction but it was also clearly real.

On this occasion Peter had a request. After years of work the Rocket Lab team had nearly completed the development of their electron rocket and were almost ready to launch. There was just one problem. There was no regulatory regime in New Zealand to allow launches. No law, no regulations, nothing. We also hadn't signed up to any space treaties because we had never needed to. Peter had been talking to the Ministry of Foreign Affairs and Trade (MFAT), but progress had been slow. He wanted to be launching in six months. Could we be ready in time?

The officials were shaking their heads almost as soon as Beck left my office. There was a mammoth amount of work to do, Minister. It would involve getting legislation through Parliament, we'd have to sign up to all these treaties. It would need much longer.

I said we couldn't wait that long. If we were to be a government that fostered innovation, we couldn't let a bunch of paperwork hold up New Zealand's first-ever space launch. I spoke with Foreign Minister Murray McCully, and we agreed that the Ministry of Business, Innovation and Employment (MBIE) would take the lead in putting the regime together, with help from MFAT. I then had David Smol put together a small team of officials from both agencies, with the aim we would get it all done in six months. It was the regulatory equivalent of Rocket Lab's moonshot. We had no idea if we could do it, but I wanted the officials to find a way.

There were four key things that had to be done. Firstly, we needed to negotiate and sign a technology safeguards agreement with the United States Government, so that Rocket Lab could use US rocket technology in launches from New Zealand. Secondly, we had to join the UN Convention on Registration of Objects Launched into Outer Space. Thirdly, we had to draft and pass a new outer-space law for New Zealand; and fourthly, we had to set up a New Zealand Space Agency, located in MBIE. None of us had done any of that before.

The officials did a tremendous job. We didn't quite make it in six months, but then nor did Peter Beck and his team. The Outer Space and High-altitude Activities Bill had its first reading in Parliament in October 2016, and while we waited for it to pass into law we set up a contract between the government and Rocket Lab to allow for the first launch. Rocket Lab made its first test flight from the Māhia Peninsula on 25 May 2017.

The Rocket Lab launch site is on land owned by the Rongomaiwahine Iwi Trust. Peter invited me to Māhia in September 2016 to open the launch facilities and we had a wonderful ceremony in a big hangar on the remote site, way up the peninsula road. While we were waiting to start, I wandered over to talk to some of the old kuia sitting in the front row of the ceremony. I asked one what she made of it. She smiled at me and said, 'Well, we were thinking of diversifying from sheep and beef, but I have to admit I hadn't thought of rockets.'

Now that was real regional development.

LIFE COMES AT YOU FAST, and late in 2016 Mother Nature intervened again. The Kaikōura earthquake struck just after midnight on 14 November. It was really huge — magnitude 7.8 on the Richter scale. It also caused the strongest ground acceleration ever recorded in New Zealand. During the earthquake, the South Island moved six metres closer to the North Island.

The quake made a mess of the township of Kaikōura, and buried the main highway and railway lines along the coast between Picton and Christchurch under more than a million cubic metres of rubble. Many big buildings, including new ones, were damaged in faraway Wellington, while farms and wineries in Marlborough were severely shaken, as was the tourist town of Hanmer Springs. The North Canterbury village of Waiau, closest to the quake's epicentre, was torn apart.

The government swung back into gear again, with a cadence that was now eerily familiar. While you wouldn't wish for an earthquake, I think it was helpful this wasn't our first rodeo. Gerry Brownlee was by then Civil Defence Minister, and he and the PM immediately flew down to Kaikōura. The small community was completely cut off from the outside world except by air.

My responsibility was the economic impact on families and communities, and Anne Tolley and I announced an initial business support package within four days of the quake. It would be extended in scope a number of times as the impact became clearer.

The main focus of the disaster was on Kaikōura and North Canterbury, where the situation was so fragile that the armed forces were brought into evacuate locals and tourists. However, it became increasingly clear that parts of Wellington had also been hit hard, including seemingly random places like the Queensgate Shopping Centre in Lower Hutt. I went to see the impact on the Wellington wharves, and, just like Lyttelton six years earlier, the effect of the forces unleashed by the quake on huge slabs of concrete was awe-inspiring. Following a personal appeal from new Wellington mayor Justin Lester, affected Wellington businesses were quickly brought into the support package.

I was part of the second wave of ministers heading into the North Canterbury quake zone. I flew to Christchurch on the morning of 22 November, where an NH90 military helicopter waited to take me to Kaikōura. The mental images of that day will stay with me for a long time: the state of the highway on the way in, the size of the slips, the mess that was the tiny Kaikōura harbour and the damage everywhere around the town.

The resourcefulness of the locals will stay with me as well. The little Kaikōura District Council occupied a nearly new building on the main street. There were very few staff, but they were very much at the centre of things, with Mayor Winston Gray leading from the front. That day was an important demonstration of the importance of local councils when the chips are down.

The council had set up a daily community briefing at 1 p.m. in a park just around the corner from the council, and they invited me to say a few words. There were about 150 people there of all ages, seeking information and help with all the things that you need when your world is suddenly turned upside down. There was little anger, but a desire to get things sorted. Of course that was going to take some time.

From Kaikōura the army flew me down to Waiau, which was the very definition of a village flattened by an earthquake. I called in at the local town hall, where councillors and volunteers were doing their bit to support a community where most of the houses and buildings were red-stickered. In those situations, your job as a minister is to listen, support and remove blockages to getting things done. That was my role all through that day. I finished the day by heading to Hanmer Springs, where I would have meetings the next day.

There the atmosphere was different. The whole town was worried and verging on angry, fearful they had been forgotten. I was the first minister there in the week since the quakes. While Hanmer was not as hard hit as some other places, the town's businessfolk were very worried about the impact the disaster would have on their livelihoods, which revolved around tourism.

Again the damage was random. One bar which ran north to south had every bottle and glass destroyed. The one up the road running east to west had virtually no damage at all. We talked things through and I went back a number of times to stay on top of things and assist where we could, and we provided funding to promote the town to people around the country.

The biggest job was to get road access back into Kaikōura, and then to rebuild the road and the railway line. The township was completely cut off. The figures were mind-boggling. There were 85 separate landslides on the highway, and 60 bridges and 20 tunnels had been damaged on the railway line.

Taking a leaf out of the Christchurch book, we set up the North Canterbury Transport Infrastructure Recovery alliance, which included NZTA, KiwiRail and all the big civil contractors. We also funded a temporary workers' village in Kaikōura. There would have been no other way for the town to cope with the influx of people needed to rebuild the route.

The alliance was able to get the inland route between Kaikōura and Hanmer open within three weeks, and I travelled down it in those very early days. 'Open' was an interesting description, as the road remained nearly impassable in places. The visible impact of the quake ripping the land sideways was just astonishing. A huge amount of work still needed to be done, but at least people could get through.

State Highway 1 south of Kaikōura was able to open a few weeks later, but it remained very vulnerable. The railway initially opened ten months after the quake, while the highway north of Kaikōura opened a year after the quake destroyed it. The whole project to fully reinstate the two highways, the railway and the harbour took four years to complete, and cost over $1.2 billion. Nearly 9000 people worked on it, and 3000 of them stayed in the workers' village.

Such is the nature of politics that the project was completed on the next government's watch and I personally didn't get to see it finished. I will, however, never forget those early days in Kaikōura and North Canterbury, the enormity of the task, the resilience of the people, and the determination to put things back better than before.

Chapter Twenty-three
John departs,
and finance calls

THE DAY OF 5 DECEMBER 2016 had started like any other Monday. I was picked up in the Crown car around 5.45 a.m. and headed for Auckland Airport. I had my normal Monday-morning phone call with John just after 6.00, with him running through what the various media outlets wanted to discuss, and me giving my thoughts on his proposed responses. Nothing seemed amiss.

I landed in Wellington about 8.00 and decided to drop in to my apartment and do a few things before walking into the office about 9.00. At around 8.45 the phone rang. It was John again.

That was unusual. Normally we wouldn't catch up again until the pre-Cabinet meeting around 10.30. I only received a follow-up call when something had gone wrong on the morning media round, or John had said something he wanted to fess up about.

I realised straight away from his tone that something bigger was afoot. It was John's rarely used semi-ruthless tone. He was so serious that I knew instantly that by the end of this conversation, one of the two people on the call wouldn't have a job. The only question remaining was which one. I started doing a mental stocktake. Was there anything at all to be concerned about? Had I mucked up anything that was a sackable offence? I didn't think so, but in those moments you start to doubt yourself.

It all unfolded quite quickly. John had been thinking about his future and talking with Bronagh, and he'd decided that he didn't want to do another term. It was a year before the election and he felt this was the time to pull the pin so that his successor would have time to prepare for and fight the election campaign.

I began an attempt to talk him out of it, but quickly realised the decision had been made and I was wasting my time. The announcement was planned to be made publicly later that morning. Finally John told me that if Bill decided to stand to replace him, then he would support him. He told me Bill had been his long-time deputy, and in his view it would only be fair and right to endorse him as his successor.

I was still processing it all, so didn't give that part any further thought. I put down the phone and hurried into the office, my thoughts whirring. My biggest immediate concern was the election campaign next year. To say this would throw everything up in the air was quite the understatement.

I went straight to the ninth floor to see Wayne Eagleson. Only a few people knew, but Wayne was one of them. He looked a little shellshocked, but as always, preternaturally calm. He told me he'd known for a few days, as he had been booking some overseas travel for John for early next year and was having trouble getting the desired dates out of the PM. John had eventually levelled with him.

Thoughts kept racing around in my brain. The main thing was the momentousness of this change. The announcement would come as a huge surprise to the public as, notwithstanding all the challenges, the government had been sailing along well. And John had been the constant. Despite all the wear and tear of being in office, his preferred PM ratings were still in the mid- to high thirties.

This was uncharted territory. If anything, I had anticipated it would be Bill announcing his retirement in the next few months, not John. Bill was known by a few of us to have been considering retirement for some time, although he hadn't told me this directly and in recent times the talk had receded.

There is a big advantage in knowing these things even just a few hours in advance of the public. By the time the announcement was made early that afternoon, we were all moving on to the practicalities of what would happen next.

I often think back to see if I could identify any clue that John was thinking of leaving prior to that day in December. There was just the one. When he was in New York at the UN Security Council a couple of months earlier, John did two long-form interviews with Corin Dann and Paddy Gower, for *Q+A* and *The Nation* respectively. Ahead of time we had our usual chat on the phone about what questions the interviewers might ask, particularly the curveballs. One question John anticipated was whether he'd stand again in 2017 and stay for another three years. He said to me, 'Yeah yeah, I know, just stare down the barrel and say yes and yes.' He duly did so and reported back afterwards.

He has publicly said since then that those interviews and the responses he dutifully gave helped catalyse his thinking. There was something in the offhand way we discussed the answers that day that I now realise signalled his own ambivalence. But at the time I missed it.

I went to see Bill, partly to see what he was planning and partly in order to make my own call on what to do. Should I stand? I'd already had a few people ask me. I found the whole leadership thing confusing. I'd always been a team player and I liked it when the team was functioning well together. Sudden discussions about personal ambition were disorienting and off-putting.

One thing I was clear about was that I wouldn't stand if Bill decided he would. I felt the party, and indeed the country, did not need a scrap between numbers two and four over the leadership. Anyway, Bill and I were close colleagues and had become friends. Loyalty would prevent me taking him on.

A few other friends in caucus recommended I extract the price of the finance portfolio in return for supporting Bill, but I didn't have to. Bill was clear that he would be standing, and that he wanted me to be his finance minister. He announced the latter publicly at his Finance Minister's Half Year Fiscal Update presentation on the Wednesday.

Twenty-four hours on from John's resignation and the competition to be leader was starting to heat up. Judith Collins and Jonathan Coleman both threw their hats into the ring. Then just two days later it was all over as quickly as it had begun. Bill's team had done a good job of securing the public endorsement of more than half the caucus, at which point his accession was a formality.

The election of the new deputy leader was a little less smooth. Paula Bennett and Simon Bridges were both nominated, and took it to a vote in caucus a week after John resigned. I had spoken with Bill about taking on the role, but he had quite reasonably said that he didn't want deputy, finance and campaign chair to be the same person, and he wanted me to stay campaign chair.

Bill didn't declare his hand, but it was widely known within caucus that he wanted Paula in the role. She was an Aucklander, a woman and Māori, and therefore balanced the ticket well. Simon ticked one of the three boxes. He was probably more putting down a public marker for his future ambitions anyway. Simon was always in a hurry.

Paula duly won the deputy leadership and took to her promotion with trademark gusto. Her early attendances at the Kitchen Cabinet as deputy were particularly fulsome and energetic. At one stage she suggested she take over the campaign chair role before Bill gently made it clear that there was to be no change.

Politics is unique in the way in which it requires the people who work together to elect one or two amongst them to lead the team. The process by which that happens can unsettle friendships and established ways of working together. The test is whether people can complete the changes without too many bruised egos or lasting slights. I think the transfer from John to Bill achieved that, and the revised team swiftly settled down to prepare to face the public in the election in just ten months' time.

I knew we'd all miss John. He had been a great leader of the Cabinet. He was collaborative, thoughtful and gave us all the room to do our jobs.

In that context Bill was the ideal replacement. He was always more of a policy swot than John and a little less instinctive, but he was also happy to let his colleagues do their jobs. That gave us all the room to take ownership of our roles without being stifled by an overbearing prime minister's office.

For me personally, John, along with Judy Kirk, was the reason I'd gone into Parliament, and John had given me the opportunity to be a minister and perform the roles I'd been given. I will always be grateful to him for that, and we had been close confidants all the way through his prime ministership, especially around election time, but also every week in his media dealings in particular. However, I had developed into being my own person in Cabinet, and John and I quite regularly ended up on different sides in policy debates. I would miss him, but also as a result of him going I, along with everyone else, would have new opportunities.

AS A NEWLY MINTED FINANCE MINISTER, my primary job prior to the election was to collate and present my first Budget. But I had a couple of sensitive issues to deal with first: the appointment of a new

Reserve Bank Governor, and the government's plans for the future of New Zealand superannuation.

Graeme Wheeler had been Reserve Bank Governor since 2012. He was a very dry, conservative type, but I'd grown to appreciate him. Bill had regular meetings with him as Finance Minister, and I was often invited to attend in my role as Associate Finance and Economic Development Minister. Bill encouraged me to challenge Graeme on his view of the economy based on what I was seeing on the ground, especially across regional New Zealand. We had some very good, and always respectful, discussions. Sitting down with the governor and his senior team and debating monetary policy became one of the highlights of my week.

The immediate problem I had was that Graeme, for whatever reason, didn't want to be reappointed to the role. I heard later that he found it quite exhausting, particularly some of the public criticism. But that presented a dilemma. The new governor was supposed to commence their appointment in September, which would have been just before the 2017 election. While their appointment was supposed to be as apolitical as possible, it was happening right at the most political moment in the election cycle.

If Graeme had been available, and I'd wanted to reappoint him, which I think I would have, then I doubt the Opposition would have opposed the reappointment. But a brand-new governor would require more explicit bipartisan support. Graeme's logical replacement was Deputy Governor Grant Spencer, and I think he would have been an admirable successor. Grant was as dry, scholarly and careful as his boss, and I think his appointment would have served New Zealand well. But he made it clear to officials that he didn't want the permanent role either as he was nearing retirement.

The Reserve Bank is a strange beast of an organisation. It is very separate and very cloistered; in fact, probably as close to a monastery as you could imagine within the public service. It operates with quite a detached view of the world, taking its non-political role very seriously. Many people accuse it of being divorced from reality and prone to taking an overly analytical approach to the economy. Even the Treasury officials who worked with the Reserve Bank often struggled with it and, let's face it, Treasury is not exactly the headquarters of the ordinary person on the street.

I remember once witnessing a particularly pointed passive-aggressive debate between Treasury and Reserve Bank officials squared off on either side of my meeting table. In exasperation I suggested they should all go out and have a beer with one another after work. That scenario was extremely unlikely to occur for a range of reasons.

Of course, like a lot of things in the world, the Reserve Bank's perceived weakness was also its strength. Its very detachment meant that it could be trusted not to let politics get in the way of the decisions it had to make, which can be unpopular. They are the guys who often need to take away the punch bowl just as the economic party is getting started, to avoid us all getting carried away and trashing the place.

That's the reason why central banks became independent from government. It was too easy for politicians to make monetary policy decisions that were politically popular in the short term, goosing the economy in the approach to an election for example, and then having to pay the price later in the form of a huge economic hangover. You could accuse the New Zealand Reserve Bank of the time of many things, but being shamelessly populist was not one of them.

Subsequently there have been reforms designed to 'humanise' the Reserve Bank, including by making its monetary policy decisions more collectively and with the outside help of an independent committee of worthies, presumably selected because they are more in touch with economic reality than the Reserve Bank might be on its own. This has been part of an international trend which has also seen central banks' remits expand to include policy issues like combating climate change, increasing housing affordability and, in the New Zealand context, supporting the development of the Māori economy.

The poor performance of central banks in exacerbating rather than smoothing the economic impacts of the Covid-19 pandemic suggests that, at best, the jury is out on attempts to broaden the remit, popularity and connectedness of central banking. Given the wild swings in monetary policy that occurred during and after the pandemic, I think many people in hindsight might prefer a more cloistered, analytical, academic, unemotional approach to monetary policy settings.

Without the two obvious continuity choices for governor, I was left in the position of having to appoint somebody completely new, just prior to an election. I wasn't comfortable about that from a constitutional perspective, and sought advice on whether to appoint an interim governor so that after the election the new Finance Minister, likely to be either me or Grant Robertson, could make the permanent appointment away from the immediate politics of an election campaign. The advice supported that approach, and Grant Spencer accepted an appointment for twelve months as Interim Governor of the Reserve Bank of New Zealand.

It had been telegraphed to me that there was one other obvious candidate I could have appointed into the permanent role, who would likely meet the approval of the Labour Opposition. That was Adrian Orr, who at that stage headed up the New Zealand Superannuation Fund. I wasn't convinced he had the right temperament for the governor role. If Adrian was the only option, then I decided I would prefer to wait and, if given the opportunity, assess him alongside other candidates after the election.

On superannuation, our previous policy position had been abundantly clear. John had made a commitment before he'd been elected the first time that there would no change to superannuation as long as he was prime minister. That seemed a less and less tenable position as time had gone on, and the projected cost of superannuation rose with rising life expectancy. More people were living longer and longer, and because of superannuation and the health budget, more government spending was required to be directed to the elderly rather than to, say, our children's education.

John was roundly criticised throughout his premiership for not facing up to the superannuation issue, but he was right to stick with his commitment as it would have been a major breach of trust otherwise. However, he had now left, and we knew we wouldn't have much time before the media demanded an answer from Bill on whether he planned any changes to superannuation.

We decided we did need to offer a more realistic superannuation policy that at least took some steps towards solving the medium- to long-term affordability issue. I was tasked to come up with one. It wouldn't be easy. Superannuation had been a third rail for National since the broken election commitment of Jim Bolger's 1990 government. The imposition of the super surcharge tax caused a mass exodus of members from the National Party from which it has never fully recovered. That decision, along with the perceived betrayal of traditional Labour voters by the Lange / Palmer government, led to the country voting in favour of MMP.

After much deliberation, and testing of the water with Bill and senior colleagues, we announced a plan to progressively lift the age of super from 65 to 67, twenty years hence, starting in 2037 and finishing in 2040. It was deliberately set that far in the future so nobody could say they hadn't had the opportunity to plan for it. It also matched the point where projections showed superannuation would be taking an unsustainably large chunk out of the government's budget. We knew it was cautious, but we felt it was something that politicians could sign up to in a bipartisan manner so the future cost of superannuation would be manageable.

We were of course too idealistic. Both Labour and New Zealand First immediately opposed the change. That's a real pity because the public largely got on board with it right from the time it was announced. At the time of writing, there is still no government policy to change superannuation to avoid an unbearable cost being passed on to younger generations, and the demographic clock is ticking.

People often talk as if the Super Fund will solve the future superannuation problem, and it was of course set up by Michael Cullen to make it seem like he had a solution. But the fund will provide such a small contribution at almost any conceivable contribution level, that it is almost a rounding error. It is certainly a red herring.

I didn't have a huge amount of time to prepare the Budget and there was a lot to do. After six years' hard slog since the GFC we were finally back in surplus, and that of course meant ministers and departments had a long list of Budget bids they wanted prioritised. As Bill was fond of saying, it's a lot easier for a finance minister to put a Budget together when there's no money than when there is a bit of money around.

I was lucky to have effectively had an eight-year apprenticeship for the role. Latterly I'd been working with all the ministers with economic portfolios as both Economic Development and Associate Finance Minister. In effect I'd been preparing that part of the Budget with them for some years under Bill's tutelage. I was also very familiar with the big social portfolios and their spending pressures.

I decided we needed some strategic themes to organise the Budget around, and settled on four. They were: investing in better public services; making a big infrastructure investment; continuing to reduce debt; and offering some relief on taxes, particularly for low- and middle-income earners. It was a big wish list, and the Treasury Budget officials weren't optimistic we would get through all the preparatory work required in the short time available — but with a lot of hard work and a fair few weekends at the office, we did. Treasury and my office both rose to the challenge admirably.

The big-ticket items in the Budget were health at $1 billion extra a year, plus major investments in schooling, childcare, justice and other social services. All up it was a $7 billion package. We added to that an $11 billion investment in infrastructure, taking the total government investment in infrastructure over four years to $32 billion, which included a commitment to open 540 lane kilometres of new highways over the next four years.

The headline of course was the family incomes package. We settled on a combination of tax threshold changes, increases to the family tax credit for families with young children, and increases in the accommodation supplement, all to give a real lift to low- and middle-income families. As a result of the Budget, over 1.3 million families would be better off by an average of $26 a week, while many received more than $40 a week.

Key to the changes was a bid to lift people's after-tax incomes to provide a greater reward for their hard work. We decided to drop the in-work tax credit, which was effectively a benefit payment for low-income people in work in lieu of tax reductions. That was more than offset by a lift in the bottom tax threshold, where people went from paying 10.5 cents in the dollar to 17.5 cents in the dollar, from $14,000 to $22,000. The next income threshold, when the tax rate lifts from 17.5 cents to 30 cents in the dollar, was moved from $48,000 a year to $52,000 a year. I wanted people to see more of their wages in their pockets. That would be good for them, and good for our economy.

Not to spoil the plot, but after the election the new government cancelled the threshold changes, and at the time of writing there hasn't been a single tax threshold adjustment since. Despite record high inflation which keeps sending wage and salary earners into higher tax rates, people are still paying 17.5 cents in the dollar at $14,000, and 30 cents in the dollar from $48,000 a year upwards. Even minimum wage earners are now nearly at the 30 cents tax rate.

Failing to adjust tax rates has resulted in an income-tax windfall for the government while at the same time squeezing the pay packet of ordinary New Zealanders. In addition, there has been the imposition of a new higher tax rate of 39 cents in the dollar for people on incomes above $180,000. All of which goes to prove the old adage that governments of the left always think they know better how to spend your money than you do.

The final theme of the 2017 Budget was to continue paying down debt for the next rainy day. New Zealand is a small, isolated country, and the stark reality is that since Britain first left us to join the European Community nobody else is going to look out for us. That means we need a more prudent level of debt than most larger countries, to ensure we can respond and support people when disaster strikes.

It is misleading when people compare our relative debt levels to that of Japan, Germany, the UK or the US. Our small size, our isolation and our propensity for natural disasters means we represent a much bigger risk to funders than most of the countries which are trotted out as comparisons, and sadly we are just not that important. There are lots of advantages to being small and not particularly significant on the world stage, but the price is having to be capable of fending for ourselves when the chips are down.

We wanted to have money set aside for the next Global Financial Crisis, the next major earthquake, or, as it turned out, the next pandemic. My personal view is that every government has the responsibility to keep debt down, and get it back down once it has risen, in order to pay for each major unexpected event.

I felt the Budget was a well-balanced package, but the proof of the pudding on such matters is definitely in the eating. The initial media coverage on Budget night was positive, and it stayed that way despite the normal forensic analysis of Budgets that occurs over the following days.

For me the most heart-warming reactions were from larger low-income families and the social-services sector. I spoke at the regular post-Budget social-services meeting in Wellington, and they were more positive than I or they had expected to be. We had surprised them on the upside. One senior practitioner told me that Bill and I had put compassion back into conservatism. While I would beg to differ with his judgement on the government's previous track record, it was high praise indeed.

Chapter Twenty-four
Election 2017

THE SHIP OF GOVERNMENT SAILED through the first part of election year 2017 remarkably smoothly, despite the loss of our previous captain. The Budget was well received. The post-Budget Colmar Brunton poll had National under Bill's leadership at 49 per cent, Labour at 30 per cent, and NZ First and the Greens each on 9 per cent. We were heading towards an election campaign where we expected to be very competitive, and with no sign of third-term-itis.

The big change from John to Bill had worked, and not cost us any momentum. In fact, if anything, we had gained some. Bill had announced the election day for 23 September back at the beginning of February. Campaign preparations were well underway.

The media was bored, and sensed the election result was a fait accompli. That certainly wasn't our position. We knew, despite appearances, that every MMP election had been close. But we were happy with how we were travelling at that point.

Labour, on the other hand, were in real difficulty. The public hadn't warmed to their leader Andrew Little at all. The Labour people didn't like the 'Angry Andy' label we had given him, but it only worked because he so often lived up to it.

Our challenge looked to be whether we could build a strong coalition again. ACT and United Future continued to look weak, and now the Māori Party was struggling as well. Virtually nobody on our side felt able to trust Winston Peters, our only other option.

We struck a small iceberg in June with Clutha Southland MP Todd Barclay admitting to having taped a staff member's conversation without her consent. It was part of a messy breakdown in an employment relationship, one where Bill had, probably ill-advisedly, tried to mediate between the parties. He knew all of them from his years as the electorate MP.

We moved into damage control, and the ninth floor worked with the party to successfully dissuade Todd from standing at the upcoming election. It was the end of Todd's political career only three years after it started. Some would say politics involves a lot of rough justice. On the other hand, clandestinely taping people without their consent is a sure way to get kicked out of Parliament.

Labour's putative coalition partners weren't in great shape either. In July, Metiria Turei admitted she had misclaimed her Domestic Purposes Benefit back in the early 1990s, and was very roundly criticised for it.

At the beginning of August everything changed. After two particularly tough polls showing Labour on just 24 per cent, Andrew Little went into a one-on-one interview at TVNZ where he mused aloud about his own ongoing role as Labour leader. From that moment, if not before, the writing was on the wall. The only remaining question was who would replace him.

I had long thought Jacinda Ardern was the only politician on Labour's front bench to fear politically. I had told Bill, and John before him, that as campaign chair I'd only see Labour becoming truly competitive if they gave the leader's job to Jacinda. There was no one else in Labour who could capture the public's imagination.

At one level it was hard to quantify why I felt that way. As an

Opposition politician Jacinda had hardly troubled the scorer in her three terms in Parliament. She had not put any of our ministers under any sort of sustained pressure, nor developed any significant policy initiatives of her own.

What she did have was presence and likeability. She talked well off the cuff and people found her easy to relate to. In that way, she was very similar to John. Her politics were very different of course, but she passed the old test of who you would be happy to have a beer with at the pub, which is so important in egalitarian New Zealand.

I had another marker too. When Annette King was unavailable for our joint Newstalk ZB slot with Mike Hosking, various other Labour front benchers would fill in. Almost all of them struggled to maintain the easy, semi-respectful rapport the slot required. They were mostly too shrill and partisan to be effective. The only one who handled it well was Jacinda. On the two or three occasions she subbed in, she sized up the situation quickly, didn't push too hard, but got her point across.

Anyway, my concern had seemed very theoretical, as Jacinda had been clear, time and time again, that she didn't want the big job. But that was then. On 1 August, eight weeks out from election day, Jacinda Ardern became leader of the New Zealand Labour Party, and the 2017 election campaign turned on a dime.

Overnight, Labour went from old, negative and backward-looking, to fresh, new and infinitely more interesting. Conversely, we were instantly repositioned from a modern-looking government to one that looked a little more shop-worn. Such is the nature of contrasts.

The Labour faithful were initially relieved they were back in the game after nine years, and then excited as it became apparent that having Jacinda as leader could have a real and immediate impact on their electoral prospects. The Labour Party's campaign launch three weeks after she became leader was positively euphoric. The media, too, showed a lot more interest in both Labour and the contest. The 2017 election had suddenly become interesting. Jacinda Ardern was a sparkly new star in the political firmament. 'Jacindamania' was born.

This was clearly a problem for us. Once a political narrative starts to build amongst the press gallery, it can be hard to shake. Labour's policies had changed, but not radically. They had simply added a new leader, who was understandably going to get a honeymoon in the role. However, the election was only a few weeks away. She had started well, and there was a real risk her honeymoon with voters could carry her over the line.

Meanwhile, there were further movements in the minor parties. Metiria Turei's issues had gone from bad to worse, and she stepped down as co-leader of the Greens. Peter Dunne had seen the writing on the wall in his Ōhāriu electorate and had decided to retire, effectively taking United Future out of the game. Such is the nature of political zeitgeists that both pieces of news were interpreted as good for Labour and bad for us.

Things were getting negative on our side of the political fence. People were starting to worry that Bill wouldn't be able to match it with Jacinda's star power. There were private worries, and I'm sure not least for Bill, that he could lose the election as he had the one fifteen years previously.

The low point for me was the day of the first TVNZ debate on the final day of August, just 24 days prior to election day. The latest Colmar Brunton poll had been provided to us for comment ahead of its release on the news that night, as part of the lead-in to the debate. While previous polls had shown a bounce for Labour, this was the first to show Labour ahead of National, by 43 to 41 per cent. We looked like we were on the skids.

Debate prep that day was hell. We had organised some rooms at the Pullman Hotel and the senior campaign team was assembled.

The focus was on getting Bill ready but, at least in the back of everyone's minds, there was a sudden, stark fear that we might lose the election. I felt for Bill and knew this would be bringing up bad memories from 2002. This was no way to prepare.

I gave him as best a campaign chair's pep talk as I could muster, and he went out to do battle. I retired across the road to Topham Guerin's Auckland offices to watch the debate and provide some instant feedback on our accompanying social-media game.

To Bill's credit he produced an excellent performance that night, especially given the circumstances. He came out not exactly swinging, but he was firm and clear, with an excellent grasp of detail. He looked prime ministerial. Jacinda performed well, but couldn't match the hype. We'd cleared that hurdle.

But the problem remained. We were doing the right things, we had a good series of policy announcements and events, and the campaign calendar was full. The campaign team was functioning well, and there were no signs of the wheels falling off. But none of it seemed to matter. As far as the media and the public were concerned, the only story was Labour's phoenix-like rise from the ashes under their new leader.

Jacinda winning the election in just eight weeks would be a fairy tale, and some days that was the only story the gallery wanted to cover. None of Labour's announcements were earth-shattering, but their momentum kept building.

As campaign chair I knew I had to do something to change the game, but what exactly?

THE 2017 CAMPAIGN WAS DIFFERENT for me because of my role as Finance Minister, and therefore finance spokesperson for the National Party. That involved more set-piece events than I had participated in during previous campaigns, like the BusinessNZ election event, the Queenstown Great Debate, the *Stuff* Finance

Debate and so on, most often up against Grant Robertson. There was even less time than usual for retail campaigning.

There was also the battle of fiscal policies. Treasury fired the starting gun by releasing their pre-election fiscal update on 27 August as scheduled. Two days later, Labour released their updated fiscal plan, which they said was in response to the pre-election fiscal update, but in reality reflected some of the changes they had made to their plans following Jacinda becoming leader.

Labour were very wary of being called out as big spenders. They took the precaution of laying out some 'Budget responsibility rules' and getting an independent (read Labour-friendly) economic consultancy, BERL, to review their numbers.

We were ready to pounce on Labour's alternative Budget. We were sure there would be issues with it, because the previous version they released was very tight, and since then they had made some extra spending commitments. How did it all add up?

It became clear quite quickly that there were some very sloppy bits in Labour's plan. They had double-counted some income tax from multinational companies which Treasury had already counted, failed to include their promise to extend paid parental leave, and mucked up the start date of their family incomes package. Those mistakes alone added to nearly $2 billion.

However, the big one was how they had treated their allowances for further Budget spending. These allowances are cumulative. If you spend $900 million in the first year, that money must also be added to subsequent years' Budgets. If you then add another $900 million allowance in the second year, the total spend over baseline in that year is $1.8 billion, and so on.

Labour had taken the correct approach in the first version of their Budget, released prior to Jacinda's ascension, but this later version ignored subsequent years. In effect, they had either made a massive multi-billion-dollar mistake, or they had included fanciful zero

Budget allowances (outside of health) for their second and third years in office. Things like police pay and the Corrections budget — in fact anything you care to name — were apparently not going to cost anything more over the four-year projection period. And there was no money at all set aside to pay for the policies of coalition partners.

There was plenty to have a crack at, and we set about feeding questions to the press gallery about the weaknesses in the numbers.

But we struck a big problem. Nobody was interested. There is only a small number of financially confident journalists in the press gallery at the best of times, and these were not the best of times. They were either too busy, didn't feel confident about engaging in the debate, or not at work. One normally reliable numbers guy, Vernon Small at *Stuff*, was even on leave during the election campaign. That may have been deliberate. He later turned up as a PR guy for one of the new ministers.

After two or three days' effort, it was clear that nobody in the press gallery wanted to question Labour's numbers. They were prepared to take them at face value, lean on the BERL analysis, and move on, continuing with their narrative of Labour's rise under Jacinda.

I was not happy. What's the point of laying out alternative policy plans at an election if they don't have to be costed in any sort of reality? My political team and I started brainstorming about how we could make the gallery take notice.

An idea took shape around holding a press conference with supporting material to debunk Labour's numbers. Such a press conference would force journalists to address the issues. We would point out the errors and correct Labour's plan. We would also add all the errors up to provide a headline number the media could digest. In short, we would do the media's work for them.

We worked across the weekend, costing and recosting Labour's numbers, and looking for the flaws in our arguments. I had four people — my political adviser Kenny Clark, my senior media adviser Anna Lillis, the PM's financial adviser and John Key's former financial adviser, then living in Washington DC — check and recheck the arguments. Finally we knew we were good to go.

The strategy was to release the information on the afternoon of Monday, 4 September. First, though, I needed to check the approach with the broader leadership team. I sat down at Monday morning's pre-Cabinet meeting with Bill, Paula, Simon Bridges, Jonathan Coleman, Amy Adams and Wayne Eagleson. We went through the material, and then I sought their approval to proceed.

I warned them that one way or another, this would be big. It could explode in Labour's faces or our own. I was confident in the accuracy of the numbers, but I couldn't tell them which way it would finally bounce. With National now behind in the polls, it could help turn the tide — or cement the trend.

Everybody supported it. They knew it was a high-risk strategy, but we needed something. I suspect there were some who were happy that it was me going over the parapet. It was a sombre meeting, but we were in business. I held the press conference in my Beehive office that Monday afternoon, accusing Labour of an $11.7 billion hole in their fiscal plans.

All hell broke loose. The journalists were apoplectic. Labour were incandescent. Grant Robertson was off the charts, at one point memorably declaring on RNZ's *Morning Report* that my accusation was an 'affront to democracy'. That was, at the very least, amusing. How dare we accuse them of not doing the numbers right! Robertson had adopted an old Labour tactic of thundering so hard that the force of his rhetoric alone might convince doubters. It certainly helped with some impressionable journalists.

Labour lost no time rounding up a group of economists and economic commentators to support their position. Most of them didn't trouble me. Many had, shall we say, a left-wing bias, including of course Ganesh Nana, then the Director of BERL and latterly Grant Robertson's hand-picked chair of the now very left-wing Productivity Commission. Another, Bernard Hickey, referred to as an economist but a journalist by trade, considered nearly every government too fiscally conservative, so he wasn't about to trouble himself with a few billion in extra spending.

The only criticism that stung a bit was when then ANZ Chief Economist Cameron Bagrie disagreed there was a fiscal hole. He had a bob each way, suggesting that Labour's numbers would be pretty much impossible to achieve, but refused to call it what it was. Cameron later recanted and said publicly that my characterisation of the problems with Labour's fiscal plan was correct.

Much later, in December 2019, the Treasury Half Year Economic and Fiscal Update immediately prior to the Covid-19 pandemic proved that, if anything, I was too conservative in my criticism of Labour's fiscal numbers. They were by then some $19 billion over their 2017 pre-election plan, not $11.7 billion. Blithely, Finance Minister Robertson blamed subsequent events and the impact of coalition agreements, both of which he was expressly warned about at the time.

The most surprising thing to me was how so few journalists bothered to read the material and come to their own conclusion. Their treatment of the issue amounted to lining up people to agree or disagree with me, rather than whipping out a calculator and checking for themselves. The maths required was fairly rudimentary.

Those few days were fairly lonely out there copping the blowback from the commentariat. We had disrupted them and upset the apple cart, and many in the media were not happy. To Bill's credit, he backed me all the way. He was happy with the numbers and happy to have the argument.

And while it was personally bruising, it was a good argument to have. At a stroke we had brought the debate back to bread-

and-butter issues, like spending, tax and debt. That was much safer ground for us given our track record, and less lucrative ground for Labour, who had until then been riding high simply on the idea of Jacinda's coronation as prime minister.

I knew our approach was working when, on a rare Sunday at home, I took Amelia down to her tennis lesson at the Albany Tennis Park. As I watched her play, I could hear some other tennis parents I didn't know about 15 metres away debating Labour's fiscal hole amongst themselves. I heard them agree that it definitely existed. Maybe it wasn't the full $11.7 billion, but it was 'definitely a worry'.

Having wrestled the agenda back to economic issues, we refused to let it go. We spent the remainder of the campaign on tax, spending and economic growth. It was ruthless but effective. I had to dissuade more than one senior minister from making announcements that would take us away from those core issues, and I didn't make myself popular in the process. But we couldn't give Labour any room to retake the initiative.

Bill campaigned exceedingly well. After that first debate he became increasingly comfortable in his own skin and fought a stronger, more prime-ministerial campaign than Jacinda, bringing all his 25-plus years of political experience to bear. He looked like he was enjoying the campaign and he was. Mary and the family were great assets as well, with their youngest son, Xavier, becoming something of a YouTube sensation with his quirky, fly-on-the-wall videos of his father's campaign.

After that first week in September, Labour slipped behind in nearly all the polls again. The last two TV1 and TV3 polls prior to election day had us nine points in front.

And so it proved. Election night 2017 was a good night for National. We had provisionally won 58 seats, only three short of a majority, while Labour had won 45 seats. We believed we had seen off Jacindamania.

It was a great party that night at the Viaduct. The next day I thanked our campaign team, who I believed were the most formidable we had yet assembled. As I said at the time, it was one thing to ride a trend to a good election result, but something all the more challenging to turn a trend in the final weeks of an election campaign.

However, despite the clear margin we had won over the second-largest party, the challenge would come in forming a government. That was all ahead of us.

Chapter Twenty-five
Coalition two-step

THE ELECTORAL MATHS DIDN'T TURN out to be as good as it looked on election night. We had anticipated losing a seat on the special votes, but in the end we lost two, one to Labour and one to the Greens. We slipped back in the numbers precisely at the time Winston Peters was getting started in his traditional Dutch auction choice of governing partner between National and Labour.

In the past Winston had made it clear he would negotiate first with the largest party, but he changed his tune this time. He was going into discussions with both National and Labour 'with an open mind'.

Our problem was a distinct lack of friends, and that was apparent throughout the campaign. We knew Peter Dunne's hasty retirement would take out United Future, and polling had told us it was unlikely that David Seymour would add to his solitary seat in the Parliament. So it proved.

The surprise, if there was one, was the electoral demise of the Māori Party, caused by the loss by my friend and colleague Te Ururoa Flavell of his Waiariki seat, which is based around the city of Rotorua. Te Ururoa was a thoughtful and dignified parliamentarian, diligently working day and night to achieve a better future for his people. I enjoyed working with him. Unfortunately, he was not prone to blowing his own trumpet, which had him on the back foot when campaigning.

The Māori seats are notoriously difficult to assess via opinion polling. One poll had Te Ururoa as safe as houses and another had him at risk, but there was little we could do either way, as the Māori Party clearly and proudly ran their own ship. I did have one inkling though that things weren't going according to plan.

As we did our by now traditional two-day leader's bus tour up the North Island to close out the campaign, our arrival in Rotorua was greeted by a frenzy of Labour supporters waving signs on street corners. They weren't campaigning for their Rotorua candidate but for Tamati Coffey, who was standing in Waiariki. I'd never seen such visible retail campaigning in a Māori seat before. I remember clocking the activity and thinking it looked a little ominous. Those images returned to me on election night.

So there we were. Despite achieving a notable plurality of seats over Jacinda Ardern's Labour Party, we were to be beholden to the mercurial Mr Peters for the right to form a government and achieve a fourth three-year term.

There is a very limited tradition in New Zealand for these sorts of coalition negotiations. In both 1996 and 2005 Winston had coalesced with the party with the largest number of seats, but he made it clear in 2017 that this may not necessarily be the case. In some MMP countries there is a constitutional requirement for the party winning the most seats to have the first opportunity to form a government, but not here.

It was clear we were off on the wrong foot with New Zealand First, as a result of three perceived slights during the election campaign. Our first mistake in Winston's eyes was targeting and winning the Northland seat from him.

While that would have definitely stung, it ironically wasn't a result we sought or expected. Our approach to Northland was very much to campaign at a local level only, to avoid giving Winston a platform to run on nationally. Given how recently we had lost to Winston in the by-election, we expected it to be a two-election challenge to win back the trust of Northland voters and regain the seat.

Our new candidate, former policeman Matt King, was instructed to do the work getting around the huge electorate and convince people one-on-one that he should be the MP. He was given precious little air support from Bill or anyone else. That he went on to win the seat was a testament to his hard slog in every corner of that vast Northland region, plus I think a sense that Winston hadn't exactly been as energetic in promoting the electorate after the by-election as he was before. It helped immeasurably that Labour didn't pull the pin on Northland this time either.

The second perceived slight was a number of references Bill and others made in the final days of the campaign to 'cut out the middle man' and give National their party vote. We'd picked up that a number of voters, particularly in the upper North Island, were preparing to chuck Winston their party vote, variously to 'keep you honest' or 'give you a coalition partner'. Very few of those voters expected Winston to jilt us at the altar, but we were worried they misunderstood the risk. While New Zealand First made much of being offended about this campaigning through the media back channels, it was never mentioned in person to us — and I suspect Winston, the old campaigner, wasn't too worried about what were quite legitimate political tactics.

The third issue was a different story. The public leaking of Winston's superannuation issues deeply offended him, and he wasn't about to let it go.

Ironically, as National Party Campaign Chair, I was just as horrified at the leak, for political reasons as well as the obvious breach of privacy. The rise and rise of Jacinda Ardern had, if anything, been more problematic for New Zealand First than it was for us. The Jacinda narrative was sucking all the air away from Winston, and his campaign had become becalmed in its wake. Winston thrives on political oxygen, and he wasn't getting any.

I was happy about that turn of events with regard to the likely election outcome, so when I saw the news break about Winston's superannuation I knew immediately it wouldn't be at all helpful to our cause.

In the week leading up to our campaign launch, which took place just after the first TVNZ debate, Winston had been very quiet. To be fair, he hadn't had much opportunity up against the Jacinda–Bill face-off and the news about Labour moving ahead in the polls. But he had been very quiet indeed, to the point that some people had been wondering privately about his health.

When *Newsroom*'s Tim Murphy started tweeting about having a huge story that was about to break, I immediately thought of Winston. And so it proved, but not in the way I anticipated.

To this day I don't know who leaked the information. I don't believe it was anyone from the National Party, and if somehow it was, then it was a rogue operator. As I say, there was nothing in it for us. If somebody had brought the information to me, I would have told them to forget about it.

Winston went as ballistic as only he can, and fair enough. I'm sure it was part self-righteousness and part showman-campaigning, but it worked and got him back on the front page. And he didn't let it go, taking a court case after the election against Anne Tolley, Paula Bennett and anyone who could have possibly known anything. It was a taxpayer-funded witch-hunt without any evidence and it didn't turn up anything.

For what it's worth, I was attracted to the theory that the leak was a revenge attack from a disgruntled Greens supporter in MSD, who was offended at the way Metiria Turei's history on the benefit was trawled through the media. We may never know the actual story.

WE WERE ALL EXHAUSTED AFTER the campaign, but there was much work to do, and we busied ourselves preparing for the coalition discussions. Part of our considerations were about who should represent National. Bill obviously, but who else? It was agreed that Gerry Brownlee and Todd McClay would be part of the team, given they were friendlier with Winston than most of us. And there was discussion publicly and privately about whether Paula as Deputy and I as finance spokesperson should also participate.

Winston started his court case against National before commencing the coalition negotiations, so I could understand the argument for Paula not participating. He was obviously gunning for her. For my part, despite some public suggestions to the contrary, I didn't have any concerns about negotiating with Winston and his crew. I had a good relationship with Shane Jones, and a cordial enough relationship with Winston himself.

Ironically, on the way down from Auckland for the first round of discussions, I ran into Winston in the security queue at Auckland Airport. We chatted for a bit, and noted Paddy Gower's ongoing breathless campaign against my role in the negotiations, most recently on the TV that morning or the night before. Winston suggested that the journalists were guilty of 'interviewing their typewriters again'. In any event it was Bill's call, and he decided both Paula and I should participate.

I was nearly not part of the negotiations for another reason. I'd gone back to Auckland after the election for a break with the family, partly to get over my by now familiar 'election cold', a hacking cough that had taken to turning up during every campaign. It seemed to be getting better with help from some time in the garden, but then I started getting cold sweats and arthritic-type pain in my joints.

The pain went from bad to worse, and on 3 October I was admitted into North Shore Hospital where the doctors decided I was experiencing what they described as a particularly ruthless viral infection. It wasn't pleasant, but also not too serious. After lots of tests and some suitable drugs, I was discharged late the next day, with orders to go home and rest.

When I headed to Wellington a couple of days later, I felt a bit like death warmed up. Wayne Eagleson confirmed I looked the way I felt. I was definitely a bit slow-moving, and my part in negotiations was a very quiet one in those first few days.

The negotiation process was quite surreal. New Zealand First had booked a conference room on the second floor of the Beehive, just over the bridge from Parliament House. The room was bare except for a meeting table with chairs down either side. The New Zealand First crew sat down one side with Winston in the middle, and we sat down the other. We tried to discuss the process and how it all might work, but Winston was happy with just starting on a long laundry list of policies they wanted to address.

The meeting unfolded as follows. They would raise a policy, we would provide our view, for or against or nuanced, there might be a bit of discussion, and then that policy would be set aside, recorded in the minutes and we'd move on to the next one.

On the first day, Winston led off with the waka-jumping legislation, New Zealand First's desire for a review into the conduct of the 2017 election, and medical marijuana. He also told us that cancelling the proposed new Parliament building was a bottom line. Other topics canvassed included Pike River re-entry, how to help young Māori get drivers' licences, reform of the Reserve Bank, the phasing out of 1080, and instituting a royalty on the export of bottled water. After a decent period of discussion, the principals agreed that was enough for one day, and we adjourned to the next.

We held two meetings a day from then until late in the week.

Each meeting settled into the rhythm of a couple of themes per meeting, with often the relevant New Zealand First spokesperson subbing in to cover off their list of asks. Taken together it was a long list, but in most cases we signalled our amenability to changing things to at least go part-way to New Zealand First's requests. We certainly weren't stonewalling. In fact some of the things we signalled our openness to would have turned the hair of some National Party members white had they learned of them.

The discussions were nearly all good-natured, and the two sides were learning to understand each other's perspectives more. At the end of the final meeting, Tracey Martin's sister, Kirsty Christison, who was recording the discussions for New Zealand First, stood up and gave an impromptu speech, saying how much she'd enjoyed the discussion and how pleasantly surprised she'd been about the way we'd conducted ourselves and how much we knew and cared. I can only presume that wasn't what she expected.

One surprise to me was Winston's historical frame of reference. He seemed particularly wrapped up in the 1990s, and sometimes it was like the last ten years had never happened. We had one discussion in particular about the economy, and Winston's theory, subsequently shared publicly, that the world was in for dark economic times.

He wanted to know how we'd respond, whether we'd be into austerity and would slash and burn the Budget — the inference being he wouldn't want to be part of a government that would do that. We tried to stand on our track record post the GFC, but he wouldn't engage with or acknowledge that at all. It was as if that was invisible to him. I suppose he was out of Parliament at the time. He wanted to relitigate the Asian political crisis of the late 1990s and the reaction of Jenny Shipley's government, as if that was the immediate precedent. I walked away from that meeting thinking he somehow wanted proof that he wasn't going into coalition with Mrs Shipley.

Actually, he seemed to want to relitigate a lot of the policy battles of the late 1990s. The plan to rebuild the forestry service was based on its dismemberment at that time. His attitude to electricity generation was all based on an antithesis to the Bradford reforms, again as if nothing had happened in the interim. I was a bit lost. This was all twenty-plus years ago and I'd come into Parliament nearly a decade after that had all finished. Yet for Winston it was clearly yesterday.

Our side would go away after each meeting and discuss what we thought, including the likelihood of any deal. It was a fairly pointless exercise but it passed the time. Most thought the talks were constructive, but the exception was Gerry. He'd decided by about day two that Winston was just leading us on, and wasn't coming with us. Gerry is a great reader of people most of the time, so when he has a hunch it's worth taking note. I've often thought about how right he turned out to be.

After the first few days of discussions of New Zealand First's asks, we decided it was a good idea to see which parts of our programme New Zealand First would support in return, as part of any coalition agreement. That was duly tabled, but not responded to, either in the meeting or later. There wasn't any real discussion of those matters at all, except for Bill and Winston's leader-to-leader meetings very late in the piece.

There were a number of back-channel meetings on some of the thorny issues. Shane Jones and I met and talked a couple of times, particularly about immigration, the one billion trees fund, and the $1 billion he wanted for his regional growth fund. They were interesting discussions. In each one I started to go through the practicalities with him.

The idea we could plant a billion trees in ten years was obviously la-la land, and I tried to talk Shane back to something that might be achievable. We discussed what New Zealand had planted for each of the previous five years, and the chances of us planting a million a year, let alone a hundred million. I then realised that practicalities weren't actually important to Shane. It was all about the bumper stickers: a billion trees; no more immigration; $1 billion for the regions. On the last matter, in the end Labour gave him $3 billion, $1 billion for each year of the parliamentary term. I don't know how they ended up there, but the ask was $1 billion all up when it left us.

Later, we often wondered whether we could have done anything differently — in order to even up the odds a little and recapture the initiative from Winston's Dutch auction. We did make some background overtures to the Greens through Todd Muller and James Shaw, and these initially seemed promising. But the trail went cold, and we heard later that Shaw had been quickly brought into line by the more leftist elements in his party.

Time was rolling on and it didn't seem we were getting very far. Either Winston was getting even more mercurial, or things weren't going our way. We heard at various points it was all finely balanced, but it would be hard to know whether that was true or designed to wring further concessions out of both sides. We knew Shane, Fletcher Tabuteau and a couple of others wanted to come with us, but also that Tracey Martin, and probably Winston, wanted to go with Labour.

So it eventually came to pass. After days of meetings, exchanges of letters and meetings between leaders, Winston came down from the mount and announced he was going into coalition with Labour and the Green Party. For the first time since 1911, more than a hundred years, the largest party in the Parliament would not be leading the government.

We were deflated and gutted, and I was gutted for Bill. He should have been prime minister, and he would have been an excellent prime minister for the times, but it wasn't to be. We knew going into the negotiations that things were at best 50:50, so in some ways we were prepared for the result. But it didn't hurt any the less for that. At least I knew from my own experience with the radio company that everything ends at some point so you have to be philosophical.

We'd talked about it ahead of time, and had decided we wouldn't do absolutely anything to keep the Treasury benches. Bill in particular did not want to sell our souls down the river. He'd made it clear he'd rather be in a fiery Opposition taking down a shaky government than the other way around. Of course, with respect to that, fate had other plans.

As to why Winston didn't choose us, it's hard to say. Subsequent events showed he spent much of his time in the three-year term stopping Labour and the Greens from doing lots of things he disagreed with. It's not hard to construct the argument that he would have been more at home in coalition with us. Certainly, many of his former supporters think so.

He made a lot at the time about choosing a government on its way up, and I think by that he meant Jacinda primarily. I also heard that he thought it would be easier to boss Labour around because they were so inexperienced, while he might be more of a third wheel to our more battle-hardened machine.

It's also true that there was some personal history between Winston and Bill. Bill had been in the National caucus back in the 1990s when Winston was expelled. Perhaps utu was part of it. After all, the 1990s still figure large in the mind of Winston Peters.

At the end of the day, only Winston can say why he made the call he made. Since he was thrown out of Parliament again in 2020, he seems to be even denying responsibility for the government he installed.

None of that would change anything of course; the decision was made. Our job was to live with it.

Chapter Twenty-six
The aftermath

NORMALLY WHEN A POLITICAL PARTY goes into Opposition it is because the electorate has just given them a metaphorical spanking at the polls. Actually, for 'normally', read 'nearly always'. There hadn't been a New Zealand election resulting in a change of government in living memory where the outgoing incumbent wasn't clearly and visibly handed a red card by the public.

In 1972, 1975, 1984 and 1990, all first-past-the-post elections, the former governing party lost at least ten seats, sometimes more than twenty. In 1999, under MMP, National went from seven seats over Labour to ten seats behind. In 2008 the fortunes were reversed; Labour went from one seat up to fifteen behind.

In all those elections the post-election playbook for the defeated party was pretty straightforward. You tuck your tail between your legs and go away and lick your wounds for a while. Nobody wants to hear from you for at least six months, so you go and work out what went wrong and put yourselves back together.

There was no playbook for what happened in the 2017 election. National, the largest party in the Parliament with a total of 56 seats, just five short of a majority on its own, found itself on the Opposition benches with ten more seats than the party leading government.

This isn't to debate the outcome. It was clear the governing coalition had the numbers to govern. But what lessons should National take from the election result? How should it behave? Was the result a rejection of its policy prescription? Was it a rejection of the personnel? How do you rebuild if no one can point to what you did wrong, beyond carelessly losing too many coalition partners?

Our initial thesis was to carry on and make the case strongly for what we believed in. That was my instinct, and the instinct of many but not all the caucus. Some clearly wanted to rethink all our positions, and indeed our personnel. It was hard not to see at least some self-interest amongst those views.

The majority view prevailed. We may have swapped from government to Opposition, but the things we had argued for clearly still resonated with a plurality of voters. We had work to do to prosecute the case against the new government.

So we picked ourselves up off the floor, dusted ourselves off, shifted former ministers over from the Beehive to the old Parliament buildings, and started taking the game to the new government. Some of us had to learn new skills. I for one had never been in Opposition, never sat on a select committee, and never asked a question in Parliament, having only answered them. It was another steep learning curve, and an unwanted one. My time on the Finance and Expenditure Committee was brief and futile. The composition of select committees in the New Zealand Parliament means they are largely an elaborate charade. They can be useful on matters of detail where the legislation is not controversial but, other than that, the government holds the whip hand.

There was initially little in the way of personnel changes in the National team. Bill was still the leader, Paula deputy, and I retained finance. We were all very combative in the House. The new government's supporters complained that they didn't get much of a honeymoon, but why should they? The electorate remained finely balanced.

The finance portfolio was where we had our first big opportunity to take the fight to the new government. Labour were hastening through their changes for Working for Families in the lead-up to Christmas, including cancelling the tax reductions already legislated for in Budget 2017.

Some on our side didn't want to put up too much of a fight. They were more of the old-school 'they won, we lost' mindset. I, on the other hand, was very keen to fight. If a lower tax burden and providing families a better return for their hard work wasn't worth fighting for, then I wondered what was. I also figured that having an early scrap would be good for team morale.

Most of the caucus agreed and stayed willingly to fight the changes through the last House sitting week and well into the weekend, under urgency. It was a good scrap, and actually quite a lot of fun to prosecute. We were always going to lose as the coalition was rock solid that early in the game, but it was right to make our point and we made it strongly.

There was however an undercurrent of slightly strange behaviour. I noticed that our Chief Whip, Jami-Lee Ross, was very protective of our back bench, almost obstructive even. I mentioned to him a couple of different times that I might call a meeting to discuss our tactics and allocate roles in the debate. He encouraged me not to trouble myself with such tasks, and leave them to him as the whip. The first time I let it go, but the second time I thought, bugger it, it had to be okay for the finance spokesperson to have a chat with interested colleagues. He let it go through, but he was clearly uncomfortable.

When I declared I planned to send a note around, thanking our colleagues for their work during the debate, he again stepped in and tried to discourage me. It was almost like he didn't want me to work too closely with the back bench at all. I tucked my observations away for future reference.

Jami-Lee had fostered the image of being a strange and mysterious individual. He fancied himself as a bit of a schemer and a bagman, a sort of National Party Frank Underwood, Kevin Spacey's character in *House of Cards*. He even had the theme music as his ringtone. Nobody took him too seriously, at least not while John and Bill were in charge, and not least because of his ringtone.

I'd never warmed to Jami-Lee. He ended up in our 2008 year group because he came in to Parliament on a by-election between 2008 and 2011. He was friendly enough, but one of those people you'd always wonder about once he'd left the room. He was supremely ambitious, constantly pestering Bill, and John before him, for promotion, which resulted in him eventually being sent up the whips track. The whips are in charge of caucus organisation and discipline on behalf of the leader. Giving someone the role of junior whip is often a good way to solve an immediate problem and keep them busy. However, eventually they graduate to senior whip, and you may discover you have given yourself a bigger problem. I worried sometimes that's where we were heading with Jami-Lee.

THE SUMMER BREAK WAS A much-needed chance to recharge for all of us. I was emotionally and physically exhausted. The year had been arduous and had clearly not turned out as we had all hoped. It was hard to work out what to be most disappointed about: the loss of the government benches, or the manner in which it happened.

Rust never sleeps, of course, and caucus members had worked out for themselves that Bill wouldn't stay long as leader. Nobody knew how long he would stay, but they all anticipated it would be no more than six months. The manoeuvring was beginning to begin. I received two out-of-the-blue calls from colleagues over the break, and I was sure that was just the tip of the iceberg.

The first visit was from my local MP Mark Mitchell, who lived up the road in Ōrewa. Mark sat me down and told me in no uncertain terms that he thought I should be the next leader of the National Party. It was completely unprompted. Mark gave me a long list of what he saw as my leadership attributes, and finished by declaring he would not support anybody else in the current caucus above me for the job.

I was naturally flattered and more than a bit surprised. Mark and I had been friendly enough, but there had been no inkling of this. Those who know Mark will know that he is capable of some charm, and he certainly used it that day. I told him that I would give it some thought, but of course it was all very theoretical at that point.

My second visitor was Todd Muller, who ostensibly came to see me about his new climate change portfolio. Todd had been in Parliament for three years, taking over the Bay of Plenty seat on Tony Ryall's retirement. We were friendly but not close.

As the conversation turned to what might happen with leadership in the new year, Todd asked whether I had any interests in a leadership role. I gave some sort of vague but open answer, and then he surprised me by volunteering that he might have an interest in stepping up. Until then I had not seen him as leadership material at all. Todd seemed a genuinely nice guy but quite a scholarly, reserved character, very much from the centrist part of the caucus. My immediate thought was that any move like that was too early for him by some margin.

Two weeks later a speculative opinion piece from columnist Matthew Hooton appeared in the *National Business Review*, suggesting that Todd Muller could be a candidate for the upcoming leadership change, and that apparently Steven Joyce fancied himself as a leader, followed by a list of disparaging comments about how bad an idea that would be.

The surprise, to me at least, was that one of my personal

conversations had made it into print. I wasn't 100 per cent sure who was responsible, but the only other individual present at my two meetings had been Gemma the dog, and she was the soul of discretion.

It was clear by late January that there were some in the caucus who were impatient to get on with a leadership change. Both of the party's set-piece events to start the year were undermined by deliberate speculation about the leadership.

The first was Bill's State of the Nation speech in Wellington on 31 January. In a strong speech he laid down a warning for the new government, declaring they should allow no deterioration of the economy or child poverty on their watch, because the Opposition would be after them. It was stirring, positive stuff, but it was overshadowed by an internal leak speculating on the future of Paula as deputy leader.

It was a classic beginner move. You want to give the leader a nudge to move on, but you don't want to overtly leak against him because he has too much mana. Instead you have a crack at his deputy, at the same time upsetting the leader's positive news day. Subtle it wasn't.

A week later we had the two-day caucus retreat in Tauranga. I had led a strong caucus team to Waitangi on 5 February, speaking on Bill's behalf, and all seemed calm there. But when we arrived in Tauranga the mood was quite feral, and more public rumours circled around. Senior heads like Gerry Brownlee, Chris Finlayson and myself were appalled at the way Bill was being treated, and we felt strongly he had earned the right to choose when and how to go. On the other hand, there were the young thrusters, who were supremely impatient to get their hands on the steering wheel.

Simon Bridges and Todd McClay were clearly involved in the agitation, but there were others as well who probably saw their chance to rise on Simon's or somebody else's coat-tails. Simon at least was smart enough to appear to remain above the fray, but others less so. At one stage at the evening caucus function, I remember being bailed up by Jami-Lee Ross and Sarah Dowie and listening politely to a long lecture on the finer points of campaign strategy. It was clear by then that Jami-Lee was corralling the back benches for Simon despite being Bill's senior whip, and saw himself as the putative power behind the throne. Their argument could more or less be summed up as 'every campaign only needs three things', repeated ad nauseam. I recall thinking clearly that life was too short.

The truth was there was a cohort of front-bench MPs who had been impatient for their turn at leadership of the party for some time. They included Simon, Amy Adams and Jonathan Coleman, with support variously from Nikki Kaye and Todd McClay. All had risen higher in the ranks when John left, and had stayed on the front bench with the change of government. A number of them were impatient with me and my various roles, and thought that with the change of government it was their turn to run the show.

There had been a deputation by some of them to Bill in early December soon after we headed into Opposition. He had given me a heads-up that a few knives were out. Frankly it didn't worry me too much. I've long been of the view that in a game like politics you stay as long as you are useful and I'd happily move on when the time came. I've never been the sort to remain where I'm not wanted.

All the public speculation had the desired effect for the plotters, with Bill bringing forward his retirement and announcing it on 13 February.

I was very sorry to see him go. I had seen enough to know he would have been an ideal prime minister for the ensuing period in our country's history. He was, to employ that much misused phrase, a true compassionate conservative. Given more time in the job he would have achieved great progress on many of the social ills facing this country. It is an absolute waste that he never had that opportunity.

TWO WEEKS WERE ALLOCATED FOR the campaign to be the next National leader. Simon Bridges was out of the starting gate immediately with help from Jami-Lee Ross and Todd McClay, followed closely by Judith Collins and Amy Adams. Broadly, Simon was of the conservative right of the caucus, and Amy was the centrist candidate supported by Nikki Kaye and Chris Bishop, while Judith was Judith. Jonathan Coleman ruled himself out.

I had to finally decide whether to run. I had been thinking about a tilt at the leadership for a couple of months, but I am one of these people who is better at advising others than themselves. It didn't help that I had kept my thoughts largely to myself, out of respect for Bill. The only people I had really mused aloud to were close colleagues Nathan Guy, David Bennett, who I knew from right back in my National Party Board days, and Gerry Brownlee.

Once Bill announced his resignation I had a number of people ask me to stand, and others who wanted to be sure I would stay in Parliament regardless. I had worked out that I didn't want to stay to do finance or probably any other job; I had already made my contribution in most of the portfolio areas I wanted to. So I decided to throw my hat into the ring, but Suzanne and I agreed that if I didn't get the role and the new challenge that came with it, then I would likely pick my moment to move on.

It was about then that things started to get a bit weird. Mark Mitchell, who had been the first to declare his support to me privately back in January, revealed publicly that he was pondering his own leadership bid. I rang him up to ask what he was doing, and he apologised and said he'd been overwhelmed with calls to stand. Fair enough.

Mark's backers were Alfred Ngaro, Denise Lee and Erica Stanford, and Nathan Guy and I met with the four of them in Ōrewa. Our initial plan was to seek to persuade them to support my candidacy, but it was clear they were committed to their course of action. We were now in the middle of a five-way fight for the job.

We all did the rounds with all the caucus colleagues, and three of the candidates — Simon, Amy and Mark — regularly spruiked their numbers to the media through their backers. Amusingly, the numbers they individually claimed added to at least 65 people in a 56-person caucus, with no one left over for Judith and me, including our own votes.

Judith, by her own admission, only had a couple of votes that she could count on, while I knew I had more than Mark but likely fewer than Amy or Simon. My best hope was to get it down to a three-way contest and go from there.

I campaigned hard, but it was clear I was on the back foot from the start because I hadn't taken time to personally cultivate caucus members while I was a minister. I had given every ounce of energy I had to my ministerial role without any thought for a political future. Suzanne and I went on a trip around the country meeting colleagues, but there was no doubt I had a lot of ground to make up. There was also a sense amongst my colleagues that we should be looking to a new generation, closer in age to Jacinda.

I'm not sure to this day what Mark was up to. The five votes he had (including his own) were all big Paula Bennett supporters. I suspect she just parked them with Mark until she knew which way the wind was blowing with Simon in terms of the deputy leadership. Mark ended up pulling out and endorsing Simon on the morning of the caucus vote, transferring those votes across. It wasn't enough votes to have Simon elected on the first ballot, but he did get over the line in the second, and Paula was duly elected as his deputy.

I wasn't too unhappy not to get there. I had given my speech in the caucus room and spoken passionately about the role and what I thought I could achieve, but I also felt misgivings internally about the commitment required.

I particularly remember a moment during the ballot which

crystallised my feelings. The four of us — Simon, Amy, Judith and myself — were waiting in a separate room to hear the results of the first ballot. The acting senior whip came in and told us that Judith was out for the second round. Judith left, and it was just the three of us waiting for the second ballot to take place.

Right at that moment I had a particularly powerful feeling of dread. What if I got the role? I would be stuck here for another three years. I'd have to lift myself to fight harder, after an arduous nine years at the top. I thought about my family, and my absence from the lives of Amelia and Tommy in particular. In another three years they would be thirteen and eleven.

I've never forgotten that feeling.

If I had won the leadership I have no doubt I would have steeled myself and delivered the role to the best of my ability, and fought hard to return National to government in 2020. You do that. You step up and you get on with it, and you get caught up in all that needs to be done. But in that quiet moment of waiting and reflection, the feeling was definitely dread. When the news came that Simon had won the leadership, I was almost relieved.

Simon, whether intentionally or inadvertently, made it even easier for me. It became clear that whatever plans he had for me, it didn't include the finance portfolio. That was to be Amy, which was a surprise because she'd never expressed much interest in the portfolio. I suspect it was more about being seen to bring the two camps together rather than anything else.

Simon and I arranged a coffee meeting in Tauranga to talk about options. He started with something approaching an apology, saying that they had targeted me because I was the big beast, and they had to get over me to get the role. I wasn't sure what to make of that, so I just heard him out. He then declared he'd like me to stay on in a kaumātua / elder statesman-type role, sitting at number ten on the benches and offering advice to the new leadership team. I thanked him but said no thanks. I didn't feel that old. If that was the offer, then it was probably time to move on.

I left that meeting with a sense of freedom. While I had decided previously that I wouldn't stay if I didn't have the new challenge of leadership, it certainly was easier if I was also not getting finance. In truth, I think I was ready to leave. I had given my all to the party and my country for the past nearly ten years, fifteen if you include the time helping to rebuild the party before entering Parliament. The grind of Opposition didn't really appeal after all of that. While I gave the party every chance of winning in 2020 if it played its cards right, maybe my race was done. Independence beckoned, the family beckoned, business beckoned. It was time to go home.

The rest is largely history. You end up dancing with the ones that brung you. Simon largely shared the spoils out amongst his supporters, and Jami-Lee Ross got the lion's share. It is of course on the public record that he exploded spectacularly, even more so than many of us guessed he might. Simon himself was not patient enough in the role, and of course Todd Muller and Judith Collins both had their opportunities. Events and personalities combined to make the 2020 election a tragedy for the National Party in many ways similar to 2002, which had coincided with my arrival in the party. The rebuild has had to start all over again with a new generation putting their shoulders to the wheel.

For my part, I gave my valedictory statement to Parliament on 27 March 2018. And then I went home, and shut the gate.

Epilogue

'DECOMPRESSION' IS THE BEST WORD I have found to describe the process your body and mind goes through when you finally stop after a long period of busyness and stress. That is not the original meaning of the word, but it covers the feeling well. When I left Parliament, I had some serious decompressing to do.

The good news was that I had gone through this process once before when leaving radio, so I recognised some of the symptoms: the bouts of random anxiety and the difficulty sleeping. But this time around, the decompression required was immense. Four years on, I was still seeing improvement and feeling better every day. Maybe that was due to the extra intensity of a political career, or maybe it was just because I was twenty years older and taking longer to adjust.

When I first made it home there was a huge backlog of property maintenance to be taken care of, and that has taken literally years to clear. I put in a lot of work resurrecting many of the gardens we'd put in so optimistically ten years previously. I threw myself into it, taking on all the gardening and mowing. With the benefit of a new ride-on lawn mower, doing the lawns was straightforward (if time-consuming) and great therapy. The gardens, on the other hand, were a massive challenge. It took me the best part of a year to get them under control, and even then I was constantly meeting myself coming back the other way. In places I had to bash my way through six-foot-high weeds.

Bill and Mary English have visited a few times since Bill and I left politics, and on the second visit Bill staged an intervention. He'd roughly calculated how many square metres of garden there were, and then consulted Google about how much garden one person can handle. It was obvious that me working in my spare time was simply not going to cut it. I moderated my gardening ambition and hired someone in to help once again. Even so, the gardening was a hugely enjoyable and therapeutic project in that first couple of years.

On the work front, I set off on a series of trips, calling on the corporate headhunters in Auckland, Sydney and Melbourne, anticipating that I would seek out some non-executive directorship roles. It was liberating and refreshing to be organising myself again, after having my time managed to the nth degree in politics. I had some great discussions with some knowledgeable people. A senior partner in one of the Sydney firms counselled me not to rush into the first things that came along, and perhaps to hang out a shingle for some project work in the meantime. It was good advice. Since then I have fallen into a range of enjoyable projects across a number of industries and sectors. My main criteria for becoming involved is when I believe that I can really add some value. I count myself fortunate that in nearly all cases so far I have been able to do so.

I had three significant pieces of work in Australia in late 2018 and 2019. The first was a project for the South Australian government, reorganising their economic agencies to be fit for purpose in helping economic growth in the state. The second was a big vocational education review for PM Scott Morrison and the Australian federal government, and the third a review of the 2019 federal election campaign for the Liberal Party. The South Australian work gave me the opportunity to learn what a wonderful city Adelaide is, and the two national projects took me on consultation journeys around Australia, giving me a new appreciation for the geographic scale and diversity of the country.

The Australian work was good for me in another way. There is an old saying that goes something like, 'When you sell a house, you don't hang around telling the new people where to put the furniture.' It applies when you sell a business, and I think it also applies with political parties. I needed to get away from the New Zealand political scene and let the next generation of people make their own decisions and their own mistakes. I happened to be in Australia when the whole Jami-Lee Ross mess blew up, and that was a healthy place for me to see it from. Another plus about Australia is that nobody knows me from a bar of soap, and the anonymity is refreshing. Of course, Covid-19 put paid to much of the Australian work for a time, but by then my New Zealand work was growing as well.

There have been some big things happening personally, too. In August 2018, my mum passed away after being sick for some time with myeloma and other ailments. I was grateful I had time in those last few months to make regular visits to Tauranga with the family and spend time with Mum and Dad. There had been precious few visits during my ten years in Parliament, but hopefully I was able to make up for some of that before she passed. Mum was proud of me for going to Parliament, but also happy when I left.

When I left politics I wrote a list of things I wanted to do, and at the top of the list was strengthening my relationships with Suzanne, Amelia and Tommy. As politicians we can kid ourselves all we like but, for most of us, the huge amount of time we spend away from home doing our jobs puts a real strain on our families. There just isn't enough time to do justice to both, and family life often suffers.

As I reflect now, I think I got out just in time for Amelia and Tommy. Amelia in particular has flourished from having her dad in her life more. We discovered a shared love for tennis, and more recently athletics, a sport Amelia loves. She has proven to be a very handy middle-distance runner, like her granddad was in his day. There is no doubt she gets that from him, rather than her dad, but she has even got me running again. This year I have been out on the Auckland cross-country circuit, running my first races since secondary school. And no, I'm not troubling the scorers.

Every now and then Amelia asks me why we didn't do things like running earlier, although I think she knows the answer.

Tommy's health has been more of a challenge. Since the autism diagnosis he has remained non-verbal, and on top of that he developed chronic epilepsy in 2019, suffering countless drop attacks, tonic-clonic seizures and myoclonic seizures from then on. With the help of the good doctors in neurology at Starship Hospital, we found a combination of drugs that kept him largely seizure-free for eighteen months, but since then we have struggled to stay on top of his epilepsy, tinkering with the medication every six to eight weeks to try to come up with a better answer. Keeping him safe has had to take priority over his development, which I'm sure creates other longer-term consequences. Frankly, if I hadn't left politics when I did I don't know whether I could have stayed on anyway, because without me at home the burden on Suzanne would be too great for any parent to bear on their own.

I think Tommy has blossomed in his own way, too, from having his dad around. There are more challenges ahead, and so far I have failed in my biggest 'Fix-It' job: helping him to prepare for living an independent life. Call it a work in progress. More broadly, I know that our little family is in a much healthier state than it was. With Tom's situation the way it is, we're not able to travel much, but we are very lucky to have the space we have at home.

I have had the opportunity to support Tommy in other ways, although I am still working out how to make a bigger contribution in the wider autism and epilepsy fields. I am currently the patron of the Minds for Minds Trust, which supports New Zealand research into autism. There is so much to learn.

I don't miss political life now. I did initially — the sense of purpose you get from politics can be addictive and hard to replicate, which I imagine is why some people stay on well past their use-by date. But, as time has gone on, I have realised I am more than comfortable with declaring my innings over when I did. I enjoyed making my contribution and I am proud of the things we achieved. We steered New Zealand safely through some challenging times, and built successfully on what was there when we arrived. I also had some wonderful experiences and found it a genuine privilege to serve. The alternative to leaving is, of course, being carried out, and there is too much else to experience in life to let any work role — however important or trivial — define you.

There is also plenty not to like in politics. The intrusiveness of media attention, the nasty personal attacks of social-media trolls, and the constant assumption that your motives are self-serving, which for most politicians couldn't be further from the truth. This is the stuff you have to grin and bear in order to be able to make your contribution and achieve things in policy areas you feel passionate about. I was happy to accept that trade-off for ten years, but I can readily understand that there are many people in the world who wouldn't or couldn't. At least I experienced little in-person nastiness. In fact, the instances of that I could count on the fingers of one hand.

Part of leaving politics involves accepting that the debates contained therein will likely go on forever, and it is the ultimate conceit to believe your participation will settle them. The world is divided broadly into collectivists and individualists, with a whole lot of people in the middle who are collectivist sometimes and individualist at other times. As the saying goes, we are a nation that likes to capitalise our gains and socialise our losses. There are not many collectivists amongst people who strive and succeed, and there weren't many individualists when Covid-19 was raging at its peak. We need both types — and both approaches — and the trick of politics is working out which systems work best in which circumstances.

National voters believe we need to encourage the entrepreneurs, the strivers and the go-getters in order to bring about prosperity for all, while Labour voters tend to think that holding hands and moving together without rewarding individual endeavour will lead to a kinder society. I'm more in the former category, of course. I think that too often in political life we prioritise collective endeavour at the expense of achieving great outcomes for people. Think of education, for example, and health, where collectivism too often leads to mediocre performance.

It is an important debate to have, and we need good people to step up and participate in it. But I think it's time for someone else to make these arguments. If I have unfinished business, it is in the policy areas — building better roads and infrastructure, and improving our universities — not in the debates between left and right. I am glad I can make my contribution through my writing these days, rather than giving all my time to the cause.

Back in the radio days, I was struggling at one point with my wider life and I went to see a therapist, as was the fashion at my age and stage. He had me perform an exercise that I am sure is common to many a therapist's toolbox, but it's one I have never forgotten. I had to draw a number of baskets on a page and label them for the different areas of my life: work, family, friends, self, fitness, and so on. He then said I was to draw seventeen balls and place them in the different baskets, with the number in each basket representing the actual time I spent on each activity in an average week. Not the quality of time, but the quantity. I forget how many balls went into the work basket, but I think I was debating whether it should be twelve, thirteen or fourteen. When I finished the drawing, he asked me to look at it and see if I could work out where I was going wrong.

I enjoyed my time in politics immensely, and the time in radio before it. But I am old enough now to know how obsessive I can be when I am provided with an all-consuming task. It is time for a more balanced life.

Acknowledgements

I WANT TO ACKNOWLEDGE EVERYBODY who has contributed in some way to the experiences I have recounted here. I have been privileged to meet and work with so many people in radio, in politics and in business that it would be a physical impossibility to name you all. From the RadioWorks team, the wider radio industry and the shareholders to the National Party, its members and officeholders, my parliamentary colleagues, parliamentary staff, the talented team who staffed my ministerial office, the officials and the voters: my thanks to you all. I would specifically like to record my appreciation for the advice and support provided throughout many of the events in this book by the most long-standing members of my ministerial staff: Anna Lillis, Kathleen Lambert and Kenny Clark.

By necessity, even a full-length book can't do justice to all the stories, contributions and efforts that sit behind the events I have tried to relate through these pages. I particularly want to acknowledge those people and stories I haven't had space to name or recount. My time in radio especially was a longer adventure, which I have only been able to loosely summarise here. Rest assured, those memories and experiences continue to be treasured.

I also want to acknowledge a few people who were directly involved in the genesis of this manuscript. While I had been considering writing my story for a long time, it was Chris Finlayson who pushed me over the line and introduced me to Michelle Hurley of Allen & Unwin. Michelle in turn exercised great patience in encouraging this would-be author to focus on getting the damned thing written.

My thanks to Wayne Eagleson and Nathan Guy for reviewing the draft and largely confirming my recollection of the political history, and to the team at Allen & Unwin, including project editor Leanne McGregor, copy editor Tracey Wogan and designer Kate Barraclough.

Thanks also to my family — Suzanne, Amelia and Tommy — who coped yet again with me being caught up in something intensely consuming with impossible deadlines. And to my dad, my sister and my brothers, for indulging my more sporadic communication over the eight months it took to write this book.